Law and Power in Russia

Making Sense of Quasi-Legal Practices

This book explores the issue of selective law enforcement, arguing that the manipulation of the legal system by powerful insiders is a distinctive feature of Putinism, reflecting both its hybrid authoritarianism and Russian legal culture. Based on extensive research including interviews with the victims of selective law enforcement, the book analyses how selective law enforcement works in Russia, discusses the link between law and power, and relates the Russian situation to examples from elsewhere and to general legal theories and ideas of political hybridity.

Håvard Bækken (b. 1983) is a senior researcher at the Norwegian Institute for Defence Studies (IFS) in Oslo. He obtained a PhD in Russian Area Studies from the University of Oslo (UiO) in 2014. Bækken has been working as a research fellow at the Norwegian Institute of International Affairs (NUPI) and guest researcher at the Norwegian University Centre in St. Petersburg and the EU–Russia Centre in Brussels. He has taught Russian politics and history at the Institute of Literature, Area-Studies, and European Languages (ILOS) at UiO, and Russian language at the Nansen Academy. Håvard Bækken has earlier publications on issues of law, power, and quasi-legal practices in Russia, as well as forthcoming publications on resurgent state patriotism and 'patriotic education' in the same country.

Routledge Contemporary Russia and Eastern Europe Series

81 **Understanding Energy Security in Central and Eastern Europe**
Russia, Transition and National Interest
Edited by Wojciech Ostrowski and Eamonn Butler

82 **Russia's Far North**
The Contested Energy Frontier
Edited by Veli-Pekka Tynkkynen, Shinichiro Tabata, Daria Gritsenko and Masanori Goto

83 **The City in Russian Culture**
Edited by Pavel Lyssakov and Stephen M. Norris

84 **The Russian Economy under Putin**
Edited by Torbjörn Becker and Susanne Oxenstierna

85 **New Conservatives in Russia and East Central Europe**
Edited by Katharina Bluhm and Mihai Varga

86 **Civil Society, Social Change, and a New Popular Education in Russia**
W. John Morgan, Irina N. Trofimova, and Grigori A. Kliucharev

87 **The Russian Economic Grip on Central and Eastern Europe**
Edited by Ognian Shentov, Ruslan Stefanov and Martin Vladimirov

88 **Law and Power in Russia**
Making Sense of Quasi-Legal Practices
Håvard Bækken

89 **Putin's Third Term as Russia's President, 2012-18**
J L Black

Series url: https://www.routledge.com/Routledge-Contemporary-Russia-and-Eastern-Europe-Series/book-series/SE0766

Law and Power in Russia

Making Sense of Quasi-Legal Practices

Håvard Bækken

Routledge
Taylor & Francis Group
LONDON AND NEW YORK

First published 2019
by Routledge

2 Park Square, Milton Park, Abingdon, Oxfordshire OX14 4RN
52 Vanderbilt Avenue, New York, NY 10017

Routledge is an imprint of the Taylor & Francis Group, an informa business

First issued in paperback 2020

British Library Cataloguing in Publication Data
A catalogue record for this book is available from the British Library

Library of Congress Cataloging in Publication Data
Names: Bµkken, Hêavard, author.
Title: Law and power in Russia : making sense of quasi-legal practices / Hêavard Bµkken.
Description: New York, NY : Routledge, 2019. | Includes bibliographical references and index.
Identifiers: LCCN 2018050583 (print) | LCCN 2018051168 (ebook) |
Subjects: LCSH: Police administration—Russia (Federation). | Police power—Russia (Federation). | Law—Russia (Federation). | Power (Social sciences)—Russia (Federation). | Sociological jurisprudence—Russia (Federation). | Law enforcement—Russia (Federation). | Russia (Federation)—Politics and government—1991-.
Classification: LCC KLB3007 (ebook) | LCC KLB3007 .B36 2019 (print) | DDC 349.47—dc23
LC record available at https://lccn.loc.gov/2018050583

ISBN: 978-1-138-57088-7 (hbk)
ISBN: 978-0-367-66443-5 (pbk)

Typeset in Times NR MT Pro
by Cenveo® Publisher Services

Contents

List of figures

List of tables

Acknowledgements

I am indebted to several colleagues who have commented on various parts of the book draft: Pål Kolstø, Bill Bowring, Sven Holtsmark, Ingerid Opdahl, and Una Hakvåg. I owe Erlend Skjeseth for helping design the figures.

I offer my thanks to all my informants, partners, and assistants in Russia. I want to express my gratitude to the staff at the Norwegian University Centre in St. Petersburg who provided me with a pleasant base of operations for my field trips in 2010 and 2011.

My sojourn in Russia has been a study in hospitality. Dozens of Russians have generously shared their time to assist me in my fieldwork, asking for nothing in return. In particular, I want to thank the organization Golos and their regional representatives who eagerly and unselfishly assisted me. I am also indebted to the Agora center in Kazan. Without the local expertise of these and other idealists, it would have been a far more difficult task to conduct field research in more than a dozen locations around Russia.

Finally, to all my interviewees – thank you again for your time and willingness to speak freely on the sensitive issues of quasi-legal practices. You are the backbone of this study.

Any mistakes or errors that might occur in the book are my responsibility alone.

Note on translation and transliteration

All translations from Russian language sources that appear in the text are my own. The transliterations from Cyrillic to Latin letters follow the BGN/PCGN system, developed by the United States Board on Geographic Names (BGN) and the Permanent Committee on Geographical Names for British Official Use (PCGN).

Russian and Ukrainian names are simplified by omitting soft and hard signs, removing the diacritics of ë, and by shortening the endings -iy and -yy to -y (Navalny, not Naval'nyy). The soft sign is also omitted in the word 'oblast' (region), understood as part of geographic names.

In reference to English language publications, Russian authors' names are displayed as in the English original (Gel'man, not Gelman). Likewise, Russian organizations with an official English name retain this spelling (Levada Center, not Levada Centre).

Rulers of tsarist Russia are spelled according to English language convention (Alexander II, not Aleksandr II), as are geographical names when such conventions exist (Moscow, not Moskva).

Introduction

This book is about the interplay between law, power, and political control in contemporary Russia. At the centre of attention is selective law enforcement, the discriminate instrumentalization of the legal system for personal or group interests. The Russian politico-legal sphere is replete with double bottoms, shady arrangements, and quasi-legal schemes. Instead of simply outlawing behaviour they see as unacceptable, the ruling elites frequently achieve their goals though the backdoor – pushing formalities in front of them as pretexts.

It seems today that the ideological gain from mimicking Western systems is declining. Indeed, the Kremlin in many respects instead exaggerates differences, facilitating an image of Russia as a unique polity. Whereas democratic rhetoric has been scaled down, however, quasi-legality has persisted. If a human rights activist or former minister is charged with embezzlement, few will take the charges at face value. Many are those, however, who will speculate about whose toes he stepped on. Few outside observers even *care* to look into the legal basis, which is not so strange considering its political subtext. The timing, the targets, and the actors involved all imply political links. From their initiation, cases of selective law enforcement follow a different trajectory than ordinary legal cases. In public debates, they are interpreted as extraordinary, and therefore carry different implications for both the legal and political spheres than would ordinary cases.

Why, then, does the system retain the modicum of legal and purported non-political procedure, even when most observers take it for granted that it is merely for show? Instead of simply outlawing unwanted behaviour or applying repression that ignores law altogether, why does the political leadership keep making, faking, and breaking the same rules? What are the constituent parts, the effects and the consequences of this quasi-legal practice, and what does it tell us about law and power in Russian politics?

The topic and contributions of the book

In this book, I seek a deeper understanding of how and why laws are being used selectively against critics of the Putinist regime, and how this practice makes sense within the broader politico-legal system. Selective law enforcement, I argue, is a practice where two logics of governance collide, the rational-legal and the patronal. Yet, these worlds do not collide by mishap. Instead, they collide on purpose, creating in the process room for ambiguity that can be bent and manipulated.

The prospective contributions of the book may be sorted in three categories: (1) new insights about selective law enforcement as a phenomenon and practice; (2) contributions to our understanding of Putinist politics and law; and (3) new perspectives on law, power, and hybrid governance in authoritarian systems in general.

- **New insights about selective law enforcement as a phenomenon and practice**

A direct aim of the book is to provide a coherent description of what selective law enforcement *is* and how it *works* – in short, to make sense of this genuinely evasive phenomenon. The book is based on a multitude of primary and secondary sources, including my own interview material from the field. With these resources, I define selective law enforcement as *mechanism of repression aimed at enforcing informal rules of political conduct through selective legal acts.* This definition has important implications, not least with regard to the aspects of promulgation and deterrence, essential to rule enforcement. It also implies that selective law enforcement is not law enforcement as such. Instead, the practice relates to the law enforcement system in a parasitic fashion, exploiting law enforcement's muscles and legitimacy for legally irrelevant purposes.

I approach selective law enforcement with a number of qualifiers. First, as hinted at by the term *selective,* the research is concerned with volatile action, or the perception of volatile action. In other words, I disregard unconscious bias in the prosecutors' minds, a topic better discussed within social psychology or behavioural science.[1] Second, I apply the term *law enforcement* in the broadest sense, in relation to both criminal and administrative proceedings, including investigative actions that are seen by targets as selectively imposed and *de facto* punitive, such as selective inspections and raids. The research concerns any legal acts initiated informally for purposes of political repression. I apply the term *broader legal system* to encompass all the official entities involved in this process. Third, while the term selective law enforcement is sometimes used to describe manipulation for economic gain, I am primarily interested in the enforcement mechanism's *political* potential. That being said, it is sometimes hard to draw a line between politics and big business in Russia, especially when we are discussing struggles over political office.[2]

Because motivations and intentions are crucial to what selective law enforcement is, this book also concerns the question of *why.* This book grapples with both the *purposes* of selective law enforcement for individual actors, the structural *incentives* behind it, and its ultimate *impact* in terms of institutionalized repression and the reproduction of the authoritarian system.

On an overarching level, I suggest that selective law enforcement in Russian politics is the product of three sets of complexities.

First, it reflects how authoritarian leaders pursue different and partly contradictory goals at the same time. Rather than pursue one goal to perfection, they want to have their cake and eat it too. They seek fair arbitration *and* political prerogatives, repression *and* legitimacy. For the elites to govern a modern economy and increasingly demanding society, they need an impersonal bureaucratic and legal system. Yet, they also want to keep their positions of power, maintain their extraction of rent, and interfere in the legal system as they please. Even if pursuit of the latter goal retards the achievement of the former, the regime has had some success in combining them.

Second, selective law enforcement is a product of all the individuals who strive to force their will upon the system and make it work for their personal benefit. If you happen to enjoy prerogative access to the purported monopoly on legitimate violence, it can be ever so tempting to direct a portion of this force towards your personal enemies. Because Putin's regime is not simply authoritarian, but also based on personal relations as much as on law, individual or group interests frequently interfere in legal processes.

Third, the interaction between multiple and contradictory ambitions on both the macro level and the micro level are all filtered through a particular legal tradition. In many situations on the ground, the 'purpose' or 'spirit' of a given law is less important than what the law can *do* if you bend and crook it. The book shows how important the tradition of formalism and instrumentalism is to the organization of selective law enforcement on the ground.

• Contributions to our understanding of Putinist politics of law

A red thread to the book is my attempt to situate quasi-legal practices within the broader context of Russian authoritarianism, legal culture, and political development. While this broader perspective permeates the whole book, it appears more condensed in the first few chapters (see below). It is my claim that we can learn something fundamental about Russian politics by examining the peculiar interactions of law and power. Looking at the shadowy world of Russian law enforcement, we may learn more about how Russia works and how legal governance is interwoven with informal politics. The enforcement is selective, yet not arbitrary. By enforcing laws selectively, but systematically, against regime defectors, dissenters, and opposition politicians, the authoritarian regime has enhanced its dominance over public life, demobilized it, and kept civil society on an extra-constitutional leash. In this fashion, the regime found a backdoor solution for suppressing dissent in spite of Russia's constitutional guarantees.

As important as it is to understand the selective instrumentalization of law for political purposes, however, Putin's regime also uses law for much more conventional tasks, much like in a democratic country. Administrative justice has been significantly refurbished under the current regime, and

Russians increasingly use courts to address their grievances. A recurring topic of this book is to highlight the dual characteristics of the politico-legal system, a dualism in which rational-legal and patronal logics of governance unfold in separate, yet interacting spheres. I present the hybridity and dualism of the Russian politico-legal system as a product of both improvisation and path dependencies – a compromise solution to dilemmas posited by the pursuit of contradictory goals.

- **New perspectives on law, power, and hybrid governance in authoritarian systems**

On a higher level of abstraction, the book discusses findings in light of mainstream approaches to authoritarian and hybrid regimes. A key endeavour of political science over the last three decades has been to theorize and classify these regimes in terms of *interactions of opposites,* whether between authoritarianism and democracy, formal and informal institutions, rational-legal and patrimonial governance, or other conceptual pairs. The study of selective law enforcement is in this regard particularly promising terrain, from which we may draw many insights. It constitutes a practice where these interactions of opposites play out in a relatively concrete fashion, if not without complexities. Once the bends have been straightened out and complexities disentangled, the study of selective law enforcement can therefore inform our approaches to institutional hybridity in general. The book also adds to a growing literature on how law actually works in authoritarian and patronal environments, a pressing matter in our times of democratic ebbing.

Law and power in Russian politics

There are two common stereotypes about law and power in Russia, popular both there and abroad. The more prevalent of the two is the myth of Russia as the homeland of lawlessness. Russian citizens are said to disregard law, dodging its application wherever and whenever they can. Tsarist Russia failed to develop a modern legal culture, and Soviet law provided mass repression and spectacular show trials. Compared to their Western counterparts, Russian judges have traditionally been little more than clerks, low on responsibility, payment, and social status. Many are those who see Russia as a country where legal nihilism abounds, counterfeits are everywhere, and the police extract bribes from guilty and innocents alike. To a degree, they are of course right. Russia is not a Rule of Law, but a rule of powerful and wealthy individuals.

On the other hand, Russia is obsessed with law, if you only care to look closer. Shops have customer rights taped on the walls, and politicians keep the constitution at their desks. In Moscow, a hyperactive Duma is producing new draft laws at great speed. Assisted by presidential decrees and dozens of regional legislatures, Russia is a veritable law factory. If Russia may be associated with informal politics and shadowy arrangements, another stereotype connects Russia to *legalism* if not legality – to an incredibly complex bureaucracy with myriads of provisions, regulations, and standards, or to metaphors of an elaborate machinery under the will of a supreme leader. Lenin had a law degree, as does Russia's President Vladimir Putin and several individuals within his closest circle. Western observers tend to neglect 'Putin the Jurist', yet this aspect of the President has been an important part of his personage (Smith 2007). Reflecting this background, he launched his presidency by putting Russia's legal system at the top of the agenda both rhetorically and substantially. Although the hype has since faded, one cannot but be baffled by the continued focus on law in a country where informal politics dominate, corruption is endemic, and personal networks are king. Even when the regime cracks down hard, it often frames it in legal terms. If Russia is not a Rule of Law, it is for a large part ruled *by* law.

Contradictory as these two stereotypes may seem, the Russian obsession with legalism is closely related to its lawlessness. Indeed, the two attributes often reinforce one another. The detailed regulations of the bureaucracy, for instance, is both a source of legal contempt and a result thereof. Russian legal formalism was from the beginning intended to *curb* interpretation, manipulation, and discretionary justice. In practice, however, Russian formalism tends to force discretion out of transparent court proceedings and into extra-legal arenas, feeding into the low-trust spiral. Those who are able to dominate the informal backyards of justice can thus influence legal practice on individual and structural levels.

The marriage between lawlessness and legalism is very visible in a myriad of activities and practices hard to grasp within the popular dichotomies of legal/illegal or formal/informal. These practices, which certainly *relate* to law, yet in a fundamentally ambivalent manner, have caused scholars many a headache. Such practices form in most areas of life where individual interests or norms clash with formal rigidities, and are thus perhaps extra prevalent where the two are not aligned. For the non-jurist, the puzzle cannot be solved by labelling the practices as either legal or illegal, since the very essence of the practices lie exactly in the ambiguous relations to these terms. Even among experts, their legal status seems to be undecided.[3] As a practice, selective law enforcement is inherently and fundamentally quasi-legal. It exploits the letter of formal rules in some way or another, yet it is necessarily based on the *inequality* under law. Some individual cases are clearly illegal, others may be semi-legal, and some even legal in a certain sense. Not in any case, however, does this disturb their quasi-legal essence.

Both Lenin and Putin learned from their studies of law to exploit the legal system to the benefit of their political agendas. From Putin's first term as president, his administration set out to make the legal system more efficient, to make law reach into people's lives – to encourage financial investments and discourage many of the criminals who had been living off the chaos of the post-communist period, including law enforcement officials. At the same time, the reforms did not close the door for the powerful groups to circumvent, manipulate, and interfere in legal affairs. In cases where the ruling elites[4] have concrete interests, they continue to employ the state's muscle for whatever purpose they see fit. In his first term as Russia's president, Putin talked frequently of *diktatura zakona* – the dictatorship of law. Yet, many of the ruling elites acted as if the declared dictator was not theirs to follow. Putin has not aimed to establish a dictatorship, but at best a *stewardship* of law: A system where law was to rule when the real dictators were busy elsewhere.

Putin himself certainly did not invent politicized justice, but his leadership effectively closed a window of opportunity to pursue another path. By persistently intervening in legal procedures, the regime signalled that it would not depart from this old Russian tradition. Whereas political power in the previous decade had been too fragmented to make systematic use of selective law enforcement in regime building, it was under Putin's presidency shaped into a tool of systematic repression of political dissent. Already in his first term as president – and in the midst of legal reform – the Putin administration signalled the continued importance of law as a tool for the powerful. In 2001, The Spanish National Court (*Audiencia Nacional*) refused to extradite the media mogul Vladimir Gusinsky on the basis that his prosecution was politically motivated. A couple of years later, the arrest and trial of oil tycoon Mikhail Khodorkovsky became a worldwide symbol of selective law enforcement. Other cases big and small came to follow. As the years went by, selective law enforcement became a hallmark of Putinism – a symbol for how the regime mixes formal and informal components of governance, personal interests and formal rules, and dazzling intrigues and dull courtrooms. Selective law enforcement came to symbolize the marriage of legality and lawlessness in contemporary Russian politics. Under Putin's leadership, a new quasi-legal order was founded, under which quasi-legal schemes were not eliminated, but gradually co-opted to serve the regime's interests.

The third wave of democracy arguably reached its peak globally somewhere around 2006. Since then, most global democracy ratings have remained relatively stable, with regard to both the number of democracies and their average ratings.[5] The more specific ratings on the Rule of Law and political rights, however, are in downright decline. On the Freedom House index, for instance, the numbers of countries with negative development have since 2006 been persistently outnumbering those with positive development. Many low and mid-income democracies are struggling with a resurgence of neo-patrimonial tendencies, leading to a more ruthless repression of dissent (Diamond 2015).

In such a situation, many political leaders are left with reform-era constitutions and legal systems that suddenly turn out too liberal, impartial, or democratic for their own taste. In the way both Tsar Alexander III (see Chapter 3) and President Putin have had to cope with a legal order too liberal to suit their political preferences, so must also dozens of today's regimes within which the Rule of Law is on the defensive. Counter-reforms may gradually bring the political and legal frameworks into alignment. Yet, an interim period of institutional awkwardness is to be expected in many countries, where nascent elites will try to circumvent and manipulate the inherited legal order for their own purposes. If we get a greater number of authoritarian regimes worldwide, we can expect a swelling number of countries where the inherited empowerment of legal actors are *de facto* undermined by informal politics.

If the numbers and quality of liberal democracies continue to decline, theories and knowledge about legal orders under authoritarian pressure are particularly valuable for understanding developments today and in the future. As Moustafa (2014, 294) suggests, it may even be a good idea to turn the tables and use models and insights from the study of authoritarian legality to better understand phenomena in established democracies (in the spirit of Pereira 2008; Law 2010; Landau 2013). The structured study of Putinist legality plays a natural part in the development of such models. Emerging from the ashes of flawed liberal reforms in the early 1990s, Russia started under Putin to build up a new system of hybrid legality. The emerging system represented a pragmatic adaptation of an inherited institutional system to fit the needs and visions of resurgent authoritarianism.

Perspectives on law, power, and selective law enforcement

Understood as a political tool, the selective enforcement of law is well known. It is one of Russia's 'open secrets'; everybody knows about this deviance from the official rules, yet only an exclusive minority is aware of the details. Both domestically and internationally, selective law enforcement is frequently commented upon in human rights discourse, mass media, and academic research with roughly the same meaning. Commentators implicitly or explicitly condemn the practice because the legal reasoning in these cases differs sharply from what they see as the *real* motive for prosecution. The moral indignation presumably stems from a feeling of being lied to, from the illegitimacy of the perceived goals, or from a combination of these aspects. In addition, the practice obviously violates the principle of equality before the law, formally in high esteem even in modern autocracies.

Most professional researchers on Russian state and society would probably agree that informal or quasi-formal arrangements are important aspects of Russian politics (Sakwa 2011; Hale 2015). Studies of repression and coercive capabilities in contemporary Russia, moreover, confirm that such arrangements are important for suppressing dissenting voices (Robertson 2011; Taylor 2011; Horvath 2013; Gel'man 2015). A few works also examine 'politicized justice' in the electoral system at some length (Popova 2012). A step to the side of political repression, there is also literature on selective instrumentalization of legal tools in the post-Communist Russian economy (Yakovlev and Zhuravskaya 2009; Firestone 2010). A rather different approach to informal practices, including their relation to Russia law, can be found in numerous works of Alena Ledeneva (2006; 2013; 2018).

Yet, there are to date no books that approach selective law enforcement as a broad phenomenon and in a systematic fashion. The few studies that address selective law enforcement in Russia at some length tend to take recourse to circumstantial evidence and journalistic (often English-language) sources. Alternatively they focus on a few well-known cases, typically with Khodorkovsky in a major role. Importantly, these works tend to lack in theoretical or conceptual ambitions (Kvurt 2007; Burger and Holland 2008; Knoops and Amsterdam 2008; Sakwa 2014; Kahn 2018). My earlier works on selective law enforcement (Bækken 2009) and electoral registration (Bækken 2015) provide rare exceptions to this rule.

In addition to the above scholars who often focus on post-Soviet countries exclusively, also comparatists have a similar understanding of selective law enforcement in authoritarian politics and governance. In their work too, however, selective law enforcement mostly figures in the background of analysis and does not get the careful attention it deserves. Perhaps the most explicit conceptualization of the practice has been formulated by Steven Levitsky and Lucan Way, who describe selective law enforcement with reference to both its coercive and hybrid qualities:

> *Competitive authoritarian governments also employ informal mechanisms of repression. For example, many of them use 'legal' repression, or the discretionary use of legal instruments – such as tax authorities and libel laws – to target opposition and the media. Although such repression is formal in the sense that it entails the (often technically correct) application of the law, it is an informal institution in that enforcement is widely known to be selective. (Levitsky and Way 2010, 26–28)*

Levitsky and Way's conceptualization of selective law enforcement is in some respects close to the one I suggest in this book. They approach selective law enforcement as a form of institutionalized repression and link it to regime politics. Moreover, they open a door for discussing selective law enforcement in relation to regime types and broader institutional characteristics. Finally, Levitsky and Way indicate willingness to approach the peculiar hybrid characteristics of the phenomenon – holding it to be formal and informal in different 'senses.' Instead of exploring the interesting implications thereof, however, they conclude their discussion by dumping the phenomenon in a large conceptual sack together with all sorts of extra-legal practices used by authoritarian incumbents. In contrast to Levitsky and Way's conceptualization, my own approach actively challenges the reduction of selective law enforcement to a façade. I also take the hybrid characteristics of selective law enforcement into more consistent consideration and grapple with the conceptual problems this hybridity stirs up. Finally, where the two comparatists allot a few paragraphs to their discussion, I devote a full book to my elaboration.

Summarized, selective law enforcement is widely recognized as an important practice, yet it lacks structured attention. On the one hand, it is hard to see how the underlying ideas in the scholarly literature differ from the concept of selective law enforcement that I suggest in this study. On the other hand, the existing literature rarely fleshes out the concept to such a degree that conclusions regarding its meaning can be firmly established. Instead, readers are left to their own interpretations and have to make inferences from the idiom's semantics and the referential environment. In short, the authors make little attempt to fix the fluid associations into a harder scientific concept that can be used in systematic research. As it seems, most authors have been content with an implicit understanding of selective law enforcement as something that is hard to describe, but instantly recognizable when spotted. However, as some credit Bertrand Russell for saying: "Everything is vague to a degree you do not realize till you have tried to make it precise". The moderate attention granted the phenomenon has so far failed to accumulate any significant knowledge as to how selective law enforcement actually works.

Beyond colloquial language and legal concepts

The Russian constitution guarantees equality before the law, but has no legal concepts to deal specifically with political prosecution. Neither does the Russian language have any concept of selective law enforcement as such. Granted, selective law enforcement may be directly translated into Russian as *izbiratel'noye pravoprimeneniye* or *izbiratel'noye primeneniye zakona*. At the very least, these terms are usually understood among my interviewees and their colleagues. Yet, the idioms are not native to the language in which Russians commonly frame their experiences with legal abuse. Reflecting the country's legal traditions, the most popular colloquial terms surrounding quasi-legal practices – such as 'administrative resources' (*administrativnyye resursy*), 'political technologies' (*politicheskiye tekhnologii*), 'telephone justice' (*telefonnoye pravo*), and 'Basman jurisdiction' (*basmannoye pravosudiye*) – do not stress the element of legality. Instead, they focus on power and manipulative skills.

My approach fully incorporates the perspective of legal instrumentality, which is so crucial to quasi-legal repression in Russia. In contrast to the Russian terms mentioned above, however, my concept of selective law enforcement has been tailored especially for the purposes of academic development, research transparency, and cross-case transferability. I stress legality to a greater degree than the native terms, because it is exactly through a careful look at the legal element that we get to differentiate legal abuse from other means of repression.

For different reasons, we should also resist the temptation to employ a foreign legal concept to substitute for the lack of a Russian one. The U.S. legal concept of 'selective prosecution' is well developed and displays significant similarities to selective law enforcement in Russia. Yet, a significant weakness of any legal approach to selective law enforcement is arguably its self-imposed disciplinarian boundaries. My own study of selective law enforcement is concerned with its social and political significance – a significance that greatly exceeds its legal relevance. In addition, a legal approach to selective law enforcement may presumably fail to see how the practice by definition is native to the twilight zone between legal and illegal practices. Selective law enforcement indeed illustrates some of the problems with making law the ultimate concept of what is right or important. Being aware of how ambiguities created by the legal system may be exploited provides a first step to understanding what selective law enforcement *is* and thus also *why it is.*

The focus on specifically legal tools allows us to ask several important questions: Why exactly is law such a popular tool of repression? In what ways is law related to power? What legal documents are utilized in the process? Which legal issue areas are most relevant? Notions like telephone justice and Basman jurisdiction do not provide a path for exploring such questions. Instead, they simply assert that the law is subordinated to power and the powerful. A closer examination of what role law plays in selective law enforcement helps us understand how the practice functions, how it relates to legal affairs, and why Western observers are so upset about it.

Even if the U.S. legal approach will not be discussed further in this book, I will occasionally quote Robert H. Jackson, then Attorney General in the U.S. and later prosecutor in the Nurnberg trials. Indeed, one of the best quotes to catch the gist of selective law enforcement in Russia today actually belongs to him. In Jackson's time, the legal concept was not entirely developed, and Jackson presumably had a broader phenomenon in mind.

> *If the prosecutor is obliged to choose his cases, it follows that he can choose his defendants. Therein is the most dangerous power of the prosecutor: that he will pick people that he thinks he should get, rather than pick cases that need to be prosecuted ... It is here that law enforcement becomes personal, and the real crime becomes that of being unpopular with the predominant or governing group, being attached to the wrong political views, or being personally obnoxious to, or in the way of, the prosecutor himself. (Jackson 1940, 19)*

We may expect selective law enforcement to be particularly popular in those authoritarian systems resembling contemporary Russia – with extended constitutional rights, a formally empowered and independent judiciary, and a degree of investment in democratic rhetoric, yet where all these are attributes are circumscribed *informally*. At the same time, the Jackson quote illustrates that selective law enforcement may take place in many societies and at different times. The quote also illustrates how the practice is not simply a question of judicial dependence and interference, but for a large part takes place in upstream law enforcement – the realm of prosecutors, police officials, special departments, pre-trial investigators, and related 'independent experts' – in interaction with external interests. Jackson also hints toward the authoritarian potential of the practice, and simultaneously to its possible personalization. As we will see, Jackson's warning from 1940 is strikingly relevant for selective law enforcement in today's Russia.

A three-layered concept of selective law enforcement

To unravel its complexity, I operate with a differentiation between the concept's basic, analytical, and operational levels. The relationship between the levels are noncausal – the components "*constitute* what the phenomenon is" (Goertz 2006, 15). Selective law enforcement, according to my definition, presupposes (or is constituted by) the components of informal selectivity, formal legal acts, and a link between them. This basic claim makes for the analytical level in the provided figure (Figure 0.1). Each of these three components in turn presupposes (or is constituted by) more basic building blocks that can be observed systematically – the operational level of the concept. Informal selectivity (in law enforcement) presupposes *selectors* and informal criteria for selection,

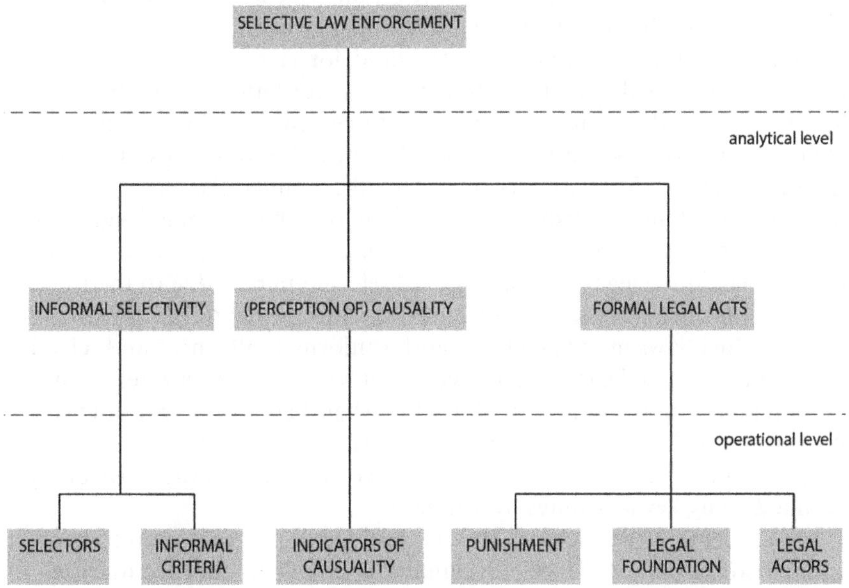

Figure 0.1 A three-layered concept of selective law enforcement.

while law enforcement presupposes a legal foundation, legal actors, and legal sanctions/punishment. The perceived link between the informal selection and the formal legal acts presupposes an indicator of causality – a pointer to why the link is perceived to be there. This is also an observable entity. Taken together, the conceptual components in Figure 0.1 form a road map for the conceptual analysis of selective law enforcement in part II of this book. The systematic examination makes us able to expand our knowledge of the core functions of the practice, identify variance, and expand the complexity of analysis.

On the methods and sources of this study

Because there is no pre-established literature to build a concept of selective law enforcement upon, I seek in this book to create a baseline for this field of study. For the same reason, I approach the topic broadly and qualitatively. The book scrutinizes the interlinkages of law and power from a multitude of angles, borrowing perspectives from law and socio-legal studies, history, political science, sociology, and anthropology. My source material includes primary and secondary literature, ranging from case files, law texts and court resolutions, via regional newspapers and NGO reports, to regime theory and the philosophy of law. As will be discussed in the next section, the book also draws extensively upon interviews with actors in the field. While the insights derived from the fieldwork indirectly inform the entire book, the interviewees' specific stories come to forth only in later chapters (especially Chapters 7, 9, and 10).

In the second part of the book, three legal issue areas get special attention. First, I dwell on Russian election law, specifically on the registration or non-registration of candidates to stand for elections. Second, I look into cases of alleged selective enforcement of legislation on extremism and hate crime. Third, I examine selective enforcement of software copyrights, including claims of abuse and their legal context. Sporadic cases from other legal issue areas add to the caseload. On all accounts, the particular cases were identified by extensive and repeated searches among English and Russian language sources, including various state, NGO, and mass media reports. The three legal issue areas were selected in part due to their popularity in quasi-legal schemes, and in part for how they highlight the different ways in which laws may open the door for informal influences and selective enforcement. To make this inquiry coherent with the interview research, the focus remains on the period of 2007-2011 when I conducted my interviews. As I argue in Chapter 7, the three case studies should be understood as peepholes into practices that have slowly evolved through the Putin era, yet retained many key attributes over time.

My concern in this book is Russia, and I will not venture into explicit comparisons. Indeed, I seek explanations partly in the peculiarities of Russian politics and legal culture. Yet, I believe this study can shed light on how authoritarian leaders may cope with legality also in other countries and at different points of time. As noted by Moustafa (2014, 293), "theorizing about law and courts in authoritarian regimes is most accurate and compelling when it is informed by 'close-to-the-ground' empirical data and … a rich knowledge of the local political ecology". Taking the local concepts into account provides an important checkpoint so as not to let artificial and rigid models from outside impede our understanding of a phenomenon examined in a cultural context. While they may be very telling, however, colloquial terms from the native environment are hardly a good foundation for academic concept development. As has been argued elsewhere, the study of today's authoritarian regimes needs research "with the explicit goal of midrange theory building and concept formation" (Morse 2012, 189). For this reason, I structure my concepts and models with the purpose of being *transferable* to other contexts.

On interviews and perceptions

During the course of two years (2010-2011) I conducted interviews in nine regional capitals and four other locations in Russia.[6] In addition, I conducted several interviews in Moscow relating to conflicts elsewhere in the country. All the interviews and examined cases are from the North-West, Central, South, Volga, and Ural federal districts. The caseload I use for my study largely consists of cases well known in the regional opposition networks. Many cases have been discussed in the local and regional press, not least online, but are unknown to most foreigners without special interest in quasi-legal repression or human rights. The interviewees can be divided into *self-defined targets* on the one hand and *experts* on the other. Various activists, journalists, and editors, representing either themselves or their organizations and media outlets, dominate the former of the two groups. The latter group consists of political scientists, lawyers, and others who work professionally on civil rights issues in Russia, in addition to experts on the specific legal issue areas and their politicization. Readers should be aware that a number of experts possibly and probably are biased. It should be mentioned that some who have experienced selective law enforcement engage in extensive information retrieval to accumulate knowledge on the topic. Experts speaking frankly on these issues, moreover, tend to eventually experience similar practices themselves. For these two reasons, the two overlap to some degree. In addition, one should be aware of the fact that political scientists in Russia may also be involved in election campaigns as consultants or may also have party affiliations of their own. In addition to the mentioned two groups of self-defined targets and experts, I refer to a small number of interviews with relatives, defence attorneys, or other sources close to the self-defined targets of quasi-legal crackdowns.

Even though I scrutinize selective law enforcement from many angles and perspectives, parts of the analysis draw strongly upon interview material and the *perceptions* of the phenomenon. This implies that the research gives ear to one side of a socio-political conflict. The conflict is also a conceptual struggle and a fight between narratives – the antagonists in my interviewees' stories would certainly not accept my framing of the issues. To lend an ear to predominantly one side in a conflict is not a problem in itself, but the ambitions of the researcher should surely be adjusted accordingly – perceptions of other people's political motivations should not be confused with the political motivations themselves. In qualitative interview research, all an observer can do is to interpret the already interpreted reality (Giddens 1976).

Perceptions of social phenomena are important. First, human beliefs about the world constitute an important part of our social and psychological reality and are worthy of attention in their own right. Second, our beliefs bear direct impact upon the 'real' world of politics and society. The impact of beliefs upon the tangible world is particularly evident when considering selective law enforcement as a mechanism to enforce informal rules. A central argument of this book is built upon the theory of deterrence, which is "first and foremost a perceptual theory. Whether a punishment threat deters depends not on the certainty, celerity, or severity of punishment in any objective sense but on the potential offender's perception" (Gibbs 2007, 371). As the argument goes, if you do not know why you have been punished, you cannot be expected to change your behaviour accordingly. In short, it is up to the punished to interpret which rule is *actually* being enforced and whether it is a formal, or rather an unwritten one. In addition, if targets of prosecution *experience* that they are being punished, the rule enforcement mechanism will function regardless of whether this punishment is officially recognized as such or not. In short, the 'perceptive' aspects of selective law enforcement are arguably as important for the outcome of the practice as are the 'substantive' ones (see Chapter 10).

Giving self-perceived targets of selective law enforcement a chance to speak of such enforcement is therefore more than a second best option. These targets possess information about their cases that we cannot expect regime insiders or law enforcement officials to have. While insiders have a powerful hand in manipulating outcomes, it remains up to the prosecuted and observers to interpret these outcomes politically. The targets also have the best overview regarding indirect consequences, such as effects of shaming, scaring away employees and partners, and so on.

The structure of this book

In addition to the Introduction and Concluding remarks, this book consists of two parts, mutually informing each other. The first part deals with the larger issues of law, power, and repression in Russia, as well as concerns under authoritarian or neopatrimonial conditions in general. For readers relatively new to Russian law and politics, Chapters 2 and 3 contain useful background material, while Chapters 1 and 4 are more theoretical in nature (details below). In the second part of the book, I present a more focused study of selective law enforcement.

The first part of the book begins with Chapter 1, where I consider the relevance of a few theoretical clusters that inform the scholarly discussion of law and power in authoritarian contexts. However ruthless they may be, authoritarian leaders cannot simply disregard formal elements of governance, least of all law. On the contrary, authoritarian governance is dependent upon many functions of law and even upon an independent judiciary. At the same time, authoritarians do not want law to 'stand in the way' of repression and rent seeking. Key to my inquiry is how authoritarian regimes attune their institutional setup to satisfy these complex demands. The chapter concludes by considering some shortcomings of institutional hybridity and quasi-legal governance, yet concludes that these arrangements are not necessarily mishaps nor attempts to fool observers. From the point of view of the regime, quasi-legality *works*, even if imperfectly.

Whereas the insights presented in Chapter 1 can provide a comparative basis and make us understand the rationality of Russia's institutional set-up, it can hardly explain the behaviour of individual actors within its law enforcement system. On the ground, most actors think little about regime types when going about their business and reproducing the patterns of quasi-legal governance. Rather, they consciously or unconsciously answer to expectations of other actors, such as their patrons, professional peers, and society. Chapter 2 therefore revisits the Russian legal tradition, adding particular emphasis on its instrumentalism, formalism, and disconnect from public morals. These tendencies have persistently shaped the interaction of law and power throughout the jagged history of Russian statehood. As will be clear in the course of this book, this legal culture continues to shape quasi-legal practices today. For a large part, the nihilistic attitudes to law that we can see among many Russians stem from a vicious circle of low expectations that are continuously reproduced by persistent abuse.

The third and fourth chapters deal with law and power in Putinist Russia from two different angles. They share a common topic, however, in discussing important tendencies of Russian politics under Putin's dominance. I show in Chapter 3 how the continuous centralization drive since the turn of the century simultaneously amassed power within the central state *and* within Putin's patronal system. The centralization drive was very broadly constituted, moving power from the regions to Moscow, but also from the legislative to the executive branch and from the executive branch to the person of the president. At the same time, Putin did much to strengthen and stabilize the Russian state. In his first period of presidency, he oversaw considerable reforms that gave a much needed boost to legal performance. The legal reforms increased the state's capacity to provide 'everyday justice' to the Russian population and reduced petty corruption in the legal system. However, the reforms hardly challenged the political prerogatives of the ruling elites. The broad centralization instead resulted in increased regime control over legal actors and thus also over quasi-legal practices. In Russia under Putin, therefore, these tools became less of an external challenge, and more of an integrated part of the political regime.

Chapter 4 grapples with Russia's politico-legal duality on a higher level of abstraction, employing the Dual State model as introduced by Ernst Fraenkel (1941). While I am not the first to employ this model to understand Putin's Russia, my analysis delves on the model's theoretical insights at greater length than previous studies. Not only does the semi-autonomous legal system grant a degree of legitimacy and efficiency to the state. Its relative empowerment also raises the cost of manipulating it for personal ends, This has under Putin limited the access to selective law enforcement to a relatively small group of insiders that possess the power and privileges to intervene. The chapter also discusses how the Russian population over time has been primed to interpret ordinary and exceptional cases as belonging to separate realms. As this book will illustrate, this has important ramifications for Russian governance.

Chapters 5 through 9 deal with selective law enforcement in more detail, bringing new evidence and concepts to the table. In Chapter 5, I examine the basic functioning of selective law enforcement and utilize various typologies and perspectives to confront its hybrid character head on. How exactly should we understand the interactions between legal and extra-legal components? The selective enforcement of law, I argue, challenges some core assumptions of mainstream approaches to institutional interactions. The discussion concludes that the informal component of selective law enforcement essentially enjoys a parasitic relation to its 'host' institution, which makes it dependent upon *both* the host's strengths and its weaknesses. In this chapter, I also lay out the mechanics of selective law enforcement as a mechanism to enforce informal rules. This approach has wide reaching implications, not least concerning rule *promulgation* and *deterrence*. In this line of argument, I also suggest that the political and legal issues of a given case can be understood as two different rule propositions. The ambiguity of the practice, I argue, stems from the overlap and conscious entanglement of these rules. By putting this ambiguity to use, manipulators can play upon both political and legal discourses opportunistically to distort and deflect criticism.

Chapter 6 introduces the readers to three legal issue areas rife with quasi-legal controversies, and familiarizes them with some specific cases and interviewees. The chapter discusses the topics of election registration, anti-extremism, and copyrights in turn, with particular stress on controversial cases and the legal provisions actually utilized in them. To ensure that the interviewees' perceptions are presented in their correct context, I review the specific legal provisions as they appeared at the time. These case studies should preferably be read as *examples* of how laws can be utilized selectively. Even if specific provisions come and go, the underlying logics of weak laws are presumably similar to that of other laws, other times, and other countries. The interviewees that claim to have been politically prosecuted are not so often complaining that they are not guilty as charged. More pervasively, they focus their criticism on what they see as double standards and not least the weak laws that make the prosecution possible. The context-rich analysis however, shows that quasi-legality can be anchored in rather different ways within different legal issue areas.

Chapter 7 continues this discussion by zooming in on the role of laws in selective law enforcement. I present a *typology of incoherence* to show various ways laws may be construed exactly for quasi-legal purposes. Common among the utilized laws is how they create a legal environment in which everyone may be framed for legal violations, at least for purposes of preliminary investigations. With regard to selective law enforcement, then, the legal formulations are important by virtue of how they open doors for backroom solutions and bend easily when pressure is added. While the incoherence of the formal framework lubricates the quasi-legal prosecution, however, it cannot by itself adequately explain the phenomenon. After all, vague or flexible laws are present in well-functioning legal systems too, without repressive consequences. In order to make sense of the practice, we therefore need to integrate the incoherence-perspective with authoritarian rationality as well as the peculiarities of the Russian legal tradition.

Chapter 8 focuses on the informal games surrounding quasi-legal repression, and how they interact with the legal pretexts. Here, I give much space to the interviewees, sorting and interpreting their original perceptions of various aspects of selective law enforcement. On some accounts, the perceptions of the interviewees are key to the practice itself. It is for instance the perception of why a case has been initiated that determine the response, rather than the actual motivations behind it. Moreover, the interviewees have the only real information as to why they came to interpret a case in this way, equally essential for the functioning of the mechanism of rule enforcement. On other issues, the interviewee statements represent informed opinions on how we may expect quasi-legal practice to take form within the power vertical and among the law enforcement actors. Their answers on who are behind the crackdowns, what their motivations may be, and how they have communicated their wishes to the legal actors cannot be considered evidence as such. Yet, considering the experience and expertise of the interviewees, their contributions are still valuable to our understanding of the practice.

Chapter 9 deals with the impact of selective law enforcement, both for the prosecuted individuals and for society at large. Unsurprisingly, the persecution brings about a range of negative effects for the involved, ranging from stigmatization and organizational recruitment problems to prison sentences and broken families. In many of the examined cases, however, no legal sanctions were ever imposed, even if the prosecution was seemingly conducted on political request. Central to understanding this fact is not only to recognize the partial autonomy of Russian courts, but also to realize how the constant quasi-legal attention works to produce punishment before a case actually reaches the courtroom. Punishment must necessarily be understood subjectively, since it is the perceptions of unequal treatment that produces the deterring effects. If the political message can be delivered successfully without formal legal sanctions, this is just as good or perhaps better for the authoritarian leaders. A pre-trial investigation may seem less outrageous to the public, but may very well be serious enough to deter most Russians from oppositional activities. Meanwhile, the activists and critics of the regime spend precious time and resources to endure what often amounts to a hailstorm of legal claims, obviously reducing their capabilities to conduct activities harmful to the regime. In this chapter, I also discuss how quasi-legality is gradually being institutionalized as law enforcers internalize the authoritarian rules of the game and eventually produce skewed enforcement patterns without the need for either repressive laws or direct commands from above. In the brief concluding chapter, I summarize my main findings and arguments and offer some remarks on the persistence of quasi-legality for the years to come.

Notes

1. As we know predominantly from U.S. research on social psychology, prosecutors and not least jurors tend to routinely discriminate on a range of extra-legal criteria such as race, social status, or general attractiveness.
2. Some scholars use the term 'selective law enforcement' with the meaning of policing or prosecution strategies under strained resources (Kleinig 1998). Within such a conception, selective law enforcement may for instance include giving priority to the more serious violations (within a legal category) before the less serious ones. A related form of selective law non-enforcement is known to take place where the small fish in a criminal network may be released on the premise that they become police informants. In these accounts, selectivity is a neutral term and does not itself indicate abuse. In a positive sense, overly harsh laws may even be compensated for through selective law enforcement.
3. Consider for instance the wavering interpretation of the legal status of corporate raiding (*reyderstvo*) in Russia in scholarly literature, represented for instance by Firestone (2010), Mesquita (2018), and Barsukova and Ledeneva (2018).
4. Field and Higley (1980, 20) define elites as "persons occupying strategic positions in public and private bureaucratic organizations". The notion of *ruling* elites underscores this aspect of elitism, favouring positions of political power instead of cultural capital, education level, etc.
5. See Levitsky and Way (2015) for a critical perspective on 'the myth' of democratic recession, and Diamond (2015) in the same issue for a contrastive approach.
6. In a few cases, I have anonymized interviewees on request. Most of the others, however, are semi-anonymized on the author's initiative. Because of the harsher political climate in Russia today than at the time of the interviews, the interviewee names do not show in the manuscript. At the same time, readers with intimate knowledge of the field can possibly recognize some of the cases. The semi-anonymized interviewees are not formally referred to in the notes or in the bibliography, but I provide the necessary information about their positions and role in the study in the main text. To make this degree of anonymization

meaningful, some journalistic articles that support and clarify issues from the fieldwork have been suppressed. As for the interviewees, I have made exceptions for a couple of internationally recognized scholars making statements within their acknowledged expertise, namely Arkady Lyubarev on regional election and Aleksandr Verkhovsky on anti-extremist enforcement.

References

Barsukova, S. & Ledeneva, A. 2018. Concluding remarks to Volume 2. Are Some Countries More Informal than Others? The Case of Russia. *In:* Ledeneva. A (ed.) *The Global Encyclopaedia of Informality. Understanding Social and Cultural Complexity. Volume 2.* London: UCL Press.

Burger, E. S. & Holland, M. 2008. Law as Politics. The Russian Procuracy and its Investigative Committee. *Columbia Journal of East European Law*, 2, 143–194.

Bækken, H. 2009. Selective Law Enforcement against Russian NGOs. Pursuing Informal Interests through Formal Means. *NUPI report.* Oslo: Norwegian Institute of International Affairs.

2015. Selections before Elections. Double Standards in Implementing Election Registration Procedures in Russia? *Communist and Post-Communist Studies*, 48, 61–70.

Diamond, L. 2015. Facing Up to the Democratic Recession. *Journal of Democracy*, 26, 141–155.

Field, G. L. & Higley, J. 1980. *Elitism.* London: Routledge.

Firestone, T. 2010. Armed Injustice. Abuse of Law and Complex Crime in Post-Soviet Russia. *Denver Journal of International Law and Policy*, 38, 555–580.

Fraenkel, E. 1941. *The Dual State. A Contribution to the Theory of Dictatorship.* New York: Oxford University Press.

Gel'man, V. 2015. The Politics of Fear. How the Russian Regime Confronts Its Opponents. *Russian Politics and Law*, 53, 6–26.

Gershman, B. L. 2008. The Most Dangerous Power of the Prosecutor. *Pace Law Review*, 29, 1–28.

Gibbs, J. 2007. Deterrence Theory and Research. *In:* Macaulay, S., Friedman, L. M. & Mertz, E. (eds.). *Law in Action. A Socio-Legal Reader.* New York: Foundation Press.

Giddens, A. 1976. *New Rules of Sociological Method. A Positive Critique of Interpretative Sociologies.* New York: Basic Books.

Goertz, G. 2006. *Social Science Concepts. A User's Guide.* Princeton: Princeton University Press.

Hale, H. 2015. *Patronal Politics. Eurasian Regime Dynamics in Comparative Perspective.* New York: Cambridge University Press.

Horvath, R. 2013. *Putin's Preventive Counter-Revolution. Post-Soviet Authoritarianism And the Spectre of Velvet Revolution.* Oxon: Routledge.

Jackson, R. H. 1940. The Federal Prosecutor. *Journal of the American Judicature Society* 24, 18–20.

Kahn, J. 2018. The Richelieu Effect. The Khodorkovsky Case and Political Interference with Justice. *In*: Kurkchiyan, M. & Kubal, A. (eds.) *A Sociology of Justice in Russia. Cambridge*: Cambridge University Press.

Kleinig, J. 1998. Selective Law Enforcement and the Rule of Law. *Journal of Social Philosophy*, 29, 117–131.

Knoops, G. J. A. & Amsterdam, R. R. 2007. The Duality of State Cooperation within International and National Criminal Cases. *Fordham International Law Journal*, 30, 260–295.

Kvurt, Y. 2007. Selective Prosecution in Russia. Myth or Reality. *Cardozo Journal of International & Comparative Law*, 15, 127–168.

Landau, D. 2013. Abusive Constitutionalism. *UC Davis Law Review*, 47, 189–260.

Law, D. S. 2010. How to Rig the Federal Courts. *Georgetown Law Review*, 99, 779–835.

Ledeneva, A. 2006. *How Russia Really Works. The Informal Practices That Shaped Post-Soviet Politics and Business*. Ithaca: Cornell University Press.

2013. *Can Russia Modernise? Sistema, Power Networks and Informal Governance*. Cambridge: Cambridge University Press.

2018. (ed.) *The Global Encyclopaedia of Informality. Understanding Social and Cultural Complexity*. London: UCL Press.

Levitsky, S. & Way, L. 2010. *Competitive Authoritarianism. Hybrid Regimes after the Cold War*. Cambridge: Cambridge University Press.

2015. The Myth of Democratic Recession. *Journal of Democracy*, 45–58.

Mesquita, M. 2018. Reiderstvo (Russia and FSU). *In:* Ledeneva. A (ed.) *The Global Encyclopaedia of Informality. Understanding Social and Cultural Complexity. Volume 2*. London: UCL Press.

Morse, Y. L. 2012. The Era of Electoral Authoritarianism. *World Politics*, 64, 161–198.

Moustafa, T. 2014. Law and Courts in Authoritarian Regimes. *Annual Review of Law and Social Science*, 10, 281–299.

Pereira, A. W. 2008. Of Judges and Generals. *In:* Ginsburg, T. & Moustafa, T. (eds.) *Rule by Law. The Politics of Courts in Authoritarian Regimes*. New York: Cambridge University Press.

Popova, M. 2012. *Politicized Justice in Emerging Democracies. A Study of Courts in Russia and Ukraine*. Cambridge: Cambridge University Press.

Robertson, G. B. 2011. *The Politics of Protest in Hybrid Regimes. Managing Dissent in Post-Communist Russia*. Cambridge: Cambridge University Press.

Sakwa, R. 2011. *The Crisis of Russian Democracy. The Dual State, Factionalism and the Medvedev Succession*. Cambridge: Cambridge University Press.

2014. *Putin and the Oligarchs: The Khodorkovsky-Yukos Affair*. New York: Tauris & Co.

Smith, G. B. 1997. The Struggle over the Procuracy. *In:* Solomon, P. H. J. (ed). *Reforming Justice in Russia 1864-1966. Power, Culture, and the Limits of Legal Order*. New York: M.E. Sharpe.

Taylor, B. D. 2011. *State Building in Putin's Russia. Policing and Coercion after Communism*. Cambridge: Cambridge University Press.

Yakovlev, E. & Zhuravskaya, E. 2009. State Capture. From Yeltsin to Putin. *In:* Kornai, J. E. A. (ed.). *Corruption, Development and Institutional Design*. International Economic Association conference.

Part I

Law and power in Russian politics

1 Law and power in authoritarian regimes

Research and perspectives

Before I turn to the specifics of the Russian case, a discussion of existing research on law and power in general is worthwhile. Not only do the findings of these studies give us a better understanding of the how law and power are related to each other in authoritarian regimes. Also, the study of selective law enforcement can contribute to developing our general understanding of this rationale. The following chapter introduces two theoretical clusters particularly relevant to our inquiry into law and power in Russia. First, it deals with regime theory and in particular with the role of informality and personal power within these perspectives. While previous debates on 'hybrid regimes' often concern 'soft' authoritarian systems, I maintain that the perspectives these debates establish are just as important for 'harder' and more consolidated authoritarian systems like Russia, as long as they retain their fundamental institutional hybridity. Second, the chapter elaborates on existent perspectives on authoritarian regimes and their relation to legal governance. Existing knowledge on how law works as a tool of authoritarian governance is vital for our discussions through the entire book. The discussion also explains why semi-autonomous legal systems, and courts in particular, can make sense for modern authoritarians or even autocrats. I conclude the chapter by briefly considering the strengths and shortcomings of hybrid governance from an authoritarian regime perspective.

Contemporary authoritarianism as interacting opposites

While informality exists in all political systems, its pervasiveness became a focus of attention within political science only in recent decades. The attention reflected the mushrooming of new states and regimes in the post-Cold War environment. The point was not so much that these regimes were now more informal than earlier. Rather, the challenges of the so-called transition processes at the time highlighted how detrimental some of the informal practices were for the functioning of the new formal institutions. As the reforms were often modelled on the findings of political science and economics, it became imperative for these disciplines to understand the reasons why they frequently failed. Scholars found some explanations within the countries themselves. Instead of embracing a full-fledged transition to a new institutional platform, they seemed to mix it with *something else*. The analysis of this 'else' became a chief undertaking in the study of many post-communist countries.

In this endeavour, a standard approach became applying ideal models as a baseline, and then looking at deviations from these models. Scholars repeatedly discussed modern authoritarianism in terms of *interacting opposites* – be it between democracy and authoritarianism, state and regime, or patrimonial and rational-legal legitimacy. In the early 1990s, the so-called diminishing subtypes conceptualizations proliferated, put together by ideal types (usually democracy) and adjectives to qualify them (Collier and Levitsky 1997). The qualifier was often tracked back to political culture, path dependencies, or informal practices and institutions that constituted the 'something else' interacting with, and often contradicting, the formal institutional order. Side by side with these regime-type classifications emerged typologies of institutional interactions, reflecting efforts to explain and sort out how different types of informal behaviour come to complement, accommodate, or subvert formal institutions.

As the deviations from democratic ideal models became more apparent and many regimes seemed to head in other directions, the branding of these political systems as 'democracies with adjectives' became less conceptually appealing. In 2002, Thomas Carothers declared the transition paradigm dead. About the same time, the academic mainstream shifted away from transition perspectives. The interaction-of-opposites-approach, however, remained the most popular point of departure. The notion of 'hybrid regimes' (Diamond 2002), and 'competitive authoritarianism' (Levitsky and Way 2002) became particularly popular and remain so today. An increasing number of scholars deserted theoretical perspectives from the post-Cold War era, and instead underscored the need to understand how these new regimes 'really work' – a phrase which over time become a catchphrase in the research on authoritarianism.

In light of the developments of Putin's third term (from 2012), more sinister terms like a 'fascist political system' (Motyl 2016) and 'personalist autocracy' (Fish 2017) appeared in the interpretive landscape. Yet, Russia remains fundamentally hybrid, institutionally speaking. Even if the Putin regime moves towards embracing full-blown authoritarianism, Russia can still boast institutions we hardly associate with old-school dictatorships. Regardless of how resilient authoritarianism may be in today's Russia, the country remains strongly influenced by the formal trappings of the post-Cold War order.

Façade theories

The post-Cold War environment was marked not only by scholarly classification of regimes according to normative ideal types. More importantly, the 'winners' of the Cold War saw in the communist collapse their chance to turn their ideals into reality in a far greater portion of the world. By an unprecedented conditionality for loans, aid, and memberships in international organizations, they aspired to shape the world in their image. In retrospect, however, these efforts have been criticized as "superficial, selective, and inconsistent" (Levitsky and Way 2010, 19). Through a formalistic and reductive approach to democratization, privatization, and the Rule of Law, "the international environment created incentives for incumbents to employ informal mechanisms of coercion and control while maintaining the formal architecture of democracy" (ibid., 27). One consequence was the emergence of what Jowitt (1996) called *mimic democracies;* "Formalistic more than formal, truce rather than true democracies, based on floundering not founding elections".[1]

Some years later, several scholars focusing on the post-Soviet politics era trotted the same conceptual path.[2] In Dmitri Furman's (2007) terms, Russia became a "counterfeit" or "imitation democracy", and its constitution a "fig-leaf". Several authors allude to the fake villages that legendary Russian statesman Grigory Potemkin according to popular myth saw constructed to impress Empress Catherine II (Riabchuk 2009; Fisun 2012, 93; Pisano, 2018). Andrew Wilson (2005) has called democracy in Russia "fake", and instrumentalized for private gain. Rather dramatically, he suggests that a major part of post-Soviet politics is put on stage by a professional class of "political technologists", experts in "faking democracy". In Wilson's (ibid., 47) words: "Politics is 'virtual' or 'theatrical' in the sense that so many aspects of public performance are purely epiphenomenal or instrumental, existing only for effect or to disguise the real substance of 'inner politics'". Shlapentokh and Arutunyan (2013, 44–49) similarly interpret much of Russian politics as "Putin's show", "false drama", "charade", "deception", and "a façade of democracy". Façade theories new and old have in common a stress on the *deceptions* in Russian politics. Furman (2007, 14) is less compromising than most: "Were it not for the self-deceit on the part of society and the deception practiced by those in power," he states, "such systems could provide no justification for their own existence".

The practice of selective law enforcement found in Russia may be seen to fit well within such an understanding of Russian conduct. If you look closer, it shows all the nastiness of a cynical power struggle, but on the outside, it is glossed with legal coating to dazzle observers. Claims of politicized justice frequently trigger responses from Russian leaders about how the individuals in question have been found guilty by an autonomous court and legal system, and that the executives cannot possibly intervene in these processes.[3] Obviously, we must understand selective law enforcement in this context primarily as a *legal* façade. Such façades need not be associated with democracy or democratic legitimacy, but would simply fake rational-legal governance and thus extract legitimacy even in cases of ulterior motivations. Some highly esteemed scholars seem to interpret quasi-legality along these lines. Alexei Trochev (2016, 123) suggests for instance that Russian "courts in criminal cases provide a legal veil for [...] reigning in political opponents". Levitsky and Way (2010, 27) interpret selective law enforcement within a framework of institutional façades, noting how selective law enforcement "can be presented to the world as enforcement of the Rule of Law rather than repression". The same understanding seems to underlie the interpretation of many cases of selective law enforcement, not least in journalistic accounts.

Regardless of how conceptually intriguing the façade interpretation of Russian politics and selective law enforcement may be, however, my research strongly indicates that quasi-legality in Russia has *not* been primarily about deceptions. Considering how endemic the window dressing is in today's Russia, and how disillusioned the population is with regard to it, one could perhaps better use façade theories to explain the origins of the Putinist system rather than its current rationale.[4] Whether we speak of so-called electoral technology, creative accounting, or selective law enforcement, most Russian and international observers are well aware that the system is rigged. More than a decade ago, human rights veteran Sergey Kovalev noted how "everybody knows everything. The very lie no longer aspires to deceive anyone, from being a means of fooling people it has ... turned into an everyday way of life, a customary and obligatory rule for living" (Myagkov et al. 2009, 9). As explored in anthropological research on endemic corruption, mutual understandings, open secrets, vague phrases, and euphemistic language games can in these settings be more prominent than straight-forward deceptions (Nuijten & Anders, 2007). At the same time, the recent years of hybrid warfare, outrageous state propaganda, and election meddling, have again intensified the narrative in which Russia play the role of the masked bandit. These developments in international politics may very well have provided new and continued momentum to this sort of regime classification.

Commonly, and correctly in my opinion, selective law enforcement is interpreted as the sending of a *signal* to other possible targets (Gel'man 2018). Yet, the façade (if we interpret it as deception), and the signal are mutually exclusive interpretations. The intention of sending signals is not to hide the political content, but on the contrary to let it shine through. If observers were unable to understand the political context of a given case, how could anyone expect them to change their political attitudes in response? In the actual cases examined in Part II of this book, there is nothing to suggest that attempts are made to hide the political content. On the contrary, law enforcers often unmistakably *flag* the cases as political, leaving all sorts of hints at the scene. The interviewees of this study reject the idea of legal façades and question whether anyone would be deceived by the thin glazing of legality proffered. Opinion polls largely confirm this view, at least in the more well-known cases. Most Russians, and particularly citizens with political influence, interpret high profile cases predominantly as politically motivated (see Chapter 2).

Because the legal wrapping is unable to cover up the political or personal content of a given case, it does not grant the case much rational-legal legitimacy in the eyes of most observers. In addition, the legal case is hardly hurting the moral integrity of a target. On the other hand, since more or less everyone recognizes that the case is in reality politically initiated and largely irrelevant for the topics of everyday justice, it does not necessarily ruin the observers' trust in the legal system completely. The crackdown signals to society that the targets have powerful enemies and thus stigmatizes the targets as *political* actors. In conclusion, even if façade theories can contribute to the explanation of the origins of many authoritarian regimes, and even if many Russian officials today continue to embrace deception as a political tool, theories of fake legitimacy seem incapable of explaining the rationale of the cases I analyse in this book.

Neo-Weberian opposites

For reasons indicated above, the post-Cold War environment played Dahl's classical definition of democracy (polyarchy) out on the margins of debates. Because even dictators have been holding elections the last three decades, researchers have sought new terms to extend or renew the discussions on authoritarianism. Instead of focusing on the Dahlian access to power, many scholars have increasingly paid attention to the legitimacy of the regime and its *exercise* of power – using a Weberian basis for regime classification (see Guliyev 2011). A number of these approaches find common shelter under the conceptual umbrella of neopatrimonialism.

The focal point of neopatrimonialism as a term is the mixture and interaction of basically opposing ideal types, in this case between Weber's rational-legal and patrimonial types of governance. For Weber, the latter signified a system in which patron-client relations, personal allegiances, and kin-ties were key. Neopatrimonialism as a concept is based on the premise that all contemporary systems of governance answer roughly to Weber's criteria of rational-legal legitimacy, yet that his distinctions remain relevant. In the literature on neopatrimonialism there seems to be a consensus that neopatrimonialism as a concept attempts to deal with political systems that mix a rational-legal bureaucratization with some elements of patrimonial (informal, traditional, personal) rule. The consensus, however, ends there (Erdmann and Engel 2007; Pitcher et al. 2009; Guliyev 2011).

Neopatrimonialism as an academic concept is associated with the scholarship of Guenther Roth (1968), and has often been employed in the study of developing countries. More recently, the term gained popularity as a tool to understand contemporary Russia (Whitmore 2010; Hanson 2011; Fisun 2012; Robinson 2012; 2017; Gel'man 2016). Robinson (2017) for instance seeks to explain post-communist developments through neopatrimonial optics, in which uncertainty and the interplay of competing logics and elite interests are key. Yet, it was exactly these mixed logics that underpinned the relative success of the Putinist system. The centralization of coercive capabilities strengthened Putin's personal power even as they strengthened the state. This points to the entanglement of the regime and the state in many authoritarian systems. In Robinson's argument, the Tandem-rule of Putin and Medvedev highlighted the differences between patronal and rational-legal logics, while the economic crisis gave these differences increased salience. Following 2012, however, Putin managed to stabilize the situation by a discursive shift from state functionality and modernization to vaguer notions "based on a cultural rather than an administrative conception of the state" (Robinson 2017, 360). While this trick may have fended off some pressure towards rationalizing and modernizing the state, it seems unable to satisfy a growing anti-corruption movement.

The normativity and general confusion surrounding terms like clientilism, patrimonialism, neopatrimonialism, Rule of Law, or corruption, made Henry E. Hale (2010; 2015; 2017) move up on 'the ladder of abstraction' (Sartori, 1970) and introduce the new concept of *patronalism* as a point of departure for analyzing personalized politics. Hale's point is largely one about the *pervasiveness* and *fundamentality* of personal politics in many societies. To him, patronalism is a "pattern of social relations" – a more pervasive phenomenon than simply a form of governance (Hale 2015, 25). Selective law enforcement is a case in point. Although this book is predominantly concerned with the practice as a mechanism of political repression, it is in reality used in all sorts of contexts, from protecting ones daughter from unwanted attention, to shutting down a competing business.

Several scholars define neopatrimonialism in terms of "conflictive modes of organization and domination" (Erdmann and Engel 2007; Robinson 2017). We could expect patrimonialist (or patronal) forces and interests within the state to eat away at rational-legal governance and vice versa. It seems, however, that this conflict of interests is not necessarily as strong in weak states, where one can boost rational-legal efficiency and legitimacy by improving the legal performance in issue areas with low political salience. Rational-legal and personal politics carry different impacts in different political spheres. Even if their boundaries are sometimes blurred, these two spheres, to use Harold J. Berman's (1963, 8) term, show a considerable degree of *compartmentalization*. As suggested in the Introduction, Putinist Russia aspires to be a *stewardship* of law, in which the law can rule relatively independently when the masters are away or unconcerned. In a sense, the ruling elites switch the state bureaucracy to 'paternal mode' on political demand, a line of thought that will be further explored in later chapters.

Authoritarianism and judicial power

Like many other things in life, law is a manifestation of power. In the naked rationality of Douglas North (1990, 59): "those who run the state will use that force in their own interest". Bluntly speaking, we would expect law to serve the people in a democracy, the oligarchs in an oligarchy, and the autocrat in an autocracy. Unsurprisingly, however, reality proves to be more complex. For one, politicians use law for a multitude of purposes simultaneously. Political leaders may for instance seek legitimacy, law and order, effective governance, third party negotiation, repression of opposition, international recognition, fair arbitration, and the institutional entrenchment of today's normative values. Authoritarian leaders, moreover, usually seek to delimit legal systems so that they cannot threaten their hold on power. These interests are not easy to pursue simultaneously, producing a situation of manoeuvring, prioritizing, and manipulating. Legal traditions and cultural patterns, moreover, are more firmly entrenched than any policy goal of the time. They influence actual legal practices to a significant degree, and may work to both advance or distort political intensions. If we add this to the fact that legal systems are not autonomous actors, but usually consist of thousands of individuals with diverse interests, aspirations, and attitudes, we get a sense of the complexity of the matter.

When the former Soviet states broke with the old system and dismissed communist ideals, their new leaders pledged to strive towards not only democracy, but also constitutionality and legal reform. As was the case for democratization efforts, scholars and politicians treated post-Soviet countries with medicine derived from Western societies (Hendley 1997). Rule of Law became the yardstick by which Western countries measured the legal systems of purported 'emerging democracies', even if some of them lacked the traditions, realistic hopes, or even ambitions to fit this template in the short- to mid-term. As a number of failed transitions would eventually show, the development toward a Rule of Law appeared evasive. In many countries where stakes were high and the future uncertain, various actors were fighting, buying, circumventing, and manipulating law, utilizing it in a struggle for power, money, and influence. This is not to say that there were no honest attempts to institutionalize human rights and democratic institutions in post-Soviet regimes. These attempts did find some strongholds. In many regimes, however, the prerogatives of the powerful tended to trump these rights in individual cases. The transition paradigm supposedly approached Russia as a 'normal country.' In reality, however, rent seeking elites were perhaps more normal than political leaders zealously protecting constitutional rights.

Even if the Rule of Law remains our ideal, we should do well to remember that legality and legalism are older and more universally recognized principles than the norms often present in a democracy. Law has been employed as an effective tool to organize elite power and govern the state longer than it has been used to protect democracy and human rights. Indeed, since law is a manifestation of power, and the powerful do not necessarily share the interests of society, we should hardly be surprised that law sometimes fails to protect the common citizen. Similarly, we should not be surprised when it proves unable to hold the power holders accountable for their actions.

Banal as this argument may seem, recognizing it goes a long way towards understanding the workings of law in authoritarian context.

Even though scholars have convincingly laid out the rationality of Rule of Law as a way of organizing society, this does not imply that other solutions are irrational. In the practical world, rationality is individual and context-based: Rational actors take into account all the circumstances they recognize as relevant in their situation. As Kathryn Hendley (1997) points out, to full-heartedly embrace law overnight would for individual Russians imply an immense leap of faith – even if they too can see the benefits of a well-functioning legal system. The ruling elites, moreover, have obvious incentives for keeping their prerogatives intact or strengthened. For many, it seemed more rational to make fortunes on the legal, economic, and political flux, than to work for socio-economic and legal equality. Some of the business elites also benefit from safety valves, which made investments in the Russian legal system less pertinent. Unlike ordinary Russians, the elites can incorporate their businesses abroad, and therefore have recourse to foreign arbitration courts more able to protect their property rights and safety of contracts than would be the case in Russia (Markus 2017).

Building on the tradition of Martin Shapiro (1981), the studies collected by Tom Ginsburg and Tamir Moustafa (2008b) made a most welcome addition to the relatively meagre literature exploring the actual functioning and meaning of law under authoritarian rule (Moustafa 2014). While the authors did not claim that these regimes could boast a Rule of Law, they also dispelled myths of how judges and courts would be completely under the heels of their authoritarian masters. In an attempt to fill the massive gap between these two ideal types, they found that limited legal autonomy makes sense "in an astonishing array of circumstances" (Ginsburg and Moustafa 2008a, 12). Shapiro (2008, 329), commenting on the book, noted that the findings reflect "not so much that courts do more now as that students of politics now see more of what courts do". Indeed, many of the mechanisms and purposes of authoritarian legality are very basic and of old origin, even if the post-Cold War order in many ways changed the formal institutional setup.

In many ways, this above line of research provides for the study of law what others have done for the study of elections. Both research fields examine how authoritarian regimes try to utilize formal institutions for the benefits they grant while simultaneously restraining their potential for regime change. To a certain extent, courts and elections serve the same purposes. They both help organize intra-regime competition, channel dissent, and give authoritarian regimes some degree of legitimacy. A well-functioning legal system also makes it easier for the political leadership to exercise social control, be it over public opinion, opposition parties, or self-interested and predatory state officials. By giving citizens channels to address state abuse locally, for instance, courts provide quality control of regime insiders, reducing classical agency problems.[5] The lack of a free press and transparent state institutions can make the seeming absence of information about local abuse of office a significant concern in authoritarian regimes. The ability of autonomous courts to regulate localized corruption is thus extra valuable in these cases. No less important, a well-functioning legal order may also strengthen the state economy through real administrative justice and a credible defence of property rights. In some settings, authoritarians may also empower the judicial system to implement unpopular policies so that the ruling elites cannot be held accountable for them. To benefit from all these functions, however, the judicial system must retain some real autonomy, or at the very least be perceived as retaining it (Ginsburg and Moustafa 2008a). Because most authoritarians, like all political leaders, want to reap the benefits of legal governance, legal autonomy thrives in the most unexpected places. Fraenkel's (1941) classical study of Nazi Germany documents that not even a totalitarian (or near totalitarian) regime 80 years ago was exempted from this rule. In Hitler's Germany, Fraenkel shows, the Nazi leadership was completely subjugating legal principles to its own political project, yet still used semi-autonomous courts to deal with a range of less salient issues. Although a ruthless dictator may have the capacity to interfere in any legal case by picking up the phone, it does not mean he or she has either the interest or willingness to do so.

If semi-autonomous courts give authoritarian leaders benefits they cannot easily discard, then they also give them headaches. Autonomous courts are unpredictable allies, which may sometimes lead to unwanted consequences. A vivid example from Russia is the case against the Nechayev group in Moscow in 1871, when the recently empowered courts shockingly acquitted what the regime saw as enemies of the state. Courts may also be turned into arenas for critics to get public attention, highlight governmental abuses, and build judicial support networks of legal experts, rights defenders, and opposition parties. These tactics sometimes yield political results even if courts eventually turn down the actual demands of the networks (Moustafa 2007). For these reasons, the liberalizing potential of autonomous courts (and elections) can contribute to the dynamics and relative openness of these regimes. Authoritarian leaders are often willing to live with this degree of uncertainty if they can achieve some benefits that would otherwise be unattainable (Hale 2015).

At the same time, authoritarian leaders usually try to minimize the loss of political control that formal institutions may imply. If we stick with Ginsburg and Moustafa's (2008a) categorization, authoritarians have come up with four main devices of regulation. First, and obvious in most authoritarian systems, judges are fundamentally vulnerable vis-à-vis the political regime. In practical life, legal actors that oppose the political order tend to get ignored or worse, ensuring a general 'core compliance' with regime interests. Second, authoritarians may tailor special rules for judicial review and/or implementation of court decisions, not least by limiting the power of judicial review to formalistic issues. In general, formalistic legal frameworks make courts stay clear of broader issues. Third, authoritarians may curb some dangers posed by autonomous courts by repressing emerging judicial support networks by legal, quasi-legal, or illegal means. Finally, authoritarian systems can make use of fragmented court systems to insulate political issues from judicial powers, a popular strategy in countries with military tribunals. By exempting more cases from general jurisdiction, authoritarians can safely empower the politically emasculated courts within their limited jurisdictional field (Pereira, 2008).

The three first methods are clearly relevant to the Russian case. Judges are highly vulnerable to the system they act in, and few will risk any sort of judicial activism. They also operate within a formalistic tradition that partly cuts them off from interpreting broader legal principles which tend to be more politically salient. With regard to the judicial review function, the lack of what Trochev (2012, 354) called *court-friendliness* is the biggest problem: Other state institutions lack both the capacity and willingness to actually implement court decisions. Russian authorities also suppress judicial support networks by using a broad set of tools. Indeed, many targets of political prosecution are lawyers and organizations that work to defend others against the same practice. Even organizations providing the background information on contentious legal issue areas, such as Golos, Sova, and Levada, experience related state pressure.[6] The forth device mentioned by Ginsburg and Moustafa is jurisdictional fragmentation. Formally, there is no fragmented system in Russia, and according to the Russian constitution (Article 111), "the creation of extraordinary courts shall not be allowed".[7] In a sense, however, the dual system remains relevant through an informal but universally recognized separation of political and ordinary legal cases – the above-mentioned compartmentalization of politico-legal affairs. Because power rather than law dictates some cases from the point of initiation, not just the courts but also the broader legal system is in practice fragmented.

Ginsburg and Moustafa do not mention selective law enforcement in their summarized findings, but this too is a mechanism to circumvent semi-autonomous courts despite a reliance on law. Selective law enforcement circumvents courts in two ways. First, the ruling elites can utilize the *upstream* law enforcement system to harass in the name of law. For practical purposes, there is not much independent courts can do to stop this. Even if judges stubbornly refuse to play along, the harassment will work just fine without judicial approval. When courts of law subsequently hold the state accountable for abuse, this rarely impacts behaviour, since processes shield individual perpetrators from harm's way. Second, courts may be sidelined when actors find substantial legal foundation for important cases. A judge given a well-prepared case may have little choice but to pass an unpalatable sentence, even if he or she knows that the case was initiated for political purposes. The functioning of this mechanism is based on pervasive legal violations, incoherent legal frameworks, or a combination of the two. According to many Russians, *anyone* may be found guilty according to Russian law.

Although we should not accept this claim at face value, it does have some merit (see Chapter 7). When laws are vague and/or possible violations are everywhere, all that is needed to get legal sanctions (or at least preliminary investigations) is the initial decision to launch an investigation.

The collection of works by Ginsburg and Moustafa came in a period where the study of authoritarian justice was on the rise. Among those who have explicitly built upon their work is Peter J. Solomon Jr. (2015), who suggests four main ways authoritarians may tailor their judicial system. First, they may favour a truly supressed judicial system of limited jurisdiction and dependent judges, like for instance that of the USSR. Second, they may choose a fragmented judicial system, where courts are independent yet emasculated by means of jurisdictional limitations. Third, they can construe systems with genuine judicial autonomy and jurisdiction, which typically makes for unstable and short-lasting arrangements (Solomon uses Russia 1864-1906 as an example). Finally, authoritarians can opt for formally independent and empowered judges with broad jurisdiction, yet *de facto* undermine them by informal means. Putin's Russia, Solomon adds, belongs to this last category.

Solomon's categorization does at least two things. First, it highlights the dimensions of court autonomy and empowerment for purposes of legal regime classification. Second, it situates historical and present Russia within this general framework. The chosen categorization illustrates how Russia's legal system, despite all its path-dependencies, is far from stagnant. The fragmented court system is the only category within which Solomon does *not* situate Russia at any point of its historical development. Yet, it is exactly the idea of fragmented jurisdiction that will serve my point of departure in discussing contemporary Russian justice in Chapter 4. In doing this, I do not challenge Solomon's classification. Certainly, Russia does not have a fragmented court system, at least not legally speaking. For reasons I have touched upon above, however, I do find the model a worthwhile point of departure for highlighting certain aspect of how politicized justice works.

The power and weaknesses of hybrid governance

Conclusively, Russia's institutional hybridity reflects both its post-Cold War origin and an institutional choice. As Graeme B. Robertson has pointed out:

> *Hybridity is neither the result of unsuccessful authoritarians who fail to impose a closed regime, nor a trick adopted in order to create uncertainty in the eyes of people trying to evaluate the regime. Nor are hybrid regimes necessarily the result of an unfinished struggle between an authoritarian state and a democratic opposition: Instead, hybrid regimes can be deliberately designed to extract the benefits of competition while minimizing the likelihood of loss of control. Hybridity may actually be preferred by*

> *incumbents as a way to manage the disunity and disorder that threaten all authoritarian political regimes. Competition may be less something that authoritarians have failed to eliminate than something they consciously allow and try to control. (Robertson 2011, 12)*

This is of course not to imply that institutional hybridity comes without costs, nor that quasi-legality is more effective than impersonal governance. For all its strengths, informal or quasi-formal rule remains unpredictable and inefficient. Even from an authoritarian perspective, the impact of informal institutions upon political life is not only for the better. In general, states are unruly things, even with established legal tools and bureaucracies. Without these stable societal foundations, no modern state can exist. When legality and bureaucracies work poorly, this fundamentally reduces a state's ability to regulate society for *whatever* purpose. It is not by chance that all modern societies have established formal bureaucracies and law as means of control, regardless of their political orientation. The inefficiency related to informal control also decreases the size of the cake off which rent seeking elites want to feed. Authoritarians try to extract the benefits of law without paying the political costs, but they cannot do so perfectly.

Quasi-legal practice may illustrate the unruliness of hybridity. Because the formal institutions are too weak to withstand short-term interests, and informal checks and balances are imperfect, the quasi-legal output does not necessarily reflect the leadership's wishes. When new weak laws appear, they are not immediately put into quasi-legal schemes to effectively crush opponents. Rather, enforcement tends to be experimental and unpredictable. As Françoise Daucé (2015, 59; 65) concluded in her research on the use of 'foreign agents' legislation, law enforcement within politically sensitive fields tends to take place in an "uncertain, improvised and arbitrary manner" leading to a "permanent unpredictability that affected both the non-profit groups and the institutions tasked with enforcing the law". Changes in anti-extremist legislation have produced similar effects (Chapter 6). The vague rules of the game creates uncertainty, and even if the system is primed for picking up political signals, these signals can easily be misread, distorted, and manipulated.

When the institutionalization of selective law enforcement brings about predictability, as I argue in Chapter 9, this is not a predictability comparable to fair and evenly enforced law. For the purposes of this book, I define selective law enforcement narrowly to highlight its political potential, but similar practices are of course taking place outside of politics too, not least in business. Quasi-legal governance, moreover, is not the result of a master plan. Rather, it is based on semi-permanent characteristics of Russian politico-legal culture, which the ruling elites sometimes find useful to play upon. The political leadership may seek to exploit the potential of quasi-legality and curb the ability of others to freeride (see Chapter 4), but it cannot perfectly control the proliferation of abuse. My argument is therefore *not* that quasi-legal enforcement is predicable, but that its unpredictability gradually diminishes as the result of accumulated experience among the players and the settling of the rules of the game (until they are changed again).

So-called legal nihilism and reliance on informal solutions among Russian bureaucrats and the rest of society makes law-based governance extremely difficult (Chapter 2). A fundamental problem relates to societal expectations when reforms are introduced. As Ledeneva (2011, 40) notes, "changes in the formal rules are simply interpreted as yet another constraint to be dealt with informally". Not only will the bureaucracy be hesitant to implement rules that threaten their own position in a corrupt economy, but other participants may also develop new schemes and techniques to counter legal initiatives that challenge their way of social navigation. Russia's modernization efforts have turned out difficult and often yielded limited gains (Ledeneva 2013; Hale 2015). Whereas the lack of implementation of court rulings is a considerable problem in itself, the issue is much more pervasive than that. According to Medvedev, 70 per cent of his orders when he was Russia's president during the 2008 financial crisis were left unimplemented. Even Putin has acknowledged that half of his formal decisions are never enforced (Trochev 2012, 367). For these reasons, rulers will have an extremely difficult time if they want to opt out of a system of informal control. When patronal logics become entrenched in this way, legal initiatives to root out corruption may be ignored and left unenforced, or even be used selectively for corrupt purposes. In this way, fighting corruption by increasing scopes of punishment becomes sort of like fighting a snowman with snowballs, every ball adding to the snowman's body. The best or only way to fight corruption effectively may paradoxically be by informal means. Indeed, Mark Galeotti (in Guillory 2016) has suggested that genuine anti-corruption motivations played a part in the 2016 elite purges – a statist adjustment to the neopatrimonal balance, yet partly by quasi-legal means.

Governing Russia without law is of course hardly a viable alternative. While models of patronal politics may give the impression that commands are smoothly flowing down the hierarchies of power to end up in effective implementation at the bottom level, this is hardly how society works. Instead, directions and information are filtered through very complex networks of power, influence, and corruption. At every level, original intentions are distorted. Even if commands in theory can be transmitted directly from higher patrons to lower levels without being distorted, there are decisive limits to how much manual management can be done in a day. Conclusively, Russian leadership is faced with doubly poor traction, where neither legal nor extra-legal measures seem to get things done efficiently. Journalistic accounts occasionally hint that not a mouse dies in Russia unless Putin has wished for it. Considering the complexity and corruptness of the system, this is hardly a viable claim. The outcome of the Putinist system is often just a shadow of the original intensions. Only when an issue reaches a high enough level of salience, can we assume it to be manually controlled by the chief patron.

On an individual level, those on the inside of a quasi-legal regime will often face the problem of ineffective governance and reduced control beyond their personal sphere of influence. In addition, they are also subjected to a more direct threat. In general, quasi-legality creates *vulnerability.* While I have argued that the elites are interested in maintaining this system, they too are vulnerable. The regime does not only employ selective law enforcement against old enemies – it also employs it to deter against defections. Individuals that fall from grace in authoritarian systems tend to fall hard, and this tendency is not restricted to heads of state. Insiders may be above the law, but the tables may be turned against them at any moment. If they lose their informal standings with the power networks, they are vulnerable not only to separation, but also may become scapegoats for the regime's wrongdoings. The ruling elites, then, have the sword of Damocles hanging over their heads in the same way as the opposition. As Ledeneva (2011, 41) points out, "the vulnerability of individuals vis-à-vis the system" is a core principle of the current state of affairs. The only real difference between opposition and insiders in this regard is that, as long as they are on the inside of the regime, the insiders *do* comply with its informal rules and are more or less safe from crackdown for that very reason.

On a general level, the stability of neopatrimonial systems are disputed. Whereas some researchers maintain that the interaction of opposite rule sets produce instability, others have concluded the opposite effect (Robinson 2012, 2017). An obvious effect of authoritarian rule is the "insulation of reforms and reformers from the pernicious influence of interest groups and public opinion" (Gel'man 2016, 462). The problem may be not only one of information, but also of willingness. There is a fundamental conflict between state building and state autonomy on the one hand, and short-term rent seeking on the other. While the political leadership may want to strengthen the state to acquire legitimacy, government efficiency, and economic development in order to extract more rents long term, this wish will always face resistance in the system (Robinson 2017).

To some degree, the scholarly disagreement on stability regards the conceptualization of regime type borders. Considering its many upheavals, Russia can easily be interpreted as unstable. Yet, its hybridity of statism and patronalism has pervaded most of its modern history. Even if political leaders, regimes, and even states, come and go, the neopatrimonial system itself seem flexible and relatively stable – it allows for great changes within. As it is culturally 'sticky', it shapes expectations beyond those of formal rules, producing a sense of predictability to the groups and individuals orienting themselves within political regimes. This is part of why Neil Robinson (2017) prefers to use the concept of a neopatrimonial *field,* Hale (2015) discusses the pervasiveness of *patronalism,* and Sakwa (2011) seeks dynamism through the Dual State model. Following Steven Levitsky and Lucan Way (2015), many regimes since the Soviet breakup interpreted as struggling democratic, then hybrid, and now authoritarian, may in fact have changed only superficially. On a positive note, this would indicate that democratic recession is also in part a measurement error. On the other hand, one could argue that a number of regimes in which democracy is faltering, also experience an increasing entrenchment of patrimonial elements (Diamond 2015).

To summarize, hybrid governance is not easy. To base a state on interacting opposites, institutional hybridity, neopatrimonialism, and quasi-legality, is a messy affair, rife with problematic issues. At the same time, hybridity is also a solution to these problems. After all, relinquishing power to the population, establishing fair elections, refraining from legal manipulation, and stopping to extract rents were presumably never initial considerations. What will be a good balance of impersonal and personal governance is for the ruling elites fundamentally a question of gains versus risk, of course immensely complicated by the personal preferences, loyalties, and dreams of said individuals. Conclusively, while institutional hybridity and contradictory logics of governance have a number of very serious setbacks, the Putinist system constitutes a compromise solution to very complex challenges. For Putin and his closest allies, Putinism has undeniably been a blessing.

Notes

1. To the author's knowledge, the term 'mimic democracy' was first used by Mattei Dogan in his studies of interwar Romania. Many years later, it was picked up by Jowitt and introduced to the post-communist context.
2. Certainly, the approach is not limited to the post-Soviet world, see Pisano 2018.
3. See for instance how Putin deflected the question of Tatyana Felgengauer on the 2017 annual broadcasted Q&A session.
4. In Levada polls, a significant (yet underwhelming) proportion of Russians states a belief in Putin's readiness for fair elections and in the trustworthiness television news, yet only 14 per cent of them believe that the political leadership and top bureaucrats always or mostly tell the truth when they refer to the state of affairs (Levada 2017, 38, 87, 120).
5. In the Russian tradition, the Procuracy has in part been performing this control-function. See Smith (1997).
6. Golos works/worked on election monitoring, the Sova Center for Information and Analysis works on xenophobia, extremism, and anti-extremism, and the Levada Center provides public opinion polls.
7. Russia does retain two layers of specialized military courts within the system of courts of general jurisdiction and a specialized court on intellectual property rights within the system of commercial (*arbitrazh*) courts.

References

Berman, H. 1963. *Justice in the USSR. An Interpretation of Soviet Law. Cambridge* (U.S.): Harvard University Press.

Carothers, T. 2002. The End of the Transition Paradigm. *Journal of Democracy*, 13, 5–21.

Collier, D. & Levitsky, S. 1997. Democracy with Adjectives. Conceptual Innovation in Comparative Research. *World Politics*, 49, 430–451.

Daucé, F. 2015. The Duality of Coercion in Russia. Cracking Down on 'Foreign Agents'. *Demokratizatsiya*, 23, 57–75.

Diamond, L. 2002. Thinking About Hybrid Regimes. *Journal of Democracy*, 13, 21–35.

2015. Facing Up to the Democratic Recession. *Journal of Democracy*, 26, 141–155.

Erdmann, G. & Engel, U. 2007. Neopatrimonialism Reconsidered. Critical Review and Elaboration of an Elusive Concept. *Commonwealth & Comparative Politics*, 45, 95–119.

Fish, S. M. 2017. What Is Putinism? *Journal of Democracy*, 28, 61–75.

Fisun, O. 2012. Rethinking Post-Soviet Politics from a Neopatrimonial Perspective. *Demokratizatsiya*, 20, 87–96.

Fraenkel, E. 1941. *The Dual State. A Contribution to the Theory of Dictatorship*. New York: Oxford University Press.

Furman, D. 2007. The Origins and Elements of Imitation Democracies. Political Developments in the Post-Soviet Space. *Eurozine.com* [online]. [accessed 05.10.2012].

Gel'man, V. 2016. The Vicious Circle of Post-Soviet Neopatrimonialism in Russia. *Post-Soviet Affairs*, 32, 455–473.

2018. Introduction. Politics of Fear. *In.* Ledeneva, A. (ed.) *The Global Encyclopaedia of Informality. Understanding Social and Cultural Complexity*. London: UCL Press.

Ginsburg, T. & Moustafa, T. 2008a. Introduction. The Functions of Courts in Authoritarian Politics. *In:* Ginsburg, T. & Moustafa, T. (eds.) *Rule by Law. The Politics of Courts in Authoritarian Regimes*. New York: Cambridge University Press.

2008b (eds). *Rule by Law. The Politics of Courts in Authoritarian Regimes*. New York: Cambridge University Press.

Guillory, S. 2016. Ossified Putinism. *Sean's Russia Blog*. 13.08.2016. Available at: http://seansrussiablog.org/2016/08/13/ossified-putinism/ [accessed 04.01.2018].

Guliyev, F. 2011. Personal Rule, Neopatrimonialism, and Regime Typologies. Integrating Dahlian and Weberian Approaches to Regime Studies. *Democratization*, 18, 575–601.

Hale, H. E. 2010. Eurasian Polities as Hybrid Regimes. The Case of Putin's Russia. *Journal of Eurasian Studies*, 1, 33–41.

2015. *Patronal Politics. Eurasian Regime Dynamics in Comparative Perspective*. New York: Cambridge University Press.

2017. Russian Patronal Politics beyond Putin. *Dædalus*, 146 (2), 30–40.

Hanson, S. E. 2011. Plebiscitarian Patrimonialism in Putin's Russia. Legitimating Authoritarianism in a Postideological Era. *In:* Adams, J. & Charrad, M. M. (eds.). *Patrimonial Power in the Modern World*. [Online]: SAGE.

Hendley, K. 1997. Legal Development in Post-Soviet Russia. *Post Soviet Affairs*, 13, 228–251.

Jowitt, K. 1996. Dizzy with Democracy. *Problems of Post-Communism*, 43, 3–8.

Ledeneva, A. 2011. Can Medvedev Change Sistema? Informal Networks and Public Administration in Russia. *In:* Kononenko, V. & Moshes, A. (eds.). *Russia as a Network State. What Works in Russia When State Institutions Do Not?* Houndmills: Palgrave MacMillan.

2013. *Can Russia Modernise? Sistema, Power Networks and Informal Governance*. Cambridge: Cambridge University Press.

Levada Center 2012. *Russian Public Opinion. 2010-2011*. Moscow: Levada Center.

2016. *Russian Public Opinion. 2012-2015*. Moscow: Levada Center.

2017. *Russian Public Opinion. 2017*. Moscow: Levada Center.

Levitsky, S. & Way, L. 2002. The Rise of Competitive Authoritarianism. *Journal of Democracy*, 13, 51–65.

2010. *Competitive Authoritarianism. Hybrid Regimes after the Cold War*. Cambridge: Cambridge University Press.

2015. The Myth of Democratic Recession. *Journal of Democracy*, 45–58.

Markus, S. 2017. The Atlas That has Not Shrugged: Why Russia's Oligarchs are an Unlikely Force for Change. *Dædalus*, 146, 101–112.

Motyl, A. J. 2016. Putin's Russia as a Fascist Political System. *Communist and Post-Communist Studies*, 49, 25–36.

Moustafa, T. 2007. *The Struggle for Constitutional Power. Law, Politics, and Economic Development in Egypt*. New York: Cambridge University Press.

2014. Law and Courts in Authoritarian Regimes. *Annual Review of Law and Social Science*, 10, 281–299.

Myagkov, M., Ordeshook, P. C. & Shakin, D. 2009. *The Forensics of Election Fraud. Russia and Ukraine*. Cambridge: Cambridge University Press.

North, D. C. 1990. *Institutions, Institutional Change and Economic Performance*. Cambridge: Cambridge University Press.

Nuijten, M. & Anders, G. 2007. *Corruption and the Secret of Law. A Legal Anthropological Perspective*. Aldershot: Ashgate.

Pereira, A. W. 2008. Of Judges and Generals. *In:* Ginsburg, T. & Moustafa, T. (eds.) *Rule by Law. The Politics of Courts in Authoritarian Regimes*. Cambridge: Cambridge University Press.

Petrov, N., Lipman, M. & Hale, H. E. 2014. Three Dilemmas of Hybrid Regime Governance. Russia from Putin to Putin. *Post-Soviet Affairs*, 30, 1–26.

Pisano, J. T. 2018. Potemkin Villages (Russia). *In:* Ledeneva, A. (ed.) *The Global Encyclopaedia of Informality. Understanding Social and Cultural Complexity*. London: UCL Press.

Pitcher, A., Moran, M. H. & Johnston, M. 2009. Rethinking Patrimonialism and Neopatrimonialism in Africa. *African Studies Review*, 52, 125–156.

Riabchuk, M. 2009. Agony of a 'Blackmail State'. Rise and (Possible) Fall of Post-Soviet Semi-Authoritarian Regimes. *In:* Lushnycky, A. N. & Riabchuk, M. (eds.). *Ukraine on its Meandering Path between East and West*. Bern: Peter Lang.

Robertson, G. B. 2011. *The Politics of Protest in Hybrid Regimes. Managing Dissent in Post-Communist Russia*. Cambridge: Cambridge University Press.

Robinson, N. 2012. Institutional Factors and Russian Political Parties. The Changing Needs of Regime Consolidation in a Neo-Patrimonial System. *East European Politics*, 28, 298–309.

2017. Russian Neo-patrimonialism and Putin's 'Cultural Turn'. *Europe-Asia Studies*, 69, 348–366.

Sakwa, R. 2011. *The Crisis of Russian Democracy. The Dual State, Factionalism and the Medvedev Succession*. Cambridge: Cambridge University Press.

Sartori, G. 1970. Concept Misformation in Comparative Politics. *American Political Science Review*, 64, 1033–1053.

Shapiro, M. 1981. *Courts. A Comparative and Political Analysis*. Chicago: University of Chicago Press.

2008. Courts in Authoritarian Regimes. *In:* Ginsburg, T. & Moustafa, T. (eds.) *Rule by Law. The Politics of Courts in Authoritarian Regimes*. New York: Cambridge University Press.

Shlapentokh, V. & Arutunyan, A. 2013. *Freedom, Repression, and Private Property in Russia*. New York: Cambridge University Press.

Smith, Gordon B. 1997. The Struggle over the Procuracy. *In:* Solomon, P. H. J. (ed.) *Reforming Justice in Russia, 1864-1994. Power, Culture and the Limits of Legal Order*. Armonk: M. E. Sharpe.

Solomon, P. H. J. 2015. Law and Courts in Authoritarian States. *In:* Wright J. D. (ed.). *International Encyclopaedia of the Social & Behavioral Sciences 2nd ed,* vol. 13, 427–434.

Trochev, A. 2012. Can Weak States Have Strong Courts? Evidence from Post-Communist Russia. In: Linnan. D. K. (ed.) *Legitimacy, Legal Development and Change. Law and Modernization Reconsidered.* New York: Routledge.

2016. Legitimacy, Accountability and Discretion of the Russian Courts. *In:* Brusis, M., Ahrens, J., WESSEL, M. S. (eds.) *Politics and Legitimacy in Post-Soviet Eurasia.* London: Palgrave Macmillan.

Whitmore, S. 2010. Parliamentary Oversight in Putin's Neo-Patrimonial State. Watchdogs or Showdogs? *Europe-Asia Studies*, 62, 999–1025.

Wilson, A. 2005. *Virtual Politics. Faking Democracy in the Post-Soviet World.* New Haven: Yale University Press.

2 The Russian legal tradition

Whereas the last chapter examined the law and power relations in Russia by looking at them in light of insights from comparative studies, this chapter deepens our analysis by looking at how the relationship between law and power has developed domestically over time. Whereas legal systems in the Western world have largely been interpreted with reference to more or less permanent ideal models (civil and common law), scholarly analysis of Russian law has been strongly flavoured by politics, political science, and international relations. This has arguably led to a fluctuating frame of analysis. According to William Partlett (2008, 7), this has contributed to poor academic memory, a weakened understanding of Russian law, and a "false impression of Russian legal evolution". I too will look at law through the lens of social science. Partlett's observations, however, remind us that legal practice is not merely a product of political institutions but part of an evolutionary cultural process. To deepen our understanding of how Russian law works today, it can be worthwhile to revisit its past – even under other political regimes.

A brief history of Russian politico-legal developments

Under the present regime, Marina Kurkchiyan (2011, 9) claims, "there is no sign of either a popular demand that law must be just or a universal expectation that lawyers must be seen to be ethical and fair". Ultimately, almost everyone expects power to trump any legal concerns. Where do these low expectations of legal performance originate? In this part of the chapter, I review the profound twists and turns on Russia's legal road and highlight some persistent phenomena. The instrumental approach to law, and the elites' pervasive interference with rational-legal logics to achieve their short-term aims are persistent variables that should be examined to understand the origins of today's 'legal nihilism.' This review does not represent a comprehensive overview of key legal reforms. However, it does give a brief introduction to some selected aspects of legal and quasi-legal governance in the not too distant past.

Law and laws in the 19th century Russia

In 1826, just following the Decembrist uprising against the rule of Tsar Nicolas I, Mikhail Speransky led a governmental committee to collect all Russian laws introduced since the reign of the 17th century Tsar Alexis. The committee gathered 35 933 enactments, no less than 46 thick volumes, before condensing the collection into a digest of 15 tomes of effective laws (Kucherov 1953/1992, 30). Speransky was rewarded the prestigious St. Andrew's order for his efforts of gathering and codifying Russian laws. However, the hours he put into this work were nothing compared to the original preparation, legislation, and implementation of all these provisions by the imperial governments. Anyone claiming that pre-industrial Russia was a lawless country should bear the 35 933 enactments in mind. The episode illustrates a real willingness to legislate and systemize rules to help govern the Russian lands. The efforts were not limited to paperwork. In the last few decades, scholars have pointed to the impact of law in a number of spheres that have tended to be ignored or underestimated in classical accounts on imperial history (Kirmse 2012).

Yet, the imperial legal system was hardly modern. In the same way as earlier efforts of codification, Speransky's tomes mainly constituted a collection of procedures, proscriptions, standardizations, and prohibitions, and lacked a legal theory to underpin their use. The governors supervised the courts, and court procedures were inquisitional rather than adversarial. Serfs, who constituted the majority of the population, did not have access to courts and were dealt justice by the gentry (Solomon 1997). The tsar had the prerogative to bestow mercy for legal violations, not based on legal norms but on "God's infinite justice" (Wirtschafter 2006, 66). The legal profession was weak, particularly so before the reforms of Tsar Nicholas I. Legal training primarily consisted of "learning to copy and fulfil chancellery formalities", and many 'legal experts' also did other administrative work (Wortman, 1976, 4). In short, law was mostly a tool of governance in a huge and autocratic state. In this sense, Russia before 1864 had plenty of laws, but no *Law*.

In a thick conception of law, tsarist Russia was underdeveloped compared with Western Europe, where various innovations like individual rights, adversarial procedure, natural law, and constitutional thinking had been gradually developing along with an increasing professionalization of the judicial craft. While legal and educational reforms in the 19th century provided a platform for Western ideas and institutional transplants to Russia, influences from Western countries tended to reach the great empire later and with less impact than elsewhere in Europe. Because the tsars wanted to rationalize its administrative apparatus, they had an incentive to import new legal tools from Western Europe. At the same time, they tended to copy legal forms, rather than fundamental principles.

For this reason, the legal reforms of the 'tsar-liberator' Alexander II in 1864 "appeared as a brilliant flash of light, illuminating the gloomy background of tsarist institutions" (Wortman 1976, 2). The reforms established for the first time a unified judicial system, and introduced to criminal justice the principle of equality of parties, jury trials, and professional advocates. The serf system had been abolished just a couple of years earlier. Reforms also curbed the wide reaching powers of the Procuracy, a state body acting as the 'tsar's eyes' combining prosecutorial powers with legal and administrative oversight (see Smith 1997). As documented by Richard Wortman (1976), the education of a professional class of jurists in the 19th century laid the foundation for a new form of legal consciousness and a sense of duty beyond that of a clerk. This new class embraced the 1864 reforms as a means to exercise real justice instead of simply matching provisions with cases. The new legal experts acquired a professional sense of duty, and brought progressive ideas and debates into Russian legal thought, not least the German concept of the *Rechtsstaat*. Suddenly, Russia enjoyed one of the more progressive legal orders in Europe, at least on paper.

The aftermath of the 1864 reforms, however, also demonstrated the reasons why Russia had not ventured on this path earlier. The reformed judicial branch was completely out of tune with the legislative and executive branches, which remained completely autocratic. As it turned out, Russian autocracy was hardly ready for these wide-reaching reforms, politically speaking. The judges started to utilize the independence granted to them. In the eyes of the tsar and his closest advisors, this amounted to undermining the foundations for autocracy, and was certainly beyond their intensions. If not exactly interfering with the sovereign's monopoly on legislation, the judges *interpreted* law, which in part was seen as the same thing. The reforms thus initiated serious tensions between executive and judicial authorities that would persist until the First World War (Wortman 1976.)

The prosecution of revolutionary dissenters in the 1870s became particularly scandalous. Eager to extract legitimacy from the judicial condemnation of terrorist acts, the legal administration of Russia decided that the trials would be held in public. In the words of the Minister of Justice Konstantin Palen: "The most candid and full presentation of all the facts should deal the greatest blow to the party sympathizing with the accused" (Wortman 1976, 279). In the subsequent trial against the Nechayev group in 1871, however, the judges acquitted 54 of the 87 individuals brought to trial (ibid., 280). The great trial of 1877 was even more outrageous from the perspective of the government. In the biggest political trial of imperial Russia, 193 alleged revolutionaries were tried for various activities in a public trial. The judges acquitted almost half of them and were lenient in many other sentences (ibid., 282). The government, evidently not ready for independent judgment, promptly arrested many of the acquitted individuals and subjected them to administrative punishment (ibid.).

In the decades following Alexander II's eventual assassination in 1881, the rulers seemed completely out of touch with the reformed judicial system. The secret police continued to deal summarily with political dissent, circumventing the courts when necessary. Limited counter-reforms also tried to revert some of the changes. Yet, the core of the reforms persisted, and the new legal system continued to live as a formal awkwardness in autocratic Russia. The reformist thinkers, even if their thoughts had limited impact on Russian politics at the time, became part of the intellectual 'silver-age' culture. Some of their contributions continue to exercise considerable influence on legal thought today (Nethercrott 2007).

From revolutionary justice to rechtsstaat in the making

Even if some old laws and legal practitioners survived the first wave of revolution, Russia's legal foundations underwent major upheavals in the first decades following the demise of the tsarist regime, and the first Bolshevik government in 1917. Whereas the old regime at least used law for window dressing and state administration, many Bolsheviks openly rebelled against law. Classical accounts generously quote Lenin's conception of law as a 'weapon' and the court as "an organ of power" (Feifer 1964, 21). At the same time, in the massive production of the Bolshevik intellectual you could find him voicing other opinions too. Lenin's relationship to law was in reality quite complicated and shifted with the political situation (Burbank 1995). However, his instrumentalist approach was a persistent feature.

When the Bolsheviks seized power, they immediately began using the courts and implementing decrees to fight any element of counter-revolution. They abolished the old legal system, and established a quasi-legal system under conditions of war. The new 'people's courts' and various 'revolutionary tribunals' lacked many vital aspects of courts, such as trained judges and a real legal foundation. Since imperial laws were abolished in 1918 and a codification of Soviet laws did not manifest until mid 1922, the judges were expected to rely on governmental decrees and their 'revolutionary consciousness.' Yet, they largely "operated within established legal procedures" (Rendle 2016, 1673). From 1919, Lenin made a decisive turn towards political hierarchy and command, and reinstated courts as an instrument of the *state*, empowered to discipline lazy proletarians as well as class enemies. In the 1920s, the regime re-established the institution of the Procuracy, with its powers of supervising legal and governmental bodies and officials.

By the end of the Civil War in 1922, most theoretical and ideational advances of the 1864 generation had been washed away from official politics and replaced with theories of Marxist origin, notably that of Yevgeny Pashukanis. While some pre-revolutionary legal mechanisms remained in place, an open embrace of Western legal norms could reportedly lead to exile or even death (Shelley 1992, 66). In the name of political expediency, the political leadership granted the *Cheka troyki* tribunals the right to pass sentence after simplified and speedy investigations without proper trial. Lenin's instrumental use of justice, however, was just one side of the coin. More than anything, he foresaw a just and self-regulating society in which law would pretty much wither away as Pashukanis theorized it would (Burbank 1995).

Joseph Stalin's (1924-53) legacy in the realm of law is also ambiguous. In Khlevniuk's (1997) conception, Stalin saw law and terror as components necessary for a unified policy of repression. He had limited tolerance for real or imagined critics, ignoring documented legal principles. In 1931, for instance, almost two thirds of new prisoners incarcerated in the rapidly developing system of GULag were never prosecuted (Rittersporn 1997, 208). The tyrannical and unpredictable leader, a number of local mini-Stalins, and a completely subjugated judiciary, all facilitated a system where legal actors turned to political signals or patronal preferences for guidance on how to apply the laws. The utilization of vaguely formulated laws against 'socially dangerous persons', 'harmful individuals', or 'counter-revolutionary agitators' increased dramatically, resulting in a growing share of 'political prisoners' in prison camps.

Repression proved hard to regulate by these means, however, as state purges became a vehicle for political manoeuvring and settling old scores. In Gabor Rittersporn's (1997) analysis, it appeared the leadership had a genuine wish to curb the proliferation of extra-judicial repression, but was unwilling to organize and pay the political cost for real judicial processes. Law enforcement agencies, in particular the NKVD, became a strong societal force, circumventing courts and squashing political attempts to constrain their powers. As extra-judicial mass-arrests and executions mushroomed, the state monopoly on legitimate violence was under serious threat. After half-hearted efforts to curb arbitrary coercion in the mid 1930s, the Great Terror of 1937-38 took repression to a new level in which both judicial and extra-judicial bodies partook. In addition, the infamous show trials of 1936-38 still stand in global history as epitomes of legal perversity. Even if they had no real autonomy under Stalin, judges were expected to keep a façade of impartiality, not least after the 1936 Constitution formally declared the courts independent.[1] Even in periods when the regime sought to judicialize repression, it evidently leaned on an instrumental notion of law. As Rittersporn (1997, 221) points out, the period "accustomed officialdom and the public alike to the notion that any use of the criminal sanction was lawful as long as it was sanctioned by legal acts".

While terror was integral to the Stalinist system, Stalin was also the architect of the centralized and hyper-bureaucratic Soviet system, giving up on Marxist visions of a world revolution and the withering away of the state. As part of his 'revolution from above', the regime bolstered administrative and legal capabilities from the late 1930s. Following the end of the Great Terror, Stalin famously declared that the "stability of the laws is necessary for us now more than ever". Indeed, not only the overburdened penal system, but also an increasingly complex economy, increased the need for predictability and practical legal solutions. With or without socialist glazing, the administration often structured the latter solutions around old-fashioned legal mechanisms. In what Robert Sharlet (1977) sees as a *de facto* counter-revolution, the influence of Pashukanis was purged in favour of Stalin's new favourite legal thinker, Andrey Vyshinsky. The regime adopted a new constitution in 1936, codified new laws and rationalized others. Notably, some of these changes took place before the Great Terror, and Vyshinsky himself is perhaps best remembered as prosecutor of the show trials. Thus, the increased emphasis on legal administration did not run counter to terror, but alongside it. Stalin or his Politburo, moreover, were certainly not willing to let themselves subordinate to legal procedures.

The next unquestioned Soviet leader, Nikita Khrushchev (1953-62), broke with some established Stalinist practices. The prerogatives of the secret police were reduced, and the special tribunals abolished. The *People's Law* of 1961 declared that "Soviet law provides for no preferences whatsoever. All are equal before the law" (Feifer 1964, 23). While Khrushchev's leadership initiated reforms, his legacy is two-faced. He fought personal interventions in legal affairs, but he was also a warm advocate for the Party's 'leading role' in society. In theory, the Party should ensure that the legal actors adhered to the Party line *in general*, yet refrained from intervening in *operational work*. Despite rampant violations in practice, this had also been the official policy under Stalin (Gorlizki 1996, 260).

Some scholars have found evidence suggesting that party interference decreased somewhat as a result of Khrushchev's initiatives (see Shelley 1986). Yet, the abolition of special courts restructured political and personal instrumentalization of the legal system, rather than eliminating it. From Khrushchev's period as secretary, political trials were conducted within the ordinary court system. The authorities signalled their status as political by the use of KGB prosecutors, vetted defence counsel, and handpicked judges (Solomon 1992b, 5). As they refused to give away their prerogatives, it reportedly became "customary for party secretaries to give instructions to legal officials orally and in the form of advice", what would eventually be known as 'telephone justice' (*telefonnoye pravo*) in Russia. The interference of party elites in law enforcement did not always relate to political preferences. More commonly, the powerful used legal actors to cover up their criminal acts, protect friends, or selectively attack rivals (ibid., 13). In this fashion, formal rules served to back up cases initiated on purely extra-legal criteria. While revolutionary justice openly challenged the idea of law, and while Stalin channelled political cases into special courts, the post-Stalinist politicized justice became increasingly similar to selective law enforcement as practiced today.

The political leadership of Leonid Brezhnev (1964-82) further rationalized the Soviet legal system. Within an authoritarian logic we are now familiar with, the goal was to find "ways to enhance the integrity, efficiency, and legitimacy of the legal system without constricting party rule" (Huskey 1992, 32). Because extra-legal interference with legal processes tended to be ignored under Brezhnev's political leadership, the practice increasingly became routine. According to Yoram Gorlizki (1997, 274), the interventions became increasingly "detached from their ideological moorings" as private motivations for abuse took over (also see Shelley 1986). One attempt to estimate the magnitude of increased interference suggests that the proportion of judges that experienced interference by politicians more than doubled in just one decade (Solomon 1992, 27, fn.4). The legal actors' systemic dependence on officials for housing and other vital services ensured their compliance with informal directives and personal wishes. Similar to Stalin, and comparable to behaviour under Putin, the Brezhnev regime strengthened the rational-legal system even as it increasingly abused it for individual and group interests.

From the 1960s to the 1970s mass repressions in the traditional sense continued to decline in the Soviet Union. The previously extensive use of force was neither useful nor efficient, and arguably dangerous to the regime. The new system of Soviet repression was more sophisticated, making use of various mass surveillance, preventive measures, selective law enforcement, and the infamous practice of sending political dissenters for forced psychiatric treatment. The new system of selective and narrowly focused repression of open dissent ensured that the country looked relatively peaceful from the outside. As noted by Vladimir Gel'man (2015, 14): "the 'surgical' repressions of dissenters sent a clear signal to other Soviet citizens: unauthorized public and political activism would cost them dearly". In short, the system of repression was gradually becoming more modern and more similar to Putinist Russia. According to Gel'man, the system was effective: Dissenters became "few in number, poorly organized, and almost completely eliminated by the beginning of Perestroika" (ibid.).

Frustration with poor legal performance led the last Soviet leader Mikhail Gorbachev (1985-91) to initiate considerable reforms to Soviet legality, ranging from technical changes to the legal system to reviewing its very foundations. The communist leadership took measures to increase judicial autonomy, to expand citizens' rights, and to regulate the use of political power. The new leadership condemned political interference in legal affairs and made it a serious criminal offence.[2] The idea of *pravovoye gosudarstvo,* that roughly translates into 'rule-based state' or *rechtsstaat,* was promoted by the state reformers, and at the very heart of the system, the new position of President had its powers defined and delimited by law, and was expected to protect and obey the constitution.

While the political developments never allowed the reforms to be fully implemented, many progressive initiatives later resurfaced in the New Russian Federation, not least in its constitution of 1993. Other initiatives originating in the 1980s, moreover, had more immediate effect on legal output. In the 1980s, the prosecuted had better opportunities to defend themselves in court than earlier and the number of acquittals and terminated criminal cases almost tripled from the beginning to the end of the decade.[3] The state prosecuted fewer dissidents through notoriously vague laws on 'anti-Soviet agitation and propaganda' and 'defamation of the Soviet state.' To an increasing degree, judicial dependence shifted from that of direct pressure of politicians toward a reliance on judicial hierarchies – a profound change that continues to influence the judiciary's political dependence today (Foglesong 1997). Social attitudes and expectations rooted in decades of instrumentalism and political interference, however, were more resistant to change.

Reform and disintegration under Yeltsin

The trend of legal liberalization did not die out with the Soviet Union. In late 1991, a group of liberal legal reformists backed by Boris Yeltsin and headed by the visionary Sergey Pashin, continued to administer legal reform through a special department in the Presidential Administration. In October 1991, the Russian parliament adopted Pashin's *Concept for Judicial Reform and Procedure* – a road map for developing Russia's legal system. The constitution of the Russian Federation, moreover, largely reflects the reformist current of late Soviet times. From 1993 onwards, Russia was constitutionally a rule-based state. The Constitution also established the Constitutional Court to review the constitutionality of new laws.

On many accounts, however, the reform agenda found itself in serious opposition to powerful groups within the legal and political bureaucracies, most importantly the Procuracy, the Ministry of Interior, and the Ministry of Justice. These conservative forces managed in practice to block or counter many changes to the legal system, even if the parliament had formally adopted Pashin's plan. Law enforcement agencies, for instance, managed to acquire sweeping powers that made certain judicial mechanisms redundant. As had been the case earlier, reform was partly thwarted by extended departmentalism (*vedomstvennost'*) among state agencies struggling to come out of the institutional turmoil unscathed. Lamenting the eventual resignation of Pashin and the elimination of his department within the Presidential Administration, a group of liberal jurists declared in 1995 the "death of judicial reform" (Huskey 1997, 338).

There are also reasons to question the solidity of the reform agenda itself. As was the case with the democratization efforts, the legal reform initiatives were criticised for being a superficial and top-down transplant of Western ideas without sufficient regard for local circumstances. A disgruntled voice within the Procuracy, for instance, criticized Pashin's concept as a mishmash of elements from Anglo-American and Continental law, ignoring Russian national traditions (in Huskey 1997, 327). Evidently, many changes lacked support within the state bureaucracy. They also met resistance in Duma, to the effect that Yeltsin instead pushed them through by means of presidential decrees. Just as important, many legislative transplants from Western countries were incomprehensive to Russian businesspersons (see Hendley 1997). While these laws had different content than what

Russians were used to, they still refurbished old expectations of inexplicable and alien regulations imposed from above. In this situation, it made good sense for legal subjects to lean heavily on existing informal networks rather than on law and legal institutions.

On a basic level, legal reform struggled to overcome deeply entrenched Soviet legacies as well as the post-communist crisis. In the first half of the 1990s, the country initiated a massive privatization process on an unsteady legal basis, giving rise to massive quasi-legal manipulation aiming for rent extraction. The wish for a rapid transition to democracy and a free market resulted in a period of institutional uncertainty that again came to strengthen informal practices detrimental to the construction of a legal order. Since the stakes were so high, the prevailing uncertainty resulted in strong incentives to seek individual short-term gains. The informal norms were also in flux, and the general disillusion with state power and legitimacy created a normative vacuum. In this crisis, a legal tradition dominated by the instrumental role of law provided a particularly poor foundation for restoring trust.

In the early post-communist period, power was severely fragmented. Moscow was standing on the unsteady feet of a president trying to establish and maintain a balance between different powerful groups, and many regions in practice had great independence from central authorities. In the realm of law, this was manifested in thousands of regional laws contradicting federal legislation, including the Constitution. The hasty and unequal privatization process also gave birth to new economic elites with the capacity to challenge state power for influence over the legal system. The general crisis lubricated legislative and judicial corruption, as did the temporary legal vacuum produced by the rapid transformation. While instrumental and cynical attitudes to law carried over from Soviet times, the informal institutions that had regulated its use and abuse had all but disappeared. Neither the state in general, nor its political leadership could amass enough power to keep control with legal abuse. While the leading figures of the regime certainly benefitted from their position and influence over legal actors, they were at the time too fragmented to streamline this influence or keep the prerogatives for themselves. In short, the fragmentation of power made the quasi-legal field up for grabs. Several negative feedback mechanisms reinforced the crisis. Extensive state capture made laws develop disorderly and often contradictory, judicial corruption served to further aggravate the attitudes to law, and the economic crisis made judges more dependent on bribes, which also contributed to undermine trust and slow down recovery.

Hendley's research on Russian 'legal nihilism' indicates that the experience of the early post-communist era had a profound and long-lasting impact on Russian legal culture. Indeed, she suggests, "the post-Soviet experience may have been more disillusioning than the Stalinist repressions" (Hendley 2012, 151). It also played valuable cards into the hand of Yeltsin's successor. First, the crisis and associated uncertainty created a massive demand for law and order allowing Putin to establish much of his early legitimacy. Since all progress is relative, the 'time of troubles' was a valuable rhetorical asset, in reference to both its historical and contemporary meaning of the term (Petersson 2017). Second, the 1990s once again fuelled societal expectations of law and courts to serve as tools for the powerful, even if access to legal structures had now largely been privatized and no longer remained in the hands of any ruling party. Since these expectations had been entrenched, it caused relatively little stir when Putin's regime started its pick and choose game of political prosecutions. When the Putin administration centralized power in the Kremlin, many perceived it as the state recapturing domains of illegitimate economic interests, rather than the state corroding the rights of ordinary Russians. To many, the subordination of law enforcement under the ruling power networks was more acceptable when they already interpreted law enforcers as 'werewolves in epaulettes' and henchmen of the mafia. When the regime clamped down on human rights organizations, it framed it as a rollback of foreign influence from the transition era. Many, moreover, perceived the quasi-legal means as normal, if not exactly legitimate. The legal failure of the 1990s thus helped legitimize both key elements of the politico-legal dualism that the Putin administration would later develop.

Russian politico-legal culture

Despite its many twists and turns, Russian legal history has displayed a significant consistency through 200 years and three different states. This is particularly true with regard to the interrelation of law and power, shaped not least by the persistent mix of statism and patronalism. While Russia's level of development, its complexity, and its proximity to Western Europe have influenced the formal institutions of the country to a significant degree, its power holders have always found ways to water down any negative consequences these institutions may have had for their own prerogatives. In this way, Russian legal practices bear the mark of the authoritarian context in which it has been developing.

Following the lead of Lawrence M. Friedman (1990, 213), I employ a broad understanding of legal culture as a set of "ideas, attitudes, expectations and opinions about law" as well as the observable practices resulting from these ideas. The below analysis, however, is primarily concerned with particular elements of this culture – in particular those assets that shape the employment of law for purposes of suppressing dissent, and inform the interpretation of this employment.

Kurkchiyan identifies three "component tiles in the mosaic of Russian legal culture". They are:

> *(a) an extreme formalism in the perception of what law is; (b) the reduction of law's social value to that of a mere instrumental role; and (c) a conflict*

> *between the formal and informal rules of Russian social institutions that continually undermines institutional performance. (Kurkchiyan 2011, 4)*

Kurkchiyan's approach may seem selective, as she defines 'legal culture' in terms of deviation from an ideal type, peppering the list with normative suggestions like 'extreme', 'mere', 'conflict', and 'undermines'. Yet, her list is in tune with my study of selective law enforcement and I will use it as a point of departure – not to define Russian legal culture, but to discuss specific aspects of this culture that come into play in quasi-legal repression. As we will see, my study confirms the high relevance of these aspects, and their historical pervasiveness provides some explanation as to why they remain in play.

According to one definition, an instrumental use of law is present when the law is "*consciously* viewed by people and groups as a *tool* or *means* with which to achieve *ends*" (Tamanaha 2006, 6). In the Russian tradition, legal instrumentalism takes two main forms. First, law is perceived as a state tool of social and political engineering rather than a safeguard for individuals. The notion that law should stand *above* the hierarchy of individuals has therefore been alien. With an instrumental concept of law as a fundament, a 'thick' conception of Rule of Law is hard to imagine; a tractor cannot steer the farmer. Second, because the Russian tradition gives high priority to legal texts at the expense of precedence or legislative intent, the legal provisions can once enacted be put in motion for whatever purpose. Among important segments of the elites, "the law has come to be evaluated in terms of its capacity to generate informal income" or otherwise entrench one's power (Barsukova and Ledeneva 2018, 488). Much because it has been interpreted in instrumental terms, Russian Law has consistently failed to be a causeway indicating where the citizens may pass safely (Kahn 2014). Alternatively, in a different metaphor, it has been a sword, rather than a shield. In its ultimate consequence, the combination of instrumentalism and particularism in legal affairs may create a situation in which "the law does not apply; it is applied."[4]

When the concept of *pravovoye gosudarstvo* resurfaced in the official discourse under Gorbachev, its proponents did not necessarily seek the subordination of the state to any principle extraneous to the state. Many have interpreted *pravovoye gosudarstvo* as "the supremacy, or reign, of enacted law rather than of law in the larger sense" (Berman 1992, 47). Even progressive Soviet experts reportedly understood the term along these lines at the time (ibid.). This may come as a surprise considering the element of *pravo* (Latin: *jus*), and not *zakon* (Latin: *lex*) in this term. William E. Butler (2003) stresses this linguistic point, and maintains that a Rule of Law interpretation would in fact be more accurate. According to the analysis of Ilja Skrylnikow (2009), mainstream Russian constitutional legal theory does indeed connect the term to a substantial and 'thick' interpretation today. Skrylnikow also points to how prominent Russian legal scholars in the 20th century connected the concept to material, and not merely formal content, and sometimes even to natural law[5]. At the same time, he also maintains that the term first and foremost signifies the primacy of *zakon* – positive law as adopted by the legislators acting on behalf of the sovereign people. As Skrylnikow concludes, there seems to be a certain ambivalence concerning the theoretical foundation for Russia's constitution (ibid.).

A further comparison of *pravovoye gosudarstvo* with Rule of Law would of course be complex, considering the dozens or hundreds of modern definitions of the latter (see Silkenat et al., 2014). The issue is further complicated, and perhaps made less salient, by how Russian constitutional theory sees the term not so much as a declaration of what Russia is and must be, but rather as a normative declaration for what it should aspire to become (Skrylnikow 2009). One could certainly ask whether this aspiration today constitutes a real endeavour.

With the notable exceptions of 'revolutionary justice' and Stalinist terrors, the Russian and Soviet legal practice has been oriented towards strong formalism, and still is today (Kurkchiyan and Kubal 2018). This implies that rules should be read to the letter, and that principles of equity, fairness, and legislative intent carry less importance. An embrace of strict formalism is a well-known phenomenon in long-standing authoritarian regimes. Indeed, scholars have pointed to a general tendency for authoritarian rulers to embrace legal formalism and positivism (Solomon 2015). The basic idea is that formalism empowers the formal rules (and legislators) in order to limit the discretion of legal actors. In the Russian case, we may trace this rationale back to tsarist legal doctrine. Empress Catherine II, for instance, feared that any interpretation or judgment beyond a mere "identification of facts and appliance of law to these facts" would develop into *de facto* legislative power that could undermine autocratic rule. The empress' *Nakaz* of 1767, an instruction to the country's Legislative Commission, indicated a strong belief in legal formalism: "Where the laws are precise and clear, the office of a judge consists only in ascertaining the Fact". The *Nakaz* even specified how the consideration of 'the spirit of the law' should be avoided at all costs: "Nothing is as dangerous as this general Axiom" (Wortman 1976, 11).

The formalism advocated by Catherine II presupposed rules that are as clear and directly applicable as possible. Yet, rules cannot accurately take account of every complexity of life and therefore tend to leave cases of doubt, where interpretation is needed after all (Schauer 1991, 218–19). To make matters worse, Russia today does not fit the empress' ideal. Like other modern legal systems, Russia's legal order is founded on a set of more general principles to tackle the complexities of modern societies. In addition, contemporary Russian legislation is frequently criticized for containing vague or unspecified legal terms. As indicated by this study, Russian formalism seems particularly unable to deal adequately with laws that are notoriously unclear to begin with, just as was the case in the Soviet Union. When underdetermined legal definitions mix with instrumentalism, formalism, and personalized politics, it makes for an unpredictable legal environment.

Within the Russian formalistic paradigm, the exercise of discretion in legal decision-making is still frowned upon as a stepbrother of corruption (Kurkchiyan and Kubal 2018). While formalistic solutions may squeeze ambiguities out of the courtrooms, however, the ambiguities do not necessarily disappear. Often, Russian judges instead have to deal with the ambiguities *outside* the legal sphere because there is no space for officially exercising direction within it. In this highly non-transparent setting, the formalist system is vulnerable to extra-legal penetration. The high level of corruption in the legal system fuels the fear of discretion in court rulings, which again forces discretionary justice into less controllable forms. In Hendley's (2011, 17) account, the result is a vicious circle "motivated by the false assumption that the written law can account for every possible circumstance".

As mentioned, it may arguably be easier to instrumentalize the rules within a paradigm of legal formalism because this paradigm to a lesser degree stresses broader legal principles and the originally intended purpose of law. My research confirms a willingness to apply a highly formalistic conception of law in individual cases, bordering on the absurd. Public display of swastikas, for instance, is a legal offense in Russia. This restriction was utilized in one illustrative case in which an activist was arrested and fined for handing out crossed out swastikas in protests against an ultra-nationalist march (Sova 2013). While a formalistic approach would (possibly) give the officials the right to behave in this fashion, the priority would make little sense from the perspective of substantial justice.

Scepticism against discretion also tends to empower *local rules* – rules with the narrowest range of applicability (Schauer 1991). These rules with highly specified applications naturally tend to be more concrete and thus easier to apply than rules that are more general. In other words, formalism may strengthen a system's tendency to enforce various sub-laws and regulations, rather than broader legal principles higher up in the legal hierarchy (see Henderson 2012). Not least for Russian judges who are vulnerable and consequently risk-averse (Chapter 3), local rules may serve as a relatively safe domain. Formalism thus threatens to turn the hierarchy of laws upside down, with the consequence that infringements against specified standards trump constitutional rights. Election registration procedures provide an example of how this preference for local rules may be instrumentalized for political purposes. In several cases, candidates have been denied registration due to purely technical, completely minor, and substantively irrelevant mistakes (see Chapter 6). The right to stand for elections is in practice less important, and any 'spirit' or 'purpose' of the law is neglected.[6] As this suggests, there is no necessary contradiction between an extra-ordinarily formalistic approach to law and a predominance of informal solutions. On the contrary, an overly formalistic state seems to encourage informal solutions because it is not itself flexible enough to tackle the complexities of everyday life. This was very visible in the Soviet Union, where the formalistic rigidity of the system encouraged the development of informal practices to fill in the gaps and mend some of the system's most glaring contradictions and dysfunctions (Ledeneva 1998).

The third and final element in Kurkchiyan's triad points to the traditional disconnect between law and social norms, not least in the minds of non-professionals. Natural law has had limited impact on the Russian legal tradition and never created common expectations that law should further some common good *beyond* the will of the sovereign. In addition, the influence of instrumentalism and formalism in practice contributed to drowning the sovereign's legislative intent. Already in the late 1800s, the famous conservative statesman and jurist Konstantin Pobedonostsev recognized how the numbers and details of provisions and standards sapped the law of moral influence.

> *We strive to emancipate the individual, but everywhere we dig pitfalls about his feet, the victims of which more often are the innocent than the guilty. When we consider the infinite multitude of laws and regulations, and the bewilderment of legislators and judges. The simple man cannot know the law. (Pobedonostsev 1992, 32–3)*

The result, lamented Pobedonostsev, was a popular conception of law as a "mysterious power, existing for a purpose inexplicable, and everywhere restricting and paralyzing the operations of life" (ibid.). Legal transplants have later contributed to the general alienation of law in the eyes of the public (Hendley 1997).

In Russian legal thought, the question about the relations between law and morals has been multifaceted. Many thinkers of the 19th century, and also the rulers themselves, did in fact associate law directly with moral and normative values. Yet, most reformers "objected to the intrusion of moral judgement into juridical affairs" (Nethercrott 2007, 62). Nikolay Taragantsev, who remains an influential voice today, advocated a rigorous separation of law and morality. Anything else, he claimed, would trespass into divine jurisdiction (ibid.).

Solomon has examined this element of Russian legal culture under the conditions of *glasnost*. Among the effects of Gorbachev's lifting of censorship was a wave of journalistic attention toward legal abuse. In 1988, the state brought a number of high-level officials, including Brezhnev's son-in-law Yury Churbanov, to court for corruption. The Churbanov case was marked by a high public profile, the suspects were commonly referred to as 'criminals', and pictures of supposed evidence were shown on television. The public was primed for a showdown against corrupt elites. As it turned out in court, however, many of the charges had no supporting evidence. The final sentences were surprisingly moderate. Many commentators celebrated the case as a rare non-political trial of a Soviet politician, yet "the public at large was puzzled, dismayed, and angered" (Solomon 1992, 267). Solomon concludes that the citizens "supported legal procedures and principles only as a means of achieving results that they considered correct. In fact, most members of the public seemed to have reserved for themselves the right to judge what was right or of wrong, and made their judgment on *moral* rather than legal grounds" (ibid., 263–4).

The response to the first Khodorkovsky trial in 2003 was similar. Although most people believed that the case was initiated for political purposes, and the legal foundations were a mere pretext, a majority also supported his jailing. Also tellingly, the numbers of respondents that agreed the Pussy Riot cases were handled in "a just, objective and impartial manner" doubled after one year of conservative policy (Levada 2016). Arguably, one would normally expect a 'moral turn' in political discourse to alter the moral rather than the legal interpretations of a case. Instead, what may seem like morally founded appreciation of legal procedures resembles what Solomon found in the Churbanov-case, where the 'wrong' moral outcome was interpreted as resulting from judicial mistakes or weak investigation (Solomon 1992a, 267). From one point of view, these reactions arguably suggest a conflation, rather than a separation, of law and morals. More importantly, however, they highlight how legal principles carry little moral authority in themselves. They are instead a means to achieve a specific and short-term or midterm goal, such as the imprisonment of a pre-defined villain. As is the case with instrumentalism, this third aspect is an element of many and perhaps all legal cultures, yet it is particularly evident in the Russian case.

Low trust and low expectations today

The traits identified by Kurkchiyan provide the backbone for what is commonly referred to as 'legal nihilism' in Russia, a well-known phenomenon in tsarist, Soviet, and post-Soviet Russia. While observers use legal nihilism in a variety of meanings, the term generally points to a pervasive neglect of law. As Denis J. Galligan (2003, 1) puts it, post-communist societies "do not take law seriously". Meaningless law was a notion reiterated by several of my interviewees, claiming for instance that "there are no Rights in Russia" and that courts are "one hundred percent subordinated". However, no modern society would completely disregard law or legal institutions, so legal nihilism must be understood relatively and approached as an *element* of legal culture.

According to Hendley (2012, 150), legal nihilism in Russia signifies a "particularistic view of law, under which citizens obey laws that strike them as fair and/or convenient" and otherwise ignore them. Such behaviour, however, would arguably suggest that the law does not *at all* influence citizens' choices. If a given rule does not constitute a reason for action, a legal subject can hardly be said to *follow* (or obey) law, even if his or her action happens to comply with it (see Schauer 1991, 113). Thus, we may add to Hendley's characterization of legal nihilism one important point: While simple non-compliance is certainly a consequence of the same disregard for law, legal nihilism also takes the form of quasi-obeying cynicism marked by the willingness to *instrumentalize, manipulate*, and *circumvent* law with full disregard for any notion of its *spirit* or *purpose*. The consequences are visible in a myriad of practices, not merely in quasi-legal governance. In this conception, the legal nihilist is not immune to incentives provided by the legal institutions. However, the legal nihilist does nothing to support law in cases in which the incentives are not immediately present.

Estimating legal attitudes

In surveys, Russians notoriously report a persistently low trust in legal institutions. The *Russian Public Opinion*, a periodical report published by the Moscow based Levada Center, documents low trust in Russian legal institutions through many years. The negative assessment of courts, for instance, is relatively stable. The proportion of respondents who believe that "a common man can get a fair trial" has remained flatly at one fourth of the sample for the period of 2006-2013 (Levada 2016, 161). With regard to polls directly relevant to selective law enforcement, only 8% believe that Russian authorities do *not* use law enforcement agencies against political opponents, while 40% believe it is a "quite common" or "common" practice (Levada 2012, 142). 64% of the respondents, moreover, believe that it is most likely or completely certain that courts are used "for political purposes in order to get rid of political rivals or persecute the dissidents" (ibid., 167). Various Levada polls (2012; 2016; 2017) on motivations and the legality of politicized cases generally support this picture.[7]

The low trust in legal institutions is constantly reproduced by continued manipulation and circumvention of law on many levels and on many arenas. Yet, there have also been reported tendencies of increased trust. On many accounts, polls show higher trust in law enforcement agencies in more recent years, for instance, at least up until 2015 (Levada 2017, 85). One should be cautious of the short-term effect of the Crimea annexation on these figures, an event that caused a patriotic boost of support to more or less every state institution. At the same time, many figures indicate a gradual progression starting even before this occurrence, for instance on the assessment of police work. *The Russian Public Opinion* also indicates that many more Russians "feel protected against the arbitrariness of the law-enforcement bodies" than was the case in the early Putin years.[8] In addition, survey results published by Hendley in 2017 indicate changes towards reduced nihilism. Whether we interpret the figures to indicate relative prevalence or absence of nihilism is a matter of perspectives, but Hendley's key point is both valid and important: In *everyday* Russia, law is not completely subordinate to power, but works to produce a degree of predictability in common disputes. Seemingly, the citizenry increasingly appreciates this.[9] Russians are more willing to use courts to solve disputes and are increasing their reliance on legal mechanisms.

The improved trust reported by Hendley and others may seem puzzling amidst continued and perhaps intensified quasi-legal repression. One could at first glance believe that the political cases reflect a general deterioration of the Russian legal system, and that these flagrant cases would strongly affect the trust in the Russian legal system. While these beliefs are not completely unfounded, two factors cushion the effects they posit. First, the Putin administration padded the legal system to deal with a greater caseload and resist petty economic interests. As will be discussed in the next chapter, legal reforms have given ordinary Russians a greater degree of everyday interaction with courts, and litigation against the state has been increasingly successful and yields greater compensations. The second cushion relates to Russia's politico-legal duality. Because Russians are able to discern between cases of high politics and everyday matters, the fabrication of evidence in a high profile case will not necessarily influence the ordinary Russian's expectation of neighbourhood police or local courts to deal fairly in everyday interactions. The ruling elites are presumably indifferent to the country's divorce settlements, traffic incidents, and petty theft. In everyday justice, therefore, authoritarian consolidation does not necessarily affect legal attitudes in a linear fashion. In our fascination or indignation over outrageous injustices, we do well not to forget that everyday life is a different matter.

The reproduction of low expectations

Despite some increased trust within the field of everyday justice, the situation remains difficult. Legal nihilism, after all, remains pervasive. To some degree, social norms seem to positively encourage illegal behaviour, not least related to corrupt practices. As Hale (2015, 19) points out, "the bureaucrat who fails to use his position to 'look out for his own' is seen as callous and even selfish, neglectful of his duties to family, friends, and community". Again, the phenomenon is deeply rooted. Brian L. Davies documents one case in early modern Russia when the citizenry chased a governor out of town because he did not accept bribes (in Hale 2015, 44). The citizens were angry because the governor suddenly shut off their access to regional policy making. It would appear the population disregarded legal principles because they see them as inferior to established customs. In this line of thought, they perceived laws as artificial transplants from high politics, conceived by elites and for reasons unknown.

Yet, these examples do not imply that everyone would want a life of legal dysfunctions if they could design everything from scratch. The negative attitudes to law among Russians are not necessarily principled in the sense that that they discard law because they see customs and informal norms as more fair or logical. The dependence on personal favours from bureaucrats also reflects the bureaucracy's consistent failure to provide goods impersonally. In the same way, the insistence to bribe the governor in Davies' example reflects a lack of other channels of influence. Sometimes even if the expectation to disregard law is formulated in positive terms, it may still be negatively derived: Illegal behaviour may result less from individual disregard for law and more from low expectations of legal performance. As for the fundamental *values* with regard to legal principles, there are reasons to believe

Russians are quite positive to the Rule of Law. The comparative surveys conducted by James E. Gibson (2003) at the turn of the century, for instance, indicate considerable support for legal principles among the Russian population. Compared to populations in other countries, like France, Poland, or Spain, Russians displayed a rather average support for legal principles. Frenchmen, for instance, were more likely than Russians to agree with statements such as "if you don't agree to a law, it is okay to break it" and "it's all right to get round the law as long as you don't actually break it". In a review of various polls from the first decade of Putinist rule, Trochev (2012) agrees, finding strong evidence for low expectations and trust, but none for disregard of legal principles in themselves.

Rather than a disdain for legal principles, therefore, Russian legal nihilism should be interpreted a spiral of low expectations. In the words of Kurkchiyan (2003), there is a 'negative myth' surrounding the workings of Russian law and legal institutions. In essence, this myth says that law does not matter in Russia; that it simply has been an extension of the will of the powerful, and that the people inhabiting Russia do not care for law and live their lives as best as they can without it. The myth gives life to the perception that you should not follow law blindly, because if you do, others will take advantage of you. If you follow the law, business competitors will get ahead. If you take your matters to court, a bribe will make your efforts in vain. The myth produces a feeling of helplessness. It purports this is how Russia *is* – that legal nihilism is part of the Russian DNA. Even former president Medvedev has asserted that legal nihilism in Russia "goes back to the dawn of time" (in Hendley 2012, 150).

Kurkchiyan does not use the word myth to imply that the situation is not real. The point is that the problem to a large degree originates in perceptions, mutual distrust, and low expectations: "People in such societies are caught in a vicious cycle" (Hale 2015, 19). In a way, the situation resembles a collective action problem where low expectations and trust within the group deter against more law-abiding behaviour among the group members. In general, Russians abhor the high-level corruption and extortionist bureaucracy they live under, but are unable to pull out of the system. At top levels, the elites have repeatedly failed to take the lead in solving these problems. As the Russian saying goes – the fish rots from the head.

While some trace legal failure back to the dysfunctionality of the Soviet system, extremely negative attitudes to law were present well before Pashukanis arrived on the scene with revolutionary fervour. In imperial, communist, and post-communist times, Russian intellectual elites and politicians repeatedly voiced their negative assessments (see Hendley 2017). Two hundred years ago, Petr Poletika, an official within the Ministry of Foreign Affairs, claimed that "the severity of the country's laws is tempered by the fact that you need not actually obey them", a phrase frequently repeated today (Hale 2015, 39, fn. 3). According to Nethercrott (2012, 61) the tsarist administrations encouraged the negative myth of lawlessness as a means to block reform, and

Hendley (2017, 11) argues that tsarist and Soviet Russia systematically suppressed more positive narratives of law. More recently, Medvedev as president also put his authority behind the negative assessments: "No other European country can boast of such a level of disregard for law" (in Hendley 2017, 13). While Medvedev intended it to be an impetus for change, the prevalence of such statements reproduced the vicious circle of legal distrust. Who would like to put his or her faith in law, when even the president says that nobody else will?

To summarize, the 'negative myth' about Russian law is founded on real and substantial shortcomings. The Soviet Union, as well as Imperial Russia before it, always retained a rule of men and never a Rule of Law. The legacy of Imperial Russia is far from identical to that of enlightened monarchies of Western Europe, and the *Rechtsstaat* was never on the Soviet agenda before Gorbachev, even if legal reform was. Law could not effectively shore up political interference and could not trump the will of either Nicholas I or Stalin. The institutional shortcomings and repeated abusive practices fuelled the myth's reproduction, causing ever more disaffection, proverbs, and jokes about law and power within and outside Russia's borders. At the end of the day, for many Russians it seems sounder to utilize social networks and informal contract enforcement than to gamble on some abstract state mechanisms that never worked properly. This is true for governors and the governed alike.

Notes

1. On the blatant contradictions between Soviet law and Soviet reality, see Ioffe (1985).
2. Yet, according to Louise Shelley (1986) the Gorbachev administration did not resist the temptation to selectively instrumentalize courts to purge conservative state officials from the state administration.
3. Yet, the acquittal rates remained far below one per cent for the entire period. The percentage of terminated proceedings increased most significantly between 1984 and 1988, from 2.2 to 6.5 per cent of cases. For details, see the official statistics provided in Foglesong (1997, 314, fn.1).
4. Derived from the Russian phrase "*zakon ne deystvuyet, a primenyayetsya*", see also Paneyakh (2002).
5. As determined by nature, the law of nature is implied to be universal, existing independently of the positive law of a given state, political order, legislature or society at large.
6. For reasons I will discuss in Chapters 6 and 7, any such 'purposes' would be very hard to pinpoint, granted the laws are legislated in context and sometimes with the *intent* of selective application.
7. For relevant polls from other sources before 2010, see Trochev (2012).
8. In 2004, 15% stated they felt "fully" or "quite well" protected, whereas the proportion in 2016 was at 38% (Levada 2017, 85).
9. That being said, Hendley's research indicates that people with previous court experience are more "nihilistic and less law abiding" than those without such experience. While most court veterans evaluate the judge positively and the outcome as fair, their evaluation of individual cases does not seem to increase general trust in the system. Notably, an opposite tendency has been observed in other countries (Hendley 2016; 2017, 32–3).

References

Barsukova, S. & Ledeneva, A. 2018. Concluding remarks to Volume 2. Are Some Countries More Informal than Others? The Case of Russia. *In:* Ledeneva. A (ed.) *The Global Encyclopaedia of Informality. Understanding Social and Cultural Complexity. Volume 2*. London: UCL Press.

Berman, H. 1992. The Rule of Law and the Law-Based State (Rechtsstaat). *In:* Barry, D. D. (ed.) *Toward the Rule of Law in Russia? Political and Legal Reform in the Transition Period*. New York: M.E. Sharpe.

Burbank, J. 1995. Lenin and the Law in Revolutionary Russia. *Slavic Review*, 54, 23–44.

Butler, W. E. 2003. Jus and Lex in Russian Law. A Discussion Agenda. *In:* Galligan, D. J. & Kurkchiyan, M. (eds.). *Law and Informal practices. The Post-Communist Experience*. Oxford: Oxford University Press.

Feifer, G. 1964. *Justice in Moscow*. London: The Bodley Head.

Firestone, T. 2010. Armed Injustice. Abuse of Law and Complex Crime in Post-Soviet Russia. *Denver Journal of International Law and Policy*, 38, 555–580.

Foglesong, T. 1997. The Reform of Criminal Justice and Evolution of Judicial Dependence in Late Soviet Russia. *In:* Solomon, P. H. J. (ed.). *Reforming Justice in Russia 1864-1966. Power, Culture, and the Limits of Legal Order*. New York: M.E. Sharpe.

Friedman, L. M. 1990. *The Republic of Choice. Law, Authority, and Culture*. Cambridge (U.S.): Harvard University Press.

Galligan, D. J. 2003. Legal Failure. Law and Social Norms in Post-Communist Europe. *In:* Galligan, D. J. & Kurkchiyan, M. (eds.). *Law and Informal practices. The Post-Communist Experience*. Oxford: Oxford University Press.

Gel'man, V. 2015. The Politics of Fear. How the Russian Regime Confronts Its Opponents. *Russian Politics and Law*, 53, 6–26.

Gibson, J. L. 2003. Russian Attitudes towards the Rule of Law. An Analysis of Survey Data. *In:* Galligan, D. J. & Kurkchiyan, M. (eds.). *Law and Informal Practices. The Post-Communist Experience*. Oxford: Oxford University Press.

Gorlizki, Y. 1997. Political Reform and Local Party Interventions under Khrushchev. *In:* Solomon, P. H. J. (ed). *Reforming Justice in Russia 1864-1966. Power, Culture, and the Limits of Legal Order*. New York: M.E. Sharpe.

Hale, H. E. 2015. *Patronal Politics. Eurasian Regime Dynamics in Comparative Perspective*. New York: Cambridge University Press.

Henderson, J. 2012. Law as Regulation. In: Kurkchiyan, M. (ed.). *The Russian Socio-Legal Tradition. Report and Analysis of a Workshop Held at Wolfson College, Oxford 19 April 2012*. Oxford: Foundation for Law, Justice and Society.

Hendley, K. 1997. Legal Development in Post-Soviet Russia. *Post-Soviet Affairs*, 13, 228–251.

2011. A Reflection on Russian Courts. In: Kurkchiyan, M. (ed.). *Constructing Legal Culture through Institutional Reforms. The Russian Experience. Report and Analysis of a Workshop Held at Wolfson College, Oxford, 28 September 2011*. Oxford: Foundation for Law, Justice and Society.

2012. Who Are the Legal Nihilists in Russia? *Post-Soviet Affairs*, 28, 149–186.

2016. Justice in Moscow? *Post-Soviet Affairs*, 32, 491–511.

2017. *Everyday Law in Russia*. Ithaca: Cornell University Press.

Huskey, E. 1992. From Legal Nihilism to Pravovoe Gosudarstvo. *In:* Barry, D. D. (ed.). *Toward the Rule of Law in Russia? Political and Legal Reform in the Transition Period.*

1997. Russian Judicial Reform after Communism. *In:* Solomon, P. H. J. (ed). *Reforming Justice in Russia 1864-1966. Power, Culture, and the Limits of Legal Order*. New York: M.E. Sharpe.

Ioffe, O. S. 1985. *Soviet Law and Soviet Reality*. Dordrecht: Martinus Nijhoff.

Kahn, J. 2014. The Law is a Causeway. The Metaphor & the Rule of Law in Russia. *In:* Silkenat, J. R., Hickey, J. E. & Barenboim, P. D. (eds.). *The Legal Doctrines of the Rule of Law & the Legal State (Rechtsstaat)*. Cham: Springer.

Khlevniuk, O.V. 1997. The Politburo, Penal Policy, and 'Legal Reforms' in the 1930s. *In:* Solomon, P. H. J. (ed.). *Reforming Justice in Russia 1864-1966. Power, Culture, and the Limits of Legal Order*. New York: M.E. Sharpe.

Kirmse, S. B. 2012. 'Law and Society' in Imperial Russia. *InterDisciplines*, 2, 103–134.

Kucherov. 1953/1992. Courts, Lawyers and Trials Under the Last Three Tsars. *In:* Zile, Z. (ed.). *Ideas and Forces in Soviet Legal History. A Reader on the Soviet State and Law*. New York: Oxford University Press.

Kurkchiyan, M. 2003. The Illegitimacy of Law in Post-Soviet Societies. *In:* Galligan, D. J. & Kurkchiyan, M. (eds.). *Law and Informal practices. The Post-Communist Experience*. Oxford: Oxford University Press.

2011. The Distinctive Features of Russian Legal Culture. In: Kurkchiyan, M. (ed.) *Constructing Legal Culture through Institutional Reforms. The Russian Experience. Report and Analysis of a Workshop Held at Wolfson College, Oxford, 28 September 2011*. Oxford: Foundation for Law, Justice and Society.

Kurkchiyan, M. & Kubal, A. 2018. Administerial Justice. *In:* Kurkchiyan, M. & Kubal, A. (eds.). *A Sociology of Justice in Russia*. Cambridge: Cambridge University Press.

Ledeneva, A. 1998. *Russia's Economy of Favours*. Cambridge: Cambridge University Press.

Ledeneva. A. 2018 (ed.). *The Global Encyclopaedia of Informality. Understanding Social and Cultural Complexity. Volume 2*. London: UCL Press.

Levada Center 2012. *Russian Public Opinion. 2010-2011*. Moscow: Levada Center.

2016. *Russian Public Opinion. 2013-2015*. Moscow: Levada Center.

2017. *Russian Public Opinion. 2016*. Moscow: Levada Center.

Nethercrott, F. 2007. *Russian Legal Culture before and after Communism. Criminal Justice, Politics, and the Public Sphere*. London: Routledge.

Paneyakh, E. L. 2002. Neformal'nyye instituty i ispol'zovaniye formal'nykh pravil. Zakon deystvuyushchiy vs zakon primenyayemyy. *Working Paper*. Available at: http://ecsocman.hse.ru/data/006/680/1219/017.PANEYAKH.pdf, [accessed 06.12.2017].

Partlett, W. 2008. Re-Classifying Russian Law. Mechanisms, Outcomes, and Solutions for an Overly Politicized Field. *Columbia Journal of East European Law*, 2, 1–51.

Petersson, B. 2017. Putin and the Russian Mythscape. Dilemmas of Charismatic Legitimacy. *Demokratizatsiya* 25 (3), 235–254.

Pobedonostev. 1992 Reflections of a Russian Statesman (late 1800s). *In:* Zile, Z. (ed.). *Ideas and Forces in Soviet Legal History. A Reader on the Soviet State and Law*. New York: Oxford University Press.

Polanskii. 1927/1992. 'Revolutionary Tribunals'. *In:* Zile, Z. (ed.). *Ideas and Forces in Soviet Legal History. A Reader on the Soviet State and Law*. New York: Oxford University Press.

Rendle, M. 2016. Quantifying Counter-Revolution. Legal Statistics and Revolutionary Justice during Russia's Civil War, 1917-1922. *Europe-Asia Studies*, 67, 1672–1692.

Rittersporn, G. T. 1997. Extra-Judicial Repression and the Courts. Their Relationship in the 1930s. *In:* Solomon, P. H. J. (ed). *Reforming Justice in Russia 1864-1966. Power, Culture, and the Limits of Legal Order*. New York: M.E. Sharpe.

Schauer, F. 1991. *Playing by the Rules. A Philosophical Examination of Rule-Based Decision-Making in Law and in Life*. Oxford: Clarendon Press.

Sharlet, R. 1977. Stalinism and Soviet Legal Culture. *In:* Tucker, R. C. (ed.). *Stalinism. Essays in Historical Interpretation*. New York: W. W. Norton & Company.

Shelley, L. I. 1986. Soviet Courts as Vehicles for Political Maneuver. *Soviet Union/Union Sovietique*, 13, 163–186.

1992. Legal Consciousness and the Pravovoe Gosudarstvo. *In*. Barry, D. (ed.). *Toward the Rule of Law in Russia? Political and Legal Reform in the Transition Period*. New York: M.E. Sharpe.

Silkenat, J. R., Hickey JR, J. E. & Barenboim, P. D. (eds.). 2014. *The Legal Doctrines of the Rule of Law and the Legal State (Rechtsstaat)*. Cham: Springer.

Skrylnikow, I. 2009. Understanding the Rule of Law in Russia. In: Koetter, M. & Schuppert, G. F. (eds.). Understandings of the Rule of Law in Various Legal Orders of the World. *Rule of Law Working Paper Series*, 8. Berlin.

Smith, G. B. 1997. The Struggle over the Procuracy. *In:* Solomon, P. H. J. (ed). *Reforming Justice in Russia 1864-1996. Power, Culture, and the Limits of Legal Order*. New York: M.E. Sharpe.

Solomon, P. H. J. 1992a. Legality in Soviet Political Culture. *In:* Lampert, N. & Rittersporn, G. T. (eds.). *Stalinism. Its Nature and Aftermath*. Houndmills: Macmillan.

1992b. Soviet Politicians and Criminal Prosecution. The Logic of Party Intervention. *In:* Millar, J. R. (ed.). *Cracks in the Monolith. Party Power in the Brezhnev Era*. New York: M.E. Sharpe.

1997. Courts and Their Reform in Russian History. *In:* Solomon, P. H. J. (ed). *Reforming Justice in Russia 1864-1966. Power, Culture, and the Limits of Legal Order*. New York: M.E. Sharpe.

2015. Law and Courts in Authoritarian States. *In:* Wright J. D. (ed.). *International Encyclopaedia of the Social & Behavioral Sciences 2nd ed*, vol. 13, 427–434.

Sova. 2013. Inappropriate Enforcement of Anti-Extremist Legislation in Russia 2012. *SOVA Report*. Available at: http://www.sova-center.ru/en/misuse/reports-analyses/ [accessed 06.12.2017].

Tamanaha, B. Z. 2006. How an Instrumental View of Law Corrodes the Rule of Law. *Legal Studies Research Paper Series*. St. John's University, School of Law.

Trochev, A. 2012. Can Weak States Have Strong Courts? Evidence from Post-Communist Russia. *In:* Linnan. D. K. (ed.) *Legitimacy, Legal Development and Change. Law and Modernization Reconsidered*. New York: Routledge.

Wirtschafter, E. K. 2006. Russian Legal Culture and the Rule of Law. *Kritika. Explorations in Russian and Eurasian History*, 7, 61–70.

Wortman, R. S. 1976. *The Development of a Russian Legal Consciousness*. Chicago: University of Chicago Press.

3 The creation of a new quasi-legal order

The previous chapters looked at law and power in both a comparative and a historical light. However, the remainder of the book will focus on Russia under the regime of Vladimir Putin from the year 2000 to 2018, including the period between 2008 and 2012 when he was formally prime minister. The following chapter lays out the regime's relation to law in this period as a continuous development towards a more centralized system, where the state and Putin's patronal hierarchy were built and centralized simultaneously. By means of this dual undertaking, the regime increasingly came to control legislative processes, law enforcement structures, and the judicial system. This development was fundamental to the construction of a quasi-legal order in which selective law enforcement was refined as a tool of governance.

Centralization and Putinism

After 18 years of dominating Russian politics as both president and prime minister, Vladimir Putin entered another period of presidency in 2018. If he remains in power until 2024, Putin will be the longest sitting leader of Russia since Stalin. Albeit not as powerful as sometimes suggested, Putin has exercised considerable influence over the shaping of Russia during this time. For its special traits distinct from earlier periods in history, scholars have increasingly adopted the term 'Putinism' to describe the particular system developed in his period of dominance from the year 2000. While some aspects of the system have been more or less permanent since Putin's first inauguration, Russian politics changed dramatically under his rule. Putinism as a term may therefore be better suited to define a *process* rather than a set of systemic features fixed in time. On the surface, things have changed, but the driving forces and dynamics beneath the surface have ensured that the *direction* of development has been relatively stable.

Albeit with varying intensity, the period of Putin's dominance has been marked by political centralization processes and authoritarian drift from its very start and up until the point of writing. Today's Russia is formally a democratic and 'law-based state' (*pravovoye gosudarstvo*), as codified in the first paragraph of the Russian constitution. There is, however, a consensus among academics that Russia today cannot considered a proper democracy, nor can it be counted as a genuine *rechtstaat*. On the Freedom House index, Russia's ratings have been declining every single year[1] since the organization started the reporting project in 2003 (Freedom House 2007, 2017).[2] As for the law-based state, it was never really established. While the Putin administration has taken several steps to improve the chaotic legal situation inherited from the Yeltsin administration, it has simultaneously undermined the credibility of the legal system by repeatedly exploiting it for various particularistic (personal and network) purposes.

As the Putin regime was able to acquire and centralize more power, it continuously reinvested this newfound influence in the pursuit for even more power – extending its ambitions of control and ensuring that the centralization drive maintained its momentum. When the regime's patronal system infiltrated the state by means of personal appointments at the top level, the process was soon extended and replicated on lower levels. When Putin acquired control over the Procuracy, he used it to weaken rivals; when the Kremlin increased its influence over regional elites, it made use of their political machines to produce votes and control legislatures; when the Kremlin came to dominate legislatures, it enacted further laws to entrench its position by changing election laws, assisting state capture, and rubber-stamping further centralization measures. As the political regime increased its influence over finance, industry, and mass media, it made active use of these new assets. Even ideas were co-opted and made a part of the centralization process (Laruelle 2009). In this fashion, Putin's Russia has in two decades changed from a loosely coordinated oligarchy and evolved in the direction of a hypercentralized autocracy.

The pervasive centralization is arguably the most central feature of how Russian law and power relations have developed since the turn of the century. The centralization was in this respect twofold. First, state power was amassed to more efficiently organize rational-legal governance, create a unified legal space, and provide a modicum of law and order to the Russian Federation. Between 2000 and 2018, the central authorities regained and consolidated their dominance over legislative power, law enforcement structures, and the judiciary. The process, however, was disturbed by a second and simultaneous centralization of power, namely the consolidation of elites within the state structures. The period saw the emergence of a new super-elite, with combined financial, political and bureaucratic capacities unheard of in the Yeltsin era. Formal institutional centralization was not only designed to increase state power *per se*, but even more so to regulate the informal access to this very power. Because the formal structures were centralized, it became easier to safeguard them from outside pressures, and also easier to manipulate them from within. Thus a new quasi-legal order was established.

Centralizing legal capabilities

The Russian president has wide-reaching powers within the legal realm as recognized by the Constitution. In addition to being the chief executive and head of state, the president is formally the guarantor of the Constitution of the Russian Federation, of human and civil rights and freedoms. He can issue decrees and directives with the force of law, as long as they are not in contradiction with existing laws. He may also submit draft laws to the State Duma, and enjoys limited rights to dissolve the legislature or veto individual draft laws. Within the judicial field, the president has the power to submit candidates (to the Federation Council) for judges to the constitutional and supreme courts, as well as for the office of procurator general (who appoints his own subordinates). The president also appoints the judges to all other federal courts. He can issue pardons, has legal immunity, and can declare martial law in case of emergency.

Beyond these extensive formal powers, Russia has under Putin's presidency introduced a number of extra-constitutional bodies with impact on legislative and judicial affairs. The Presidential Administration, which had already been criticized as overblown under Yeltin, gradually grew into an extra-constitutional mammoth with a myriad of relevant departments. In Putin's first period as president, a State-Legal Department, a Department of Cadres and State Awards, a Commission on the Evaluation of Nominees for Judicial Posts at Federal Courts, and a Council on Justice Enhancement Issues were all created by presidential decree with impact on judicial affairs (Popova 2012, 141). With regards to the legislative branch, the National Council and the Council for Implementation of Priority National Projects are both chaired by the president and involve members of the legislative branch. These administrative powers, however, are just the tip of the iceberg when it comes to *de facto* regime control and oversight over the production, implementation, and enforcement of law.

One of Putin's greatest projects has been to centralize the state machinery. During his first year in power, Putin and his administration abandoned the loose federative model adopted by Yeltsin. One of the first major undertakings of the Putin administration was to reinstate the unified legal space (*yedinoye pravovoye prostranstvo*) within the federation – bringing all regional laws into line with federal laws. In this process, the Procuracy played an essential part. It pointed out thousands of illegal acts by regional legislators and brought to attention at least 60 regional constitutions and charters violating federal law (Smith 2007). Whereas the Procuracy had been an unreliable tool for Yeltsin's government, it found under Putin its old role as 'the eyes of the tsar' – formally independent but often perceived as the "investigatory arm of the Presidential Administration" (ibid., 6). Its contribution in Putin's quasi-legal 'deoligarchation' campaign did not go unnoticed (Smith 2007; Burger and Holland 2008). At the same time, the Procuracy received two formidable shaves under the Putin presidency, first by a delimitation of its prerogatives in the new Code of Criminal Procedure in 2002, and most importantly when a significant part of its mandate was transferred to the new Investigative Committee in 2007.

Another related initiative of the Putin administration was to establish seven federal districts as an extra-constitutional administrative layer between the federation subjects and the central authority.[3] These 'super-districts' from the year 2000 are managed by presidential plenipotentiaries (*polpredy*) – Putin's personal appointees – and used for executive control. While their official mandate is limited to overseeing the activities of federal agencies in the regions, this task is in practice extensive. As soon as they were set up, the plenipotentiaries facilitated the consolidation of a unified legal space and regained central control over regional branches of law enforcement agencies. Law enforcement bodies, including the FSB, were eventually reorganized along the lines of the federal districts, and other institutions like the National Guard have since followed (Robertson 2011, 152).[4] This contributed to a centralized system of coordination where the shortest route between two regions (or agencies) became through the centre (Petrov 2011, 86). In the first periods of Putin presidency, legal actors on higher levels, including police, prosecutors, and court chairpersons were rotated horizontally and thus became less dependent on their regions. Before the 2000s, this system had been limited to higher FSB officials This process of uprooting law enforcement helped to centralize control over law enforcement, and diminished regional leaders' ability to govern through 'their own' (*svoi*) people.

Another important way to increase central control with the regions was through governors. Already in the year 2000, governor affiliation with the legislature had been challenged by removing their automatic representation in the Federation Council (the legislature's upper chamber). A bit later, the governors were instead incorporated into the advisory body of the State Council, another extra-constitutional arrangement established through presidential decree and chaired by Putin himself. The most crucial tool to subordinate governors was however the abolition of gubernatorial elections in 2004/2005. After this change, Russia saw a steady increase in the number of new governors representing United Russia (*Yedinaya Rossiya*) and without prior connection to the region appointed to them, not unlike higher law enforcement officials (Reuter 2010, 300; Rochlitz 2014, 106). Whereas the governors had earlier represented the regions vis-à-vis Moscow, they arguably switched to represent Moscow vis-à-vis the regions (Petrov 2011, 81). When gubernatorial elections were eventually reintroduced in 2012, this basic tendency was not reversed. Instead, the now entrenched incumbents were usually re-elected, and harassment and various means of legal and quasi-legal filtration turned competitive gubernatorial elections into a rarity. The next three years after the reintroduction of elections, eighty one per cent of appointed (see below) or elected governors represented United Russia (Reuter 2017, 273). Since 2013, the regional legislatures have been given the authority to abandon elections altogether and instead pick one of three choices presented by the president. Under Medvedev's presidency, also municipal reforms were criticized for reducing local self-governance and contributing to unnecessary centralization (Petrov 2011).

In Moscow, the parliament was brought under control by the establishment of a party of power United Russia to support the power vertical. Whereas earlier Kremlin backed parties were arguably intended to impede the regional elites from creating a strong electoral block (Reuter 2017, 123), President Putin's administration had by 2003 the confidence and support to create a genuine ruling party, joining forces mostly with elites of central Russia. After its first elections in 2003, United Russia managed to secure legislative control by inviting formally independent candidates into their Duma faction. By continued co-optation of independents into its faction, it had by 2004 gained a supermajority of 310 out of 450 seats. As late as 2003, however, it only held a legislative majority in seven regions. This was soon to change dramatically, as governors started to join the nascent powerbase. Between 2003 and 2007, most regional legislatures saw a similar drift towards United Russia dominance, not least since much of the regional elites now joined the fold. By 2005, more than half of Russia's governors were members of United Russia, and two years later only eight governors were *not*. The party made sure that Russia's major enterprises enjoyed privileged positions on federal party lists. Local elites within industry, agriculture, mass media, health, education, and so forth were similarly invited on local lists (ibid., 127–32).

Once the party had secured its dominant position in legislatures, it made sure to use its power and regime support to maintain it. It was surfing on the popular approval of Putin, who openly supported the party but was never a member even when he became chairman in 2008-2012, and employed a broad repertoire of electoral manipulation. Over the next years, the United Russia dominated Duma also changed the formal rules of the game. Single member constituencies were abolished, as were minimum turnout requirements and the option to vote 'against all.' In the next Duma elections of 2007, United Russia managed to secure enough seats to form a supermajority with more than two thirds of the representatives. The number of parties represented in the Duma were reduced from twelve (and 67 independent representatives) to four. United Russia's control over the Duma was in reality even greater, as the few remaining opposition parties took a highly appeasing stance in the Duma. Indeed, many came to think of them as a quasi-opposition and even as Kremlin stooges (Wilson 2005). In 2008, the Duma approved Putin's Bill to extend the term of presidency to six years.

The regime experienced a setback in 2011, when legislative elections gave a less favourable result for United Russia than many had expected. Despite serious electoral manipulations, Russia's dominant party lost 77 seats and has not managed to regain the same level of electoral support since. At the same time, the regime's control over the Duma majority was not really disturbed. The considerable protest movement that mobilized around the 2011 Duma elections, however, posed a more serious challenge to the status quo. The protesters gathered mainly under slogans of free and fair elections, but the origins of the movement were more complex. In the mid term, years of economic crisis, combined with the relative opening up of the political field, had produced in the citizenry both the motivation for change and the perception that such change was possible. A long term perspective upon the protests should also consider other sources of discontent (Robertson 2013). In short, the electoral fraud and blunt presentation of Putin's comeback and Medvedev's quiet withdrawal, with clear overtones of a prearranged deal, put into motion frustrations built up over time. While the protest movement remained relatively modest in size, it was larger than generally anticipated in Russia. For its size, longevity, and middle-class elements, it was seen as potentially significant by most observers and not least by the Kremlin itself. The protests peaked in winter and maintained some of their steam into early spring.

The Kremlin reacted to the Russian 'winter of discontent' by an initial "panicky retreat, then efforts to eliminate sources of uncertainty thought responsible for the challenge" (Petrov et al. 2014, 18). Up until 2011, new parties had become continuously harder to register, effectively keeping out minorities as well as underpinning the constitutional ban on regionally based parties. To claim official registration, an aspiring party had to document a huge base of support and not least organizational capacity. Two demands were particularly difficult to satisfy, the total number of signatures, and a requirement for geographical distribution. After the 2012 protests, however, the rules were suddenly turned on their head, including a dramatic reduction in the number of required signatures. Single-mandate districts were reintroduced. Apparently, the authorities had found a clever way to appease some protesters without risking a negative effect on control.[5] So far, opening up and permitting small parties to register has not resulted in any viable challengers establishing themselves. Except for three individuals that gained seats on single-mandate districts in 2016, the same four same parties have been represented in the Duma since 2007, and the sudden relaxation of registration rules served to split opposition votes and allow more votes go to waste. Thus, United Russia could in the 2016 elections regain the supermajority it had temporarily lost, even if garnering just above half of the electorate's votes. It also continued to expand its organization on the level of municipal districts, and created a 'party school' to streamline and develop new cadres (Reuter 2017, 274–5).

Despite its almost complete control over the legislatures on both federal and regional levels, United Russia has never introduced to Russia anything resembling one party rule. The party has no real political agenda of its own, and instead assures that Putin's policies as president run smoothly through parliamentary controls. Its hegemonic position is thus not utilized to make parliamentary politics forceful, but to the contrary to emasculate its abilities to counterbalance the executive branch of power. In addition, it became an important vehicle to organize, co-opt, and control the ruling elites, not least in the regions (Reuter 2017). If we are to summarize the reorganization of legislative power, it is clear that influence has gravitated towards Moscow and towards the president in a centralization process with both formal and informal components.

The regime's efforts to control the judicial branch are more complex, and will be considered in more detail below. As for now, suffice it to say that several moves were taken to increase the judiciary's formal dependence upon the other branches, but also to increase its power to resist interventions from outside the state. The composition of the Judicial Qualification Collegiums is an example of the former. This system of collegiums responsible for judicial selection and judges' career advancement were long considered as important guardians of judicial autonomy. Until 2002, they consisted exclusively of judges. From that time, however, one third of the members have been representing 'the public', appointed by the regional legislatures. In addition, the president of the Russian Federation is entitled to one representative in both the federal collegium and in every regional collegium (Schwartz and Sykiainen 2012, 977–9). Reportedly, "applicants for judicial office must in addition also collect and submit more than a dozen authorizations, including from the prosecutor's office, police, intelligence services and other law enforcement bodies" (ICJ 2014). As a consequence of this system, Maria Popova (2012, 135) argues, the collegiums "actually serve as monitors for the federal executive of judicial behaviour at the district court level". Another controversy regards the highest-level courts, which have been subjected to several controversial changes under Putin. Between 2005 and 2008, the Constitutional Court moved to St. Petersburg, and was from 2010 brought into more direct control by means of chair appointments. In 2014, the former Supreme Commercial Court was abolished and merged with the Supreme Court. The authorities also decided to move the new Supreme Court to St. Petersburg to make it a 'city of courts.' Because many of the senior members would in practice refuse to move along with the court, it was interpreted by many as a de facto counter reform to make the Supreme Court more compliant and less competent.[6] Even a geographical decentralization then, can be the harbinger of further centralization (Solomon 2014).

Co-opting and coordinating the political elites

If the centralization of state power under Putin is well known, so is also the amassment of personal power under his rule (Hale 2017). Throughout his whole career as politician, Putin has step by step concentrated the country's power networks towards a single-pyramid system of patronal governance under his personal leadership. One of the first moves in this regard was Putin's mass assignments of his own people to positions of power. Whereas

Putin for a few years kept resources and positions aside for representatives of the old regime, he had by the end of his first term created a new administration of new and old figures, but whose primary loyalty belonged to him. In this patronal system of governance, many different interest groups and power networks or 'clans' have their say, but Putin himself remains the supreme arbiter. As is to be expected in a patronal system, the loyalty-based recruitment of personnel was replicated further down the hierarchy, ensuring a steady flow of pro-regime actors into the state structures (Ledeneva 2011; 2013; Reuter and Robertson 2012). The long term consequence of recruiting based on loyalty instead of competence, is not only poor bureaucratic performance but also a state populated by individuals "keen to seek [commands], read signals and display compliance before the command is even given" Ledeneva (2013, 240). This is not least true for Russian law enforcement structures.

United Russia proved useful to organize and coordinate the ruling elites. As is highlighted in comparative research, dominant parties may serve to co-opt, monitor and control elites and to "routinize patronage flows and the distribution of political appointments" (Reuter 2010, 302). United Russia was created top down and is highly centralized. The central organization is heavily involved in the process of candidate nomination to regional legislatures and governors, and also participates in regional election campaigns. Whereas the party was built up by co-opting regional elites of many breeds, it shifted around 2007/2008 towards stronger internal discipline and career advancement. In 2008, the party launched an extensive purge of free riders, hinting to its role in monitoring and streamlining elite commitment for the decade to come (Reuter 2017, 178). The semi-competitive elections for Russian legislatures complemented the effects of dominant party politics in this regard (see Zavadskaya et al. 2017).

Elite defection from the Putinist system is notably rare, not least in consideration of the economic crisis from 2008-2009 and the political crisis of 2011-2012. The elites that were co-opted into Putin's new super elites had multiple incentives for sticking to the system instead of challenging it, involving both carrots and sticks. We have already discussed some of the mechanisms that deter defectors. In addition, there are important habitual and emotional ties involved in Russian patronal culture that serve to bind elites together in political clanship (see Ledeneva 2011). Most crucially, however, Putin's regime did not only regulate the access to legislative and bureaucratic office, but also redistributed property and access to rents. Efforts were made to consolidate control over both the access to – and the exercise of – power and reflected a wish to monopolize, or at least regulate, rent seeking capabilities. In a simplified model of corruption, the rent flow goes from various economic actors outside the state (the corrupters) and into the pockets of office holders (the corrupted), who in turn betray their formal obligations to the state. The concentration of power in many authoritarian systems, however, seems to merge financial and political elites into new super elites. This is also what happened in Putinist Russia as financial, political, and other forms of power gravitated towards the same informal networks. As Pastukhov (2002, 66) noted even well before the authoritarian turn, the "Russian shadow spheres are formed not next to and contrary to the state but, instead, within the state's own functioning machinery and in collaboration with it". Today, this is much more evident. From their insider positions, the ruling elites can instrumentalize their advantages more efficiently for whatever purpose they see fit. In a sense, they are serving as both corrupters and corrupted at the same time – both caretakers and predators of the state. In this and other systems, the distribution of rents is indeed a large part of what keep the system together.

Whereas bureaucratic positions in themselves give access to rents, the Putin regime has also redistributed access to big firms of strategic significance. Also here, the centralization is two faced. On the one hand, many companies have been transferred to direct governmental control, particularly those within the sectors of fossil fuels, transport and communication, and the military-industrial complex. On the other hand, the companies' boards have also been filled with people with patronal bonds to Putin. Whereas regional elites have been granted some influence over these companies, Putin's directorate has been overwhelmingly Moscow based (Kryshtanovskaya and White, 2011). Even if Putin officially denounced the oligarchy of the late 1990s Russia, evidence suggests that the level of state capture in Russia remained equally high after Putin came to power, but that decision-making increasingly favoured large governmental companies (Yakovlev and Zhuravskaya, 2009). Michael Rochlitz (2014) in his research also documents a connection between regime entrenchment and corporate raiding. His findings indicate that the more loyal a regional leader is and the more votes he is able to produce for the federal elites, more raids are likely to take place. As indicated by the extra-ordinary personal wealth of his closest associates, Putin's power shuffles did not represent a deoligarchation as much a *reoligarchation*. By 2011, no other city had as many dollar billionaires as Moscow (Kelly 2011).

Centralizing state violence

To keep the increasingly authoritarian regime secure, the Putin administration became more dependent upon repressive capabilities, and particularly those capabilities able to nip dissent and emerging alternatives in the bud. For fear of losing their base of popular support and discrediting their rule at home and abroad, most authoritarians today prefer avoiding coercion that is too harsh or too widespread. At the same time, since revolutions or decisive protests are always a possibility, dissent cannot be allowed to spread. In Robertson's (2011) analysis, political systems like Putin's Russia are particularly vulnerable to public protests. Its relative openness both reduces its capabilities for large-scale repression and allows for a degree of opposition coordination, yet the regime's stability largely hinges on a common perception of invincibility. If street protests are able to undermine the cohesion of the ruling elites, loyalty-faking can suddenly turn into mass defections. 'To beat or not to beat' can thus very well be an existential question from an authoritarian regime perspective.

To solve the dilemma of coercion, Putin's regime has developed a rich variety of *low intensity coercion* tools – indirect ways to keep potential threats under control that also limit the need for *high intensity* coercion (see Levitsky and Way 2010, 58). That being said, old-fashioned blunt violence is not alien to Russian authoritarian rule. More common than taking political prisoners, however, is making oppositional activities unattractive and inconvenient by a less intensive but consistent harassment by legal, quasi-legal, and illegal means. On their lowest level of intensity, we could interpret these tools as part of a strategy of *demobilization* or *disengagement* rather than downright repression (see Petrov et al., 2014). In comparison with many comparably authoritarian regimes, communist and post-communist Russia has since the 1970s been able to keep the number of political prisoners remarkably low (Gel'man 2015).

In order to make this system work, however, the state's repressive apparatus did not only have to fulfil its tasks of maintaining law and order. In addition, it was required to operate extra-constitutionally in more or less sophisticated schemes, reducing its capacity to fulfill its formal obligations. Brian D. Taylor (2011) maintains that more than increasing real state capacity, Putin's purported state building increased the capacity to harass opposition and critics (also see Robinson 2017). From being loose cannons with predominantly local loyalties and sources of informal income, the law enforcement agencies have gradually shifted to work in the interests of the executive (Figure 3.1). In the words of Arkady Vaksberg, the new patronization of law enforcement under the regime transformed them into "zealous executors of political orders" (Ledeneva 2006, 24). Conforming with Moscow's interests to a greater extent than before, they do both ordinary and exceptional law enforcement tasks – working part-time for the formal state and part-time for the informal regime. For a large part, the centralization of the law enforcement agencies did not necessarily make these agencies more accountable to the population. Instead, access to their power shifted from disorganized elite groups towards the more coordinated super elite. One example from my research on alleged abuse of copyrights legislation (Chapter 6) may illustrate this shift. Whereas copyrights had earlier been used as pretext in extortion schemes and between rival businesses, the practice was co-opted by state interests and reinvented as a political tool. The corrupt actors were the same, one of my interviewees believed, but they now served new masters within the power vertical. As we have seen from the evolvement of corporate raiding in Russia, actors within the state have also become chief actors in quasi-legal schemes for economic gain (Rochlitz 2014).

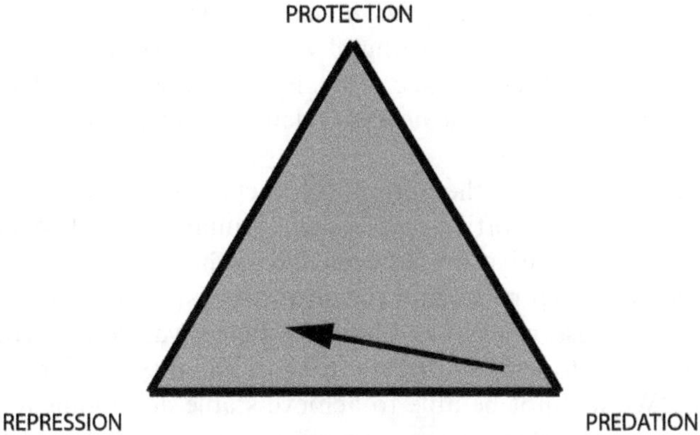

Figure 3.1 Tendency of law enforcement under Putinism (adapted from Taylor 2011, 179).

From an authoritarian governance perspective, the Kremlin's attempts to limit open dissent was largely a success story up until Putin's third term. As pointed out by Robertson (2011, 199), the various and sophisticated tools of repression, co-optation and counter-mobilization "put Russian at the cutting edge of contemporary authoritarian regime design and have made it a model for other authoritarians". In recent years, however, protests have become more frequent and articulated. Indeed, the sentencing of Navalny to yet another prison term for organizing unsanctioned rallies in October 2017 became in itself a major factor contributing to protests in dozens of Russian locations (The Guardian 2017). How these new challenges to the regime will affect the Kremlin's repressive toolbox remains to be seen. As far as legalistic responses are concerned, the regime has in broad terms done more of the same, utilizing a combination of repressive laws, harsh punishments, and selective law enforcement, but perhaps with an extra emphasis on curbing street protests.

Legal reform under Putin

No modern state and no modern regime can be strong without law. As a public official and jurist, Putin knew this, and he knew that a decade full of legal failures had created a popular demand for legal reform. While it was partly his own decision to pursue this agenda, Putin faced enormous pressure to address Russian disintegration and to boost economic growth. If the nascent regime was to survive, it had to save state integrity first (see Robinson 2017). On a range of issues, the new president therefore built his image on being the opposite of his commonly despised predecessor. Putin presented himself not only as man of action, but also as a man of stability, law and order, and a strong state. Especially in the first period of Putin's presidency, then, he pushed to fore the rhetorical sledgehammer of the 'dictatorship of law' (*diktatura zakona*). Although we in retrospect may interpret this term as a warning of what was to come, many observers initially took the new focus at face value. No doubt, Russia had a desperate need for law and order, and the new president appeared to have the will and energy to implement change.

When Putin introduced the notion of a dictatorship of law, it was clear that he did not focus on lofty principles and human rights. The term rather implies the reign of positive law, as legislated by the state itself – the unquestionable rule of written rules, and the accurate distribution of punishment for violators of these rules. The narrative Putin was constructing firmly linked the dictatorship of law directly to state stability, efficiency, and centralization: "We will not be able to achieve stable development without a truly independent legal system and an effective system of law-enforcement bodies". In his mind, "a single executive power vertical" was not contrary to this vision, but an extension of it (Putin 2000).

In some aspects, the rhetoric was more than empty promises. The first years of Putin's reign as president saw substantial legal reform, with the provision of everyday justice to the common citizen of Russia. Many of these reforms were of Putinist origin, while others were introduced previously but sufficiently funded only under Putin's presidency. If we are to believe Solomon (2008a, 3), the decision to invest in the judicial system depended largely on Putin's personal initiative. For instance, he pushed through a new and progressive Code of Criminal Procedure despite considerable opposition within the law enforcement structures, and personally intervened to keep reforms on track (Smith 2007). Through a set of measures, the new Code did amongst other changes increase the influence of judges and delimit the powers of law enforcement agencies to make raids, detain suspects, and interrogate them without defence advocates present (ibid.).

The process of consolidating a unified legal space improved both the general functioning and the prestige of the national court system. Other measures served to underpin the judicial branch more directly. The Russian state also used considerable resources to strengthen the financial situation of the judiciary, both to decrease judicial dependence on corrupting interests and to raise the prestige of judges. Salaries were increased appreciably, court buildings were improved, and courts were allocated better "staff support, facilities and equipment in order to enhance their independence, effectiveness, and prestige" (Smith 2010, 144). Central to these reforms was strengthening the total capacity of the legal system. A central tool to this end was the establishment of justice-of-the-peace courts, 'neighbourhood courts' structured on an idea from the 1864 reforms and with jurisdiction over most cases of low complexity and limited punishment. The law authorizing this new judicial level came in 1998, but it took some time to enact. Five years later, 6470 new courts had been authorized, and by 2011, the numbers were up to 7957. By this year, the justice-of-the-peace courts reportedly dealt with almost all administrative claims, three quarters of civil claims, and half of all criminal claims (Hendley 2017, 136-137). They contributed to more than a doubling of cases dealt with in Russian courts in less than a decade, and freed up capacity at the remaining courts of general jurisdiction (Hendley 2009, 241). While trust in legal institutions remains low in the population, the citizens are nonetheless willing to use them to an increasing extent. Thanks to their capacity and not least their accessibility, Hendley (2012, 337) memorably called the justice-of-the-peace courts "the unsung heroes of the Russian judicial system". Solomon (2008a, 31) also praises the efficiency of the Russian judiciary, claiming that even before they were computerized (see below) "the bulk of cases were processed more quickly in Russia than in Western countries".

The chances of winning litigations against the state are also high, not least for firms. The Constitution's Article 53 holds the state accountable to compensate for "damage caused by unlawful actions (inaction) of bodies of state authority and their officials", and procedures to underpin the obligation were adopted during Putin's presidency with the active participation of Russian judges (Trochev 2016). Since these changes were introduced, the amount of successful cases, as well as the compensation awarded to these litigants, has increased greatly. Indeed, courts of general jurisdiction rule overwhelmingly in favour of the citizens and award them on average three to four times greater compensations than government initiated lawsuits against individuals (ibid.). The same tendency is visible for commercial courts. Importantly, those who represent the Russian state in most of these cases, have no personal connections to the judge or the individual state agencies that are brought to court. When nobody in particular is held personally responsible for a violation, judges seemingly feel much freer to rule against the authorities (Trochev 2014).

Other positive developments include greater computerization of the courts, measures to increase transparency, initiatives to improve juvenile justice, and attempts to reduce the system's dependency on harsh prison sentences, although we have witnessed a considerable backlash with regard to the latter point (Paneiakh 2016). Later improvements include measures to increase transparency and public knowledge of the judiciary's work, for instance by granting courts the means to keep press secretaries and publish decisions online. The commercial courts tend to get particularly favourable analysis in the Russian context for their professionalism and competence (Bocharov and Titaev 2018). They have also been at the forefront of judicial modernization, including automation, transparency, and accessibility (Solomon 2014). Research on legal professionalism among the Russian judiciary also indicates clear changes for the better (Panina and Bierman 2013, Kurkchiyan 2018). Acquittal rates in criminal justice remain low, but did in fact double from 0.4% to 0.8% between 1992 and 2013 (Trochev 2014, 7). Jury trials have been somewhat controversial, but contributed to increased acquittal rates before their field of jurisdiction was narrowed down in 2008 and again in 2013.

In general, judicial reform under Putin has tended to favour the common citizen. According to INDEM Foundation corruption surveys, 'everyday' judicial corruption decreased greatly, even as business-related corruption has increased. One report suggests that the percentage of citizens who offered bribes in a "corruption-prone situation" in Russian court cases was cut from 60% to 30% between 2001 and 2010. The estimated proportion of judicial corruption in the everyday corruption market also went markedly down (Rimskii 2013). Despite serious shortcomings, the Putinist reforms of everyday justice contributed to a situation where "freed from direct external interference and from the burden of trying to guess the preferences of publically powerful actors, judges decide cases in accordance with the *bona fide* interpretations of the law" (Popova 2017, 68).

Channelling court dependencies

The World Justice Project's Rule of Law index, measuring a large number of variables since 2012, indicates mildly positive developments in Russia despite increasing authoritarianism. The ratings of corruption in criminal justice remain stable, and with regard to administrative justice, Russia scores comparatively well. There is, however, one very notable exception to this slight progress, namely the subcategory for "improper government influence" in the criminal justice system. For this variable, Russia has been dropping dramatically and the scores are appallingly low (World Justice Project, 2018). The figures once again highlight the politico-legal duality of the system. For all the legal reforms, the legal system is still easily penetrable for actors with sufficient political clout.[7] As we are reminded of by the repeated surfacing of quasi-legal scandals big and small, political interference in legal cases has been, and still remains, a significant phenomenon. Why is a formally empowered and independent judiciary, despite progressive reforms and decreasing corruption, still so vulnerable to pressure from the executives? I will show that these two tendencies are in fact complementary, reflecting how the judiciary dependencies have been restructured rather than eliminated.

We can reasonably assume that the regime consolidation itself secures a considerable degree of what Ginsburg and Moustafa (2008) called 'core compliance' with regime interests. In a sense, the need to explain vulnerabilities may seem superfluous within a highly patronal authoritarian regime. Since the state cannot provide sufficient protection, every citizen is vulnerable to extra legal pressure. As the ruling elites have come to control more and more levers, judges naturally become less protected from power abuse, as have most other groups in society (Ledeneva 2013, 152–9). Part II of this book documents how life is by no means easy for Russian citizens who fail to cooperate with authorities and refuse to subordinate themselves to the system. The formal empowerment of courts and formal safeguards against political abuse may delimit the impact of this vulnerability in judicial affairs, but hardly eradicate it. Considering the loyalty based recruitment patterns, one would also expect the judiciary to be increasingly pro-regime, following the logics of the state bureaucracy as a whole. Court chairs reportedly tend to fill their courts with individuals known for their conformity and loyalty to judicial superiors (Trochev 2016). A survey conducted by Hendley (2016) seems to confirm that among Russian professional judges, few have ambitions to challenge the rules of the game.

As laid out in the previous two chapters, Russian judges act within a legal formalist tradition. They are unlikely to apply the constitution directly in their cases, and will instead refer to more narrowly applicable laws when handling politically motivated cases (Solomon 2008b, 227). This implies that issues of selectivity and political rights are downplayed to the benefit of lower level laws. As I will explain theoretically in Chapter 5, claims of selective law enforcement and issues regarding legal guilt are in principle separate and unconnected. Therefore, even an unbiased judge may contribute to sanctioning what originated from political motives if the case is indeed legally sound in other ways. In other words, even if the Russian judiciary had been living up to the highest ideals of neutrality and been able to work in isolation from all external influence, the legal sanctions imposed by the state would have been statistically biased. A judge without the possibility of challenging a political (or other) selection has no means to entirely eradicate the bias produced in upstream law enforcement. The exception is of course if the judge is willing to ignore the lower level questions in an attempt to actively *counter* a politically motivated case. Such judges will hardly advance far or live long within the Russian legal system, however, unless they have informal clearance for their decisions. In addition, there is the issue of lacking capacity and willingness of the state apparatus to implement court decisions, which remains a major problem for the Russian legal system (Trochev 2012). If court decisions are left unimplemented, judicial empowerment and independence is of little use. Among the cases examined, some favourable rulings were only implemented after years of foot dragging.

Even if incentives for core compliance help explain the system's low ability to resist interference, it does not explain interventions as such. We are interested in what the channels of interventions look like and where they are located; how ruling elites may actively work to sideline institutional arrangements that in theory would ensure formally empowered and independent courts. Here, two chief factors should be underscored. First, old habits die hard. Reportedly, it remains "an acceptable practice" for officials to express opinions in direct conversations with judges (Popova 2012, 133). In addition, Russian prosecutors and judges are known to keep in close contact to avoid 'misunderstandings' and acquittals that are interpreted as mistakes and a waste of resources (Trochev 2016; Hendley 2017). This dependency may serve as a bridge for political interference. Since law enforcement officials and prosecutors are easier to control than judges, and enjoy close relationships with the latter, they may serve as political probes in courtrooms. As long as these loyalties and dependencies continue, formal independence is in practice perforated: "The emergence of truly independent and effective courts requires changes in the broader culture and in the informal practices which connect to the work of the courts" (Schwartz and Sykiainen 2012, 1061). This openness to direct guidance on specific issues ensures that compliant judges can be informed on what is expected of them.

The second issue relates to the strong internal hierarchy of the judicial branch, formally a bulwark *against* informal penetration. From late Soviet times, the judicial organizations were robust, and Putinist reforms have since consolidated, but also penetrated, the existing hierarchy. Strong institutions within the judicial branch may seem appropriate to Russia, considering its high level of corruption and issues of political interference. As the argument goes, securing bureaucratic accountability within the organization will protect the judges from extraordinary pressure from local interests. Indeed, this was in part why this structure was established in the late Soviet period (Foglesong 1997). Early Putinist court reforms partly succeeded in curbing the ability of elements outside the state structures to interfere with court procedures. At the same time, the strong and hierarchical judicial system has proved a very practical institutional setup for the central regime. It produces a bolster against petty corruption, and also serves as a channel for political dominance. Whereas the political probes into the legal system are top-down, the judicial system also contains mechanisms to pick up sensitive cases (if they are recognized as such) on the bottom level and transfer them upwards.

There are reasons why this dependency has become prominent. First, the workings of internal judicial institutions remain highly non-transparent, dominated by unclear procedures and vague criteria for appointment, promotion, and disciplinary measures. These fluid rules of the game make the careers of ordinary judges in Russia highly dependent on chairpersons, who in turn are dependent on their superiors (Schwartz and Sykiainen 2012). If judges make a wrong or careless step, it would be easy to block their further promotion, or even punish them by a formal pretext. In this fashion, the mechanism of selective law enforcement is also at work within the judiciary, with the same effect of increasing vulnerabilities and strengthening informal dependencies. As a result, judges have strong incentives to make an all-things-considered evaluation of the situation and base their ruling on what they believe their superiors would have done, instead of considering the legal issue independently (see Scheppele 2010). As Trochev (2016, 124) points out, the increased status of judges under Putin has made the profession more attractive, which means they have more to lose and plenty of recruits waiting to fill their place if they step out of line.

The strong hierarchical dependence within the organization leads individual judges to lean heavily on advice from court chairpersons in politically salient cases (Popova 2012, 137). Reportedly, the chairpersons are more politically aware than lower judges and "have the know-how and are able to intercept and interpret hints dropped by the Kremlin, the local administration, or an influential official, politician or businessman" (Ledeneva 2013, 151). In this way, political issues move up the hierarchy for decision-making before they are considered in first instance courts. It seems reasonable to assume that the more important the case, the higher up in the hierarchy a decision will be made. At the higher level of the system, the federal executives carry greater influence upon the judiciary, through the appointment of judges and through the above-mentioned special departments in the Presidential Administration closely connected to the judiciary. In addition, the Presidential Administration reportedly runs parallel evaluation processes on judges, and in practice impacts judicial career management (Popova 2012, 139–43). The political questions can thus float up in the hierarchy until they reach an appropriate level, and a decision can be transmitted back down. What can be positively cast as a strong judiciary with strong institutions, can therefore also contribute to the judiciary's politicization and exposure to informal interests, as long as these interests carry sufficient political weight.

How independent Russian judges are today compared to earlier will thus greatly depend on how we understand independence. Most importantly for our purposes, we must ask: independence from *what* and independence from *whom?* Although formal insulation locally, demands for transparency, and increased wages may have reduced the judges' dependence on illegal sources of income, both formal and informal mechanisms have simultaneously made them more dependent on federal executives and the political regime. It seems fair to conclude that courts consequently have become harder to privatize for outsiders, yet at the same time more accessible for political heavyweights. The analysis suggests that the Russian judiciary is vulnerable to political pressure through at least three mechanisms: general incentives towards 'core compliance'; a tradition of informal guidance, either directly or through middlemen; and a politicization of the judicial hierarchy. In the same ways as the political leadership realigned the previously predatory police with regime interests, strengthened informal bonds of loyalty within the state bureaucracy, co-opted financial elites, and centralized the flows of corruption, it also *rearranged* judicial dependencies, rather than removing them. In a pattern we are now familiar with, both formal and informal centralization mechanisms reflected regime consolidation – the gradual entrenchment of Putinist rules of the game.

Suppressing alternative visions of law

The centralization of power under Putin took place at the expense of actors in various roles, such as the legislative branch, the regional elites, and the political opposition. In addition, the regime has persistently been counteracting potential challengers within the political domain by attacking uncooperative elites, suppressing political opposition, and subordinating mass media to the best of its abilities. To safeguard its control over the quasi-legal field, it also became important for the ruling elites to keep alternative visions of legal order suppressed. While the Kremlin has utilized a number of tools to control civil society, curb independent media, and dominate the streets, the most central tool for stomping out challengers of the quasi-legal order has been a straightforward repression of watchdogs, human rights groups, and different minded legal actors. As is common, the means have been mixed, from repressive laws and selective law enforcement, to violent attacks and killings with impunity.

From about 2005, the top-down pressure on NGOs concerned with legal issues and human rights increased considerably. In 2006, a new extensive law on NGO activity received considerable attention, and was followed up by a sustained campaign of co-optation, isolation, and coercion (Bækken 2009). Selective law enforcement and low intensity coercion has since been commonplace, with the occasional burst of more dramatic violence. As is well known, the political leadership under Putin frequently questions the agenda of human rights groups, typically linking them to foreign interest and interference in Russia's sovereign domain. This was a central aspect of official rhetoric in the 'post-orange' period, and soon grew to become the chief narrative to discredit the human rights agenda and isolate them from Russian society (Horvath 2013). From 2012/2013, the stigma was infamously formalized when organizations financed from abroad were officially required to register as 'foreign agents' (*inostrannyy agent*). Because most organizations concerned with human rights are dependent on at least partial financing from abroad, this requirement hit this group hard.

The situation of 'different-minded' lawyers and judges in Russia has also been worsening. 'Troublemakers' are filtered out from the judiciary by various means elaborated above. Lawyers can be subjected to some of the same quasi-legal decision-making of internal organizations, not least through the Bar Chambers and their Qualification Boards, which have the power to reject admission or disbar controversial members. Lawyers also risk more severe problems, especially in political or other high-profile cases. Major problems for Russian lawyers include persistent harassment, intimidations, and physical attacks, including killings. While the Russian state has special safeguards for lawyers, these are evidently not always effective in practice. Abusive or criminal behaviour against lawyers, moreover, is sometimes a subject of impunity. In addition, journalists, scholars, or other individuals who align their conduct with judicial support groups, human rights organizations, and critical lawyers, may fall victim to similar punitive repertoire.

The repression of the human rights community has had multiple effects on law and power relations in Russia. First, it boosted control over the quasi-legal domain by hampering the capacity of watchdogs. Many of the said organizations provided legal counselling free of charge, typically in cases when the individuals were subjected to dubious processes. Second, the active suppression of judicial support networks reduced their capacity for legal activism. Some of the repressed organizations seek to hold individual office holders, and not least law enforcement officials, legally accountable. Others use courtrooms to question the legality of official policy. This judicial review function is formally well developed and accessible in Russia, but by keeping these organizations busy and suppressed, law enforcement agencies or informal interests curb their ability to utilize it. Third, the sustained campaign reduced these organizations' impact on legislative processes through hearings and lobbying, a sphere in which where many NGOs also had a strong engagement. Finally, the persecution and stigmatization of human rights organizations for more than a decade led to a polarization in public discourse between 'patriotic' and 'foreign' narratives of law, making it hard for human rights organizations and similar groups to find public audiences. The suppression of these NGOs weakens an important challenger to the Russian tradition of instrumentalist formalism – a backbone for the quasi-legal order.

A new quasi-legal order

Russia is widely known for its pervasive informal practices, and the law enforcement and judiciary are certainly not exceptions. Despite the various positive tendencies we have pointed out, the overall picture of the legal system remains relatively bleak. Political interventions, however, are a minor concern for most actors within the Russian legal system. In everyday affairs, most judges are much more tangled up in various inter-dependencies and cross pressures on local levels than they are in political games. Legal actors deal with these concerns to the best of their abilities, pulling whatever levers they have to satisfy the demanding environment and legitimize their actions for themselves as well as for others. The senior judges and court chairs today typically belong to the generation who received their law degree during the Brezhnev era. Whether we can expect significant changes in informal practices when this generation leaves office remains to be seen, but it seems fair to assume that the strong position of this generation has helped the retention of old habits within the judiciary with regard to both ordinary and extraordinary cases (Trochev 2016, 125).

In addition to the everyday navigation between different concerns, Russian legal actors may participate in various 'private' practices of a quasi-legal or illegal nature. Law enforcement officials occasionally provide protection (*krysha*) for businesses, or collect, store, and/or sell compromising material (*kompromat*). Legal actors, including judges, also participate in schemes of varying legitimacy to appropriate physical or financial assets. According to the estimates of one Moscow based NGO, 15% of Russian business entities experienced "groundless criminal proceedings" between 2000 and 2010 (Mesquita 2018, 299). The practice of corporate raiding, which was originally based on criminal networks and private security companies, has gradually developed into less violent forms that involve government officials "with the assistance of a vast network of judges, law enforcement, lawyers, accountants, journalists and others" (Mesquita 2018, 297). 'Commissioned prosecutions' (*zakaznyye dela*) in extortion schemes, and 'intellectual property squatting' to abuse loopholes in patent or trademark laws, are examples of other abuse practices that directly reflect the post-Soviet conditions of capitalism and weak formal rules (Firestone, 2010).

Other practices are more old-fashioned and have carried over from Soviet times, such as various forms of 'telephone justice' related to either selective law enforcement or selective law *non*-enforcement – for economic gain or for directly punitive purposes. Since most of these practices are based on improvisation and their definitional borders tend to be fluid, no list of quasi-formal practices can be exhaustive. Common to many of them, however, is how they reflect power relations and an instrumentalization of the state, as well as opportunism and vulnerabilities among legal actors. What may appear as manifestations of a semi-permanent politico-legal culture can thus be manipulated and played upon by powerful elites. Whereas none of the mentioned practices are unique to Putin's period, therefore, they have taken on new significance and meaning in light of regime politics.

To summarize, the Putin regime has managed to centralize control over many political tools that under Yeltsin remained fragmented. This is true with respect to legislative and judicial powers, as well as to law enforcement and other bureaucratic agencies, ranging from the FSB and the Procuracy to electoral committees. In part, centralization took the form of increased cohesion within the state structures, with more power being amassed in Moscow and regional autonomy being reduced. Also, power was transferred from the legislative to the executive branch, not least to the office of the President. While sometimes forgotten in political analysis, this was not all for the worse. The Putin administration enacted much needed legal reforms and halted federal disintegration. In the lives of common Russians, law became more accessible and petty corruption within the judiciary decreased.

At the same time, the patronal system associated with President Putin gathered force and infiltrated the very same state structure that had been strengthened. Regional elites were co-opted into a nascent super-elite, and co-ordinated through the United Russia party and various central agencies, not least through the Presidential Administration. In this way, informal interests could instrumentalize and expand the newly acquired powers and use the state's legal machinery for purposes related more to extracting rents and retaining power than enforcing the law. In part, control was used to keep the opposition at bay by quasi-legal means – to control the supply-side of elections, to muffle critical voices, and to demobilize the population by making organized criticism unpleasant or downright dangerous. Since 2000, Russia has seen the construction of a new quasi-legal order, where legal abuse has increasingly favoured the entrenched super elites. As noted above, this does not mean that decisions are all determined by higher-ranking officials, nor that all the quasi-legal acts favour the Kremlin. As Peter Rutland (2018, 276) has argued, "Putin has *not* succeeded in creating a consensual, unified elite that would be a viable successor to the Soviet and Tsarist service class". Elite alignment is not perfect. Rather, it signifies a direction, process, or development within the politico-legal sphere. As will be elaborated on in the next chapter, the consolidation of quasi-legal repression coincided with increased rational-legal governance, and the two development trends are not as contradicting as they seem.

Notes

1. Strictly speaking, the rating remained at the same level between 2011 and 2012.
2. While Freedom House ratings have been criticized as being biased towards US friendly countries (Steiner 2016), the *direction* of development should still be a fair index of authoritarian drift.
3. The number of federation districts was increased to eight in 2010 when North Caucasus became a separate district, and again in 2014 with the annexation of Crimea.
4. Russia's military districts were established along similar lines in the late 1990s, years before the new federative layer appeared in civilian affairs.
5. Yet, an opinion poll on the new election laws showed that a majority believed the changes were intended to make Russian elections less competitive (Levada 2016, 165).
6. The actual relocation has been postponed at least two times and is not likely to take place before 2022 (see Kommersant 2017).
7. What exactly is sufficient clout depends on the level and degree of interference.

References

Bocharov, T. & Titaev, K. 2018. When Business Goes to Court. *In:* Kurkchiyan, M. & Kubal, A. (eds.). *A Sociology of Justice in Russia*. Cambridge: Cambridge University Press.

Bowring, B. 2005. Russia in a Common European Legal Space. Developing effective remedies for the violations of rights by public bodies: compliance with the European Convention on Human Rights in 2004. *In:* Hober, K. (ed.). *The Uppsala Yearbook of East European Law*. London: Wildy, Simmonds and Hill.

Burger, E. S. & Holland, M. 2008. Law as Politics. The Russian Procuracy and its Investigative Committee. *Columbia Journal of East European Law*, 2, 143–194.

Bækken, H. 2009. Selective Law Enforcement against Russian NGOs. Pursuing Informal Interests through Formal Means. *NUPI report*. Oslo: Norwegian Institute of International Affairs.

Firestone, T. 2010. Armed Injustice. Abuse of Law and Complex Crime in Post-Soviet Russia. *Denver Journal of International Law and Policy*, 38, 555–580.

Foglesong, T. 1997. The Reform of Criminal Justice and Evolution of Judicial Dependence in Late Soviet Russia. *In:* Solomon, P. H. J. (ed.). *Reforming Justice in Russia 1864-1966. Power, Culture, and the Limits of Legal Order*. New York: M.E. Sharpe.

Gans-Morse, J. 2012. Threats to Property Rights in Russia. From Private Coercion to State Aggression. *Post-Soviet Affairs*, 28, 263–296.

Gel'man, V. 2015. The Politics of Fear. How the Russian Regime Confronts Its Opponents. *Russian Politics and Law*, 53, 6–26.

Ginsburg, T. & Moustafa, T. 2008. Introduction. The Functions of Courts in Authoritarian Politics. *In:* Ginsburg, T. & Moustafa, T. (eds.) *Rule by Law. The Politics of Courts in Authoritarian Regimes*. New York: Cambridge University Press.

Hale, H. E. 2015. *Patronal Politics. Eurasian Regime Dynamics in Comparative Perspective*. New York: Cambridge University Press.

2017. Russian Patronal Politics beyond Putin. *Dædalus*, 146 (2), 30–40.

Hendley, K. 2009. 'Telephone Law' and the 'Rule of Law'. The Russian Case. *Hague Journal on the Rule of Law*, 1, 241–262.

2012. The Unsung Heroes of the Russian Judicial System. The Justice-of-the-Peace Courts. *Journal of Eurasian Law*, 5, 337–366.

2016. Evaluating the Prospects for Young Lawyers to Remake Putin's Russia. *Russian Politics*, 1, 450–477.

2017. *Everyday Law in Russia*. Itaha: Cornell University Press.

Horvath, R. 2013. *Putin's Preventive Counter-Revolution. Post-Soviet Authoritarianism And the Spectre of Velvet Revolution*. Oxon: Routledge.

ICJ, 2014. Russian Federation. Appointment and Promotion of Judges, Security of Tenure. *International Commission of Jurists Report* [online]. Available at https://www.icj.org/cijlcountryprofiles/russian-federation/russian-federation-judges/russian-federation-appointment-and-promotion-of-judges-security-of-tenure/ [accessed 18.2.2018].

Kelly, L. 2011. Moscow is Now the Billionaire Capital of the World. *Reuters*. 9.3.2011. Available at https://www.reuters.com/article/us-billionaires-russia/moscow-is-now-the-billionaire-capital-of-the-world-idUSTRE7287NA20110309 [accessed 11.10.2018].

Kommersant. 2017. Pereyezd Verkhovnogo suda v Sankt-Peterburg otlozhen do 2022 goda. *Kommersant*. 19.9.2017. Available at: https://www.kommersant.ru/doc/3415237 [accessed 21.3.2018].

Kurkchiyan, M. 2018. The Professionalisation of Law in the Context of the Russian Legal Tradtion. *In*: Kurkchiyan, M. & Kubal, A. (eds.). *A Sociology of Justice in Russia*. Cambridge: Cambridge University Press.

Laruelle, M. 2009. *In the Name of the Nation. Nationalism and Politics in Contemporary Russia*. Houndmills: Palgrave Macmillan.

Ledeneva, A. 2006. Behind the Façade. 'Telephone Justice' in Putin's Russia. *In:* Mcauley, M., Ledeneva, A. & Barnes, H. (eds.). *Dictatorship or Reform. Paper Collection*. London: Foreign Policy Centre.

2011. Can Medvedev Change Sistema? Informal Networks and Public Administration in Russia. *In:* Kononenko, V. & Moshes, A. (eds.). *Russia as a Network State. What Works in Russia When State Institutions Do Not?* Houndmills: Palgrave MacMillan.

2013. *Can Russia Modernise? Sistema, Power Networks and Informal Governance*. Cambridge: Cambridge University Press.

Levada Center. 2016. *Russian Public Opinion. 2012-2015*. Moscow: Levada Center.

Levitsky, S. & Way, L. 2010. *Competitive Authoritarianism. Hybrid Regimes after the Cold War*. Cambridge: Cambridge University Press.

Mendras, M. 2012. *Russian Politics. The Paradox of a Weak State*. London: Hurst & Company.

Mesquita, M. 2018. Reiderstvo (Russia and FSU). *In:* Ledeneva. A (ed.) *The Global Encyclopedia of Informality. Understanding Social and Cultural Complexity. Volume 2*. London: UCL Press.

Paneiakh, E. L. 2014. Faking Performance Together. Systems of Performance Evaluation in Russian Enforcement Agencies and Production of Bias and Privilege. *Post-Soviet Affairs*, 30, 115–36.

2016. No Room. What Has Changed in Russia's System of Repression During the Past Year. *Russian Politics and Law*, 54, 404–413.

Panina, D. & Bierman, L. 2013. The Development of Legal Professionalism in Russia. An Institutional Perspective. *Critical Perspectives on International Business*, 9, 106–128.

Pastukhov, V. 2002. Law under Administrative Pressure in Post-Soviet Russia. *East European Constitutional Review*, 11, 66–74.

Petrov, N. 2011. Who is Running Russia's Regions. *In:* Kononenko, V. & Moshes, A. (eds.). *Russia as a Network State. What Works in Russia When State Institutions Do Not?* Houndmills: Palgrave MacMillan.

Petrov, N., Lipman, M. & Hale, H. E. 2014. Three Dilemmas of Hybrid Regime Governance. Russia from Putin to Putin. *Post-Soviet Affairs*, 30, 1–26.

Popova, M. 2012. *Politicized Justice in Emerging Democracies. A Study of Courts in Russia and Ukraine*. Cambridge: Cambridge University Press.

2017. Putin-Style 'Rule of Law' & the Prospects for Change. *Dædalus*, 146, 64–75.

Putin, V. 2000. *Annual Address to the Federal Assembly of the Russian Federation*. Available at: http://en.kremlin.ru/events/president/transcripts/21480 [accessed 08.12.2017].

Rimskii, V. 2013. Bribery and the Judiciary. *Russian Politics and Law*, 51, 40–7.

Reuter, O. J. 2010. The Politics of Dominant Party Formation. United Russia and Russia's Governors. *Europe-Asia Studies*, 62, 293–327.

2017. *The Origins of Dominant Parties. Building Authoritarian Institutions in Post-Soviet Russia*. Cambridge: Cambridge University Press.

Reuter, O. J. & Robertson, G. B. 2012. Subnational Appointments in Authoritarian Regimes. Evidence from Russian Gubernatorial Appointments. *Journal of Politics*, 74, 1023–1037.

Robertson, G. B. 2011. *The Politics of Protest in Hybrid Regimes. Managing Dissent in Post-Communist Russia*. Cambridge: Cambridge University Press.

2013. Protesting Putinism. The Election Protests of 2011-2012 in Broader Perspective. *Problems of Post-Communism*, 60 (2), 11–23.

Robinson, N. 2017. Russian Neo-patrimonialism and Putin's 'Cultural Turn'. *Europe-Asia Studies*, 69, 348–366.

Rutland, P. 2018. The Political Elite of Post-Soviet Russia. In: Best, H. & Highley, J. (eds.) *The Palgrave Handbook of Political Elites*. London: Palgrave Macmillan

Sakwa, R. 2011. *The Crisis of Russian Democracy. The Dual State, Factionalism and the Medvedev Succession*. Cambridge: Cambridge University Press.

Scheppele, K. L. 2010. Declarations of Independence. Judicial Reactions to Political Pressure. *In:* Burbank, S. B. & Friedman, B. (eds.). *Judicial Independence at the Crossroads. An Interdisciplinary Approach*. Thousand Oaks: SAGE in cooperation with the American Academy of Political and Social Science.

Schwartz, O. & Sykiainen, E. 2012. Judicial Independence in the Russian Federation. *In:* Seibert-Fohr, A. (ed.). *Judicial Independence in Transition. Strengthening the Rule of Law in the OSCE Region*. Heidelberg Berlin: Springer.

Smith, G. B. 2007. The Procuracy, Putin, and the Rule of Law in Russia. In: Feldbrugge, F. J. M. (ed.). *Russia, Europe, and the Rule of Law*. Leiden: Martinius Nijhoff.

2010. Legal Reform and the Dilemma of Rule of Law. *In:* White, S., Sakwa, R. & Hale, H. E. (eds.). *Developments in Russian Politics 7*. Houndmills: Palgrave Macmillan.

Solomon, P. H. J. 1987. The Case of Vanishing Acquittals. Informal Norms and the Practice of Soviet Criminal Justice. *Soviet Studies*, 39, 531–555.

2008a. Assessing the Courts in Russia. Parameters of Progress under Putin. *International Journal for Court Administration*, 1, 26–32.

2008b. Judicial Power in Authoritarian States. The Russian Experience. *In:* Ginsburg, T. & Moustafa, T. (eds.). *Rule by Law. The Politics of Courts in Authoritarian Regimes*. New York: Cambridge University Press.

2014. The Unexpected Demise of Russia's High Arbitrazh Court and the Politicization of Judicial Reform. *Russian Analytical Digest*, 17.04.2014

Steiner, N. D. 2016. Comparing Freedom House Democracy Scores to Alternative Indices and Testing for Political Bias: Are US Allies Rated as More Democratic by Freedom House? *Journal of Comparative Policy Analysis. Research and Practice*, 18, 332–349.

Taylor, B. D. 2011. *State Building in Putin's Russia. Policing and Coercion after Communism*. Cambridge: Cambridge University Press.

The Guardian, 2017. More than 100 arrests in anti-Putin protests across Russia. *The Guardian. 7.10.2017*. Available at: https://www.theguardian.com/world/2017/oct/07/more-than-100-arrests-in-anti-putin-protests-across-russia [accessed 21.3.2018].

Trochev, A. 2012. Suing Russia at Home. *Problems of Post-Communism*, 59, 18–34.

2014. Accountability and Discretion of the Russian Courts. *Russian Analytical Digest*, 17.04.2014.

2016. Legitimacy, Accountability and Discretion of the Russian Courts. *In:* Brusis, M., Ahrens, J., Wessel, M. S. (eds.) *Politics and Legitimacy in Post-Soviet Eurasia*. London: Palgrave Macmillan.

Wilson, A. 2005. *Virtual Politics. Faking Democracy in the Post-Soviet World*. New Haven, Yale University Press.

World Justice Project 2018. *Rule of Law Index 2017-2018*. Dataset available at: https://worldjusticeproject.org/our-work/wjp-rule-law-index/wjp-rule-law-index-2017-2018/current-historical-data [accessed 19.2.2018].

Yakovlev, E. & Zhuravskaya, E. 2009. State Capture. From Yeltsin to Putin. *In:* Kornai, J. E. A. (ed.). *Corruption, Development and Institutional Design*. International Economic Association conference.

Zavadskaya, M., Grömping, M. & I Coma, F. M. 2017. Electoral Sources of Authoritarian Resilience in Russia. Varieties of Electoral Malpractice, 2007-2016. *Demokratizatsiya*, 25, 455–480.

4 The politico-legal duality of Putinism

In this chapter, I provide an interpretation of the institutional tensions in Russia to complement the perspectives discussed in Chapter 1. By means of my approach, I seek to make sense of the curious coexistence of legal reform with increased authoritarian repression that we found in the previous chapter. I arrive at a model where I lay out the politico-legal compartmentalization in Russian politics in terms of *pragmatic dualism*, focusing on the instrumental benefits of the 'dual state' (see below) but acknowledging its historically contingent genesis. What appear to be contradictions can in fact make sense when seen from the perspective of contemporary authoritarian and neopatrimonial governance. Within this model, the Russian aspirations as reflected in its constitution are not necessarily fake, but they are only relevant within one of the two spheres. From the perspective of the dual state, universal rights and procedures are not universal after all, but they reflect a default commitment in cases where no political prerogatives have interest in interfering.

As a launching pad for my discussion, I use Ernst Fraenkel's (1941) model of the dual state, which I will refer to frequently below. Because of the potential controversy inherent in any references to the Third Reich, which provides the background for Fraenkel's research, I must underscore that I use the comparison purely to explore theoretical issues of dual jurisdiction and draw no moral or ideological parallels between the regimes in Nazi Germany and today's Russia.

The history and chief characteristics of the dual state

Fraenkel introduced the model of the dual state in the book bearing the same name, published for the first time in English translation in 1941. Fraenkel based his model on research from pre-war Nazi Germany after the Reichstag Fire Decree in 1933 until about 1938. In this period, he was himself practicing as an attorney at a Berlin Court of Appeals. In 1938, Fraenkel emigrated to the U.S. but returned after the war to become one of the founding fathers of political science in Germany. Much of the appeal in his work stems precisely from his ability to explore the issues of law and power in concert and interaction. In brief, Fraenkel's work deals with how the Nazi regime in the 1930s eliminated the *Rechtsstaat* in Nazi Germany and established a quasi-legal system that was to take its place.[1] In this emerging system of dual jurisdiction, the Nazis enjoyed uncontested prerogatives unchecked by legal principles. At the same time, considerable spheres of administration remained under rational-level governance. Fraenkel dubbed these sizeable pockets of rational-legal control 'the normative state'. He accredited the continued existence of the normative state to the *self-restraint* of the prerogative state and the necessity of keeping the German capitalist economy afloat. For its richness in conceptual innovation and theoretical insight, Fraenkel remains worthwhile to read and incorporate in today's analysis of law under duress.

In 1977, Fraenkel's work was picked up by Robert Sharlet in a study on legality and legal culture under Stalinism. Sharlet was careful to point out several important differences between the forms of dual governance under the two regimes, but convincingly explained why the parallel is illuminating in the Soviet case. Stalin's regime reserved the right to execute control over legal cases that were found to be of political importance, amongst others through special tribunals for political crimes. In a way comparable to Nazi Germany, the increasing scope of what could be regarded as 'political in the broad sense' had tragic consequences. In the regime's effort to 'normalize' the Soviet Union from the mid-1930s, Stalin headed a large-scale reform program to strengthen the rationality, professionalism, and functioning of the legal system. The state that emerged, Sharlet (1977, 155) argued, was "a dual system of law and terror". Where Nazi Germany built upon (and built down) an existing normative state, Stalin's administration instead had to re-establish rational-legal control more or less from scratch, considering its appalling state after two decades of revolution, war, and terror.

The dual state, I will argue, has more recently re-emerged in a new form. In the same fashion as Stalin and other Soviet leaders, Putin has strengthened the legal system's ability to provide everyday justice, while simultaneously promoting loyal figures to positions of power in order to increase his informal leverage. In this way, both the Stalinist and the Putinist periods witnessed seemingly contradictory tendencies of building and dismantling rational-legal governance at the same time. Both were state builders, yet also pyramid builders – working to coordinate the most important informal networks into single-pyramid systems. The incompatible goals of the regime and corresponding conflict between legal rules and political prerogatives have in Russia de facto split the politico-legal system into two distinct subsystems. The jurisdictional border between the two spheres was more clear-cut in Fraenkel's Germany than it could ever be within the muddy institutional landscapes of today's Russia. Yet, as I will argue, the idea of dual jurisdiction is appropriate to illuminate exceptionalism in Russia – how some cases are treated differently than the ordinary. As already argued, the mental division between ordinary and political cases survived from the

Stalin era and into the politicized justice of the Brezhnev era, where political salience was flagged by handpicked prosecutors and extensive background checks. The Russian population has thus been long primed to separate between ordinary and extraordinary cases, and the regime keeps dropping signals to reproduce this understanding (see Chapter 8). The dual state of Stalinism has been formally buried, but it continues to haunt Russian politico-legal affairs from its grave.

I am not the first to point out the usefulness of the dual state model to Putinist Russia. Hendley has been explicitly referring to Fraenkel's and Sharlet's works for over a decade. She contends that "the legal system [under Putin] is best conceptualized as a dual system, under which mundane cases are handled in accordance with the prevailing law, but under which the outcomes of cases that attract the attention of those in power can be manipulated to serve their interests" (Hendley 2007, 99). Hendley primarily intends to show how the non-political part of the legal system works and does not attempt to hide her revisionist project to counter the mainstream condemnation of Russian quasi-legal practices. For Hendley, a frequent reference to legal dualism thus becomes a framework within which she can examine the functioning of the Russian legal system on lower levels, without rejecting that a very different logic prevails in political cases initiated from above. As Hendley (2007, 99) points out: in Russia today "justice is possible and maybe even probable, but cannot be guaranteed". How you judge the system largely depends on whether you focus on the probable justice, or on the lack of guarantees. The dual state model lets us appreciate both aspects, without losing sight of the overarching political project.

A different approach to connect Fraenkel to Putinist Russia resulted in the theoretical framework of Richard Sakwa's (2011) book on the *Dual State and the Crisis of Russian Democracy*. In his adaptation of Fraenkel and Sharlet's thoughts, Sakwa (2011, 37–45) makes a series of quite wide reaching changes. Important for our purposes, Sakwa's reconceptualization produced some key insights that I will pick up on below. This work has also become a point of reference for others with a more jurisdictional approach, including Alexei Trochev (2016), whose interests in the model seem closer to those of Hendley. In our specific context, we should also mention Geert Jan Alexander Knoops and Robert R. Amsterdam (2007) who, albeit briefly, refer to the dual state model when characterizing Putinist Russia and the prosecution of Khodorkovsky in particular.

In Fraenkel's original model, the dual state is constituted by a normative and a prerogative state.[2] By the normative state, Fraenkel (1941, xiii) understood "an administrative body endowed with elaborate power for safeguarding the legal order as expressed in statutes, decision of the courts and activities of the administrative agencies". The prerogative state, by sharp contrast, is "that governmental system which exercises unlimited arbitrariness and violence unchecked by any legal guarantees" (ibid.). After the implementation of the Reichstag Fire Decree, the prerogative state gradually secured the exclusive jurisdiction to decide what were to be considered political threats and therefore exempted from the ordinary legal system. At the same time, "insofar as the political authorities do not exercise their power, private and public life are regulated either by the traditionally prevailing or the newly enacted law" (ibid., 57). The coexistence of these two jurisdictional spheres with conflictive logics yet complementary outcomes, constitutes the dual state in a nutshell.

In Russia and elsewhere, there is a considerable gap between formal laws, not least the constitution, and the informal rules of authoritarianism. Yet both elements contribute to regulate political life. In Chapter 1, I touched upon several approaches to authoritarian governance taking this observation as a point of departure. Whether we interpret the tensions as between state and regime, democracy and authoritarianism, patrimonial and rational-legal governance, or the Rule of Law and the rule of men, we seem to deal with largely overlapping issues. The dual state model deals with largely the same tensions in terms of two jurisdictional spheres – those of the rational-legal order and of the arbitrary forces in the political leadership, respectively. Presumably, it is Fraenkel's considerations of these tensions that make his model appeal to Sakwa. In the same way as for instance Hale (2015) or Robinson (2017), Sakwa veers away from classic regime labels in order to provide a more dynamic framework to interpret Russian politics. By means of the dual state model, the totality of the Russian experience can be grasped without underplaying neither the constitutional and liberal elements, nor the authoritairan and extra-constitutional particulars. Sakwa's approach may thus be seen as an effort to integrate the original dual state model with mainstream approaches to Russian politics. He is ambitious in his approach: "The tension between the two pillars is the matrix through which the Russian political landscape can be understood".

In line with my approach to quasi-legal repression, I will address the commonly accepted regime tensions as emanating from two *rule sets* – the coexistence of contradictory formal and informal rules under the same political leadership (Chapter 5). Perhaps better than neo-Weberian approaches, the idea of the dual state captures the gist of political and legal exceptionalism – how the regime switches at will between two modes of rule, a rational-legal and a prerogative. The two counterparts remain contradictive, however, since the rational-legal principle of impersonalism does not recognize the existence of extra-legal prerogatives.

This compartmentalization is part of the Russian legal tradition, even if the two realms are not entirely separated in practice. Selective law enforcement, we will see, illustrates both the separation and the conflation of the two spheres. Compared to Sakwa, my contribution is closer to Fraenkel's focus on the system's usefulness from an authoritarian perspective, and looks at how the two components of the dual state both contribute to an overarching political project. For this reason, it may be better suited to explain the rationale of selective law enforcement as an institutional choice, even if this 'choice' takes the form of gradual adjustments upon an existing institutional platform.

Dual state building in Putin's Russia

As discussed in the previous chapter, the Russian state under Putin became much more capable of rational-legal governance. It witnessed legal reform, legalistic rhetoric, and a considerable expansion of the legal system's capacity. If we look at these developments alone, we may conclude along the lines of Gordon B. Smith (2010, 151) that Rule of Law "appears finally to be taking root" in Russia. Against the backdrop of my study, however, Smith's conclusion may seem close to absurd. Rather than being absurd, however, it shows the dangers of pointing to the normative state without appreciating the existence of its twin system. Likewise, if we consider the prerogative state and the associated repression and manipulation to be Russia's 'true face', we will reach equally unbalanced conclusions. Both subsystems, I maintain, are fundamental parts of how Putinist Russia works.

Whereas in Germany the prerogative state was superimposed on a pre-existing legal order, the Putin administration strengthened the two subsystems at the same time. The increased production of bulk justice did not stop authoritarian drift, but rather developed alongside it. The subordination and centralization of the legislative and judicial realm we saw in the previous chapter have contributed to *both* the legal and the quasi-legal modes of governance – to both subsystems of the dual state. The success stories and the scandals, then, seem to be operating side by side. If the dual state model is appropriate to explain certain characteristics of this system today, it is even better suited to describe the *development* of the Putinist state and its underlying rationale. In Putinist Russia, and particularly so in the first two periods of Putin's presidency, the politico-legal duality was rebuilt, developed, and intensified.

Contrary to what took place in Germany, the contradictions between the two rational-legal and prerogative rule sets have not been solved by formalizing separate jurisdictional channels. Instead, the two rule sets have produced a form of hybrid governance that continues to confuse observers. Scholars have tended to discuss hybrid regimes on a high level of abstraction, but hybrid governance also has concrete manifestations - one can identify various activities of legal actors as leaning towards the one or another subsystem. Taylor explains the duality in terms of 'routine' and 'exceptional' law enforcement tasks:

> *Routine ones are those that are the core functions of an organization as set out in laws and regulations, whereas exceptional ones are set by superiors but are extra-legal or even illegal. (Taylor 2011, 3)*

In other words, the state administration works part-time for the regime and part-time for the state. Russia's coercive apparatus enforces not only formal rules, but also the informal rules dictated by the interests of their patrons. In this way, the informal interests carve out an exclusive space for themselves within the state. This split in governmental practice marks the borders between the ordinary processes on the one hand, and the exceptional on the other. Since this arrangement is unwritten and the borders fluid, it gives rise to a certain blur between state and regime, and between the public and the private sphere. The two subsystems, however, are still distinct and observable.

The importance of exceptions

Selective law enforcement is not 'how Russia works.' Selective law enforcement is merely how Russia works in exceptional circumstances. The vast majority of Russians are *not* experiencing any selection, which is indeed implicit in the term itself. Selection is extraordinary. In selective law enforcement, cases are taken out of the ordinary legal system and *de facto* dealt with in accordance to different rules. The selection, then, presupposes a notion of normality to which it constitutes an exception. The degree of importance we give this limited number of cases is crucial for how we evaluate the functioning of the legal system, judicial independence, or the Rule of Law. If we employ a pragmatic outcome perspective and look at the bulk of 'produced justice', Russia has scored increasingly well thanks to the strengthening of the normative state and of administrative justice in particular. As Russians increasingly come to use the legal system for solving their disputes with both each other and the state, the picture is increasingly becoming one of a modern country. From this perspective, the occasional high profile case of blatant manipulation may be seen as an unfortunate anomaly, certainly not good but hardly providing a basis for trashing the entire legal system.

If we look closely at the exceptional cases, however, our judgment will be different. The exceptional cases show that constitutional guarantees are not guarantees after all, but merely rules of thumb. One might ponder the usefulness of universal rights if they are not universal. In Russia, moreover, we can see that the state itself is actively involved in undermining its supposed cornerstone of constitutionalism. It is only in these exceptional cases, when the two rule sets are in sharp conflict, that we find good indications of their relative power. If the exceptional cases tell us little about how the legal system is experienced by the common Russian or how it contributes to keeping law and order in society, then they are very good indications of the *potential* for informal interests to penetrate the rational-legal logic.

When Russian citizens observe a case of selective law enforcement, they often interpret it as political repression. Within the logic of rule enforcement, this indication of a *potential* is exactly what is needed to create a *threat perception* that can influence the rational risk calculation among concerned parties (Friedman 1975, 82–4). As Hendley (2009, 261) has convincingly argued, the division between political and ordinary cases, although "opaque to outsiders, is clear to Russians". Because Russian citizens understand that the political cases are *exceptional*, their occurrences will not scare people away from the legal system in fear of telephone justice. Because the population interprets the exceptional cases as *political*, however, the practice gives them incentives to keep a low political profile. For this reason, we should not consider the exceptional cases to be marginal just because they are aberrations. Quite the contrary, the exceptional cases deserve attention because they are a barometer of the underlying mechanisms and power relations in society. They show us which actors that are ultimately in charge when push comes to shove.

For the central authorities to govern by quasi-legal means and to demobilize the population by low intensity coercion, this priming of the population is paramount. While the rough meaning of a baton to the head of a protestor is easy to understand for most, selective law enforcement is a more delicate issue. This mental compartmentalization of ordinary and political cases therefore strengthens the regime's ability to signal extra-constitutional policies through selective law enforcement. Because Russians interpret the latter cases as politically salient, yet irrelevant for the system's ability to produce everyday justice, the legal duality also shelters the 'ordinary' legal system from some negative spill over effects of political trials.

Organizing exceptionalism in Fraenkel's dual state

Fraenkel devotes a considerable part of his book to describing the unfolding of events between 1933 and 1937. This rather detailed study of jurisdictional struggle is not least a story of clashes between the old legal order and the new logics of the time, a logic of 'material justice' that demanded political expediency above everything else.[3] In this period of jurisdictional strife, the tensions between the two rule sets were more visible than later. The old order put up several fights as the Nazi regime gradually forced it to retreat. After the regime had eradicated the *Rechtsstaat*, the normative state had been tamed under the political will. The tensions between the normative and the prerogative states were still present, but since the prerogative state was firmly in the lead, they did not take the form of a power struggle. Rather, they stemmed from two different and coexisting rule sets with different *ultimate reasons* for legitimacy.[4] Whereas the prerogative state played the role of a demiurge with the right to administer the deeper 'material justice', the normative state was tied to the logic of rule based administration and 'formal justice.' Importantly, the two coexisted and were allowed to coexist because the political leadership was dependent upon both subsystems to support its political ambitions. After years of eating away at the legal order, the regime halted the expansion of the prerogative state.

As explored in Chapter 1, institutional hybridity tends to create dilemmas of governance. The Nazi regime sought to solve these dilemmas by establishing two separate jurisdictional spheres, which became the two counterparts of the dual state. To decide what question belonged within what sphere, the *jurisdiction of jurisdiction* was curiously given to one of the subparts. In other words, the prerogative state could itself define what cases it had jurisdiction over. Cases that the prerogative state did not declare as politically relevant were decided upon in the ordinary legal system, by the normative state. In this way, one of the subsystems became completely subordinated, yet was by the political leaders allowed to function more or less unblemished in whatever cases the prerogative state did not take an interest. After the political regime had secured this mechanism of political control, it could safely leave normal life to rational-legal procedures. The machinery of rational legal governance thus continued to work, but was politically disarmed. Something similar could later be observed in many other authoritarian or autocratic regimes, for instance in 20th century Southern Europe under Mussolini (Italy), Salazar (Portugal), or Franco (Spain). Indeed, Solomon (2015, 430) dubs this form of fragmented jurisdiction "the Spanish solution".

In Fraenkel's model, the prerogative state defines its own jurisdictional platform to be whatever it sees as important enough at the given time. The method to achieve this was a highly questionable juggling of legal principles. In the formulation of Karl Rudolf Werner Best:

> *The task of combating all movements dangerous to the state implies the power of using all necessary means, provided they are not in conflict with the law. Such conflicts with the law, however, are no longer possible since all restriction have been removed following the Decree of February 28, 1933. (in Fraenkel 1941, 25)*

The instrument to concretize the dual jurisdiction in the Nazi Germany system was the legal concept *konflikt*, denoting a mechanism that allowed the authorities to transfer any case they saw as significant to its own domain of legally unbound jurisdiction (Fraenkel 1941, 29–30). In other words, the dual state developed two *modes* of rule – one for cases in which the regime was not a major stakeholder, and one for the *exceptions* (Figure 4.1). Despite this power to define exceptions, which became ever more arbitrary, the prerogative state never tried to take over the old system completely. Because cases that it did *not* interfere with automatically remained under the jurisdiction of the normative state, the prerogative state was always limited to a sphere of exceptions, wherever it defined its borders to go.

In Fraenkel's Germany, as well as in many other regimes ranging from the *ancien régime* in France and military regimes in Latin America to the anti-terrorist regime under George W. Bush, exceptional cases are dealt with in parallel court systems (Pereira 2008). Typically, exceptional court systems deal with purported exceptional threats to the state or nation. This limited jurisdiction serves to legitimate the existence of exceptional courts in spite of their politically dependence. If political authorities can maintain

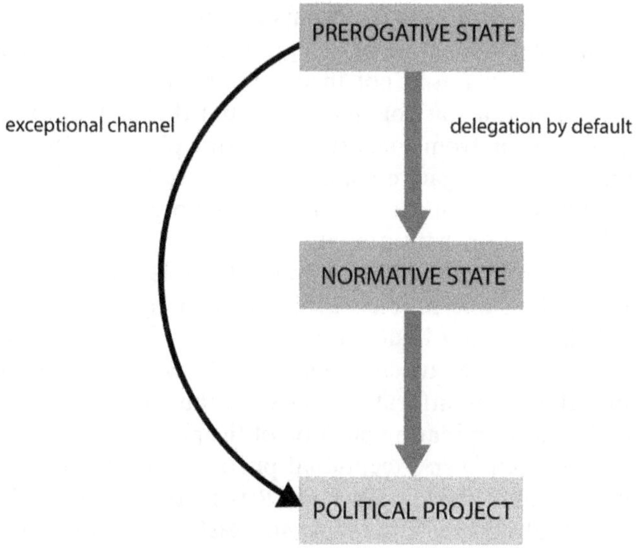

Figure 4.1 Organization of exceptionalism in pre-war Nazi Germany.

control with the special court system, they can give the ordinary subsystem considerable autonomy to ensure it works efficiently. Deciding what case belongs within each subsystem is a matter of negotiation. By means of fragmented jurisdiction, authoritarians can approach different goals within different subsystems, thus solving one of the key problems of institutional hybridity (see Chapter 1).

It is not least with regard to the organization of exceptionalism that selective law enforcement is a crucial element of Russian politics. From the Constitution of 1993, it is clear that the state should guarantee the freedoms of speech and association as well as equality before the law. By means of its repressive practices, however, the ruling elites signal their will to contain political dissent. In this process, certain targets are subjected to exceptional attention based on a rule set in which political obedience is key. If a legal case is initiated on this basis, it has been moved out of ordinary jurisdiction and will remain a political case for most purposes – for the legal actors involved, the initiators of the processes, the prosecutors, and any external observers. All of these parties will behave accordingly, making the case essentially different.

Unlike what is the case in certain other roughly comparable regimes (with regard to real civil freedoms), there are no special courts to deal with political issues in post-communist Russia, and no extralegal prerogative power has formalized. Russian courts enjoy full jurisdiction over politically sensitive cases, formally speaking. As mentioned, the constitution forbids special courts of this type. Therefore, the boundaries between the two subsystems of the dual state in Russia is informal and non-transparent, perhaps not even discernible to many outside observers. Post-Soviet Russia "has been in a permanent state of exception", Sakwa (2011, 42) notes, but the exceptions are "exercised not through constitutional provisions and some sort of defining a state of emergency, but through an informal and undeclared derogation from constitutional principles". In Russia, in other words, there is no prerogative state: "Instead we have informal behaviour … that fulfils some of the functions of the prerogative state but has no independent legal or institutional status of its own" (Sakwa 2011, 42). This insight is of profound value. It implies that selective law enforcement is a solution to the same problems shared by many other authoritarian states, namely how to coordinate political control with rational-legal rule. In other words, selective law enforcement embodies the efforts to satisfy both the formal and the informal rules simultaneously. This perspective makes room for the dominating position of the political authorities to utilize the state for their own exceptional purposes, while also illustrating the relative strength of the legal order in Russia as pointed out by Sakwa. As Sakwa (2011, 3) observes, the most successful Russian politicians are those who are able to understand and manipulate both rule sets (also see Ledeneva 2006).

In post-Soviet Russia, selective law enforcement became a solution to solve the contradictions created by institutional hybridity, weaving together the fabrics of formal and informal politics. On the one hand, selective law enforcement indicates the relative autonomy of the normative order and its ability to shape the strategies of the ruling elite. Even in exceptional cases, the political leadership cannot easily step out of the legal sphere entirely. At the same time, selective law enforcement is also a manifestation of the political leaders' refusal to bow to the constitutional order.

The counterparts in Russia's dual governance "are discreet subsystems, but the two are not insulated and hence Russian politics today is a dyadic order in which the two are in constant interaction, the essence of its hybridity" (Sakwa 2011, 41). The pervasive grey-zones in coercive practices with regard to legal/illegal and formal/informal dichotomies may thus in part originate in the fact that the formal institutions do not in themselves reflect the real balance of power in society; the *de facto* power enjoyed by the ruling elites is greater than what the laws purport. I therefore propose that quasi-legal harassment can be understood as a way to organize exceptionalism in a state in which neither exceptionalism or extra-legal harassment is formally approved of.

The jurisdiction of jurisdiction and the exceptional switch

Similar to Fraenkel's Germany, the exceptionalism in Russia is without clear boundaries. Even though the jurisdiction in Germany was delineated through the mechanism of *konflikt*, the prerogative state could move the boundary between the two 'states' at will. In Germany, the prerogative state was paradoxically *de jure* above law. In Russia, the interference with legal processes is informally constituted and thus not regulated by a formal mechanism of jurisdiction. The political leadership may nonetheless (or precisely because of this) be said to have an *unbounded* jurisdiction. While the practice is not grounded in any legal rights, the political leadership *takes* the prerogative to interfere with constitutional guarantees. The unbound character of Russian exceptionalism is reflected in the possibility of Russian authoritarian leaders to interfere in *every* sphere of life. Since this power is not channelled through a legal mechanism similar to *konflikt*, it may in fact be easier for the state connected elites to appropriate areas that were relatively undisturbed in Fraenkel's Germany, such as property rights. Indeed, the Putinist regime largely subordinates economic developement to the distribution of rents to the ruling elites. Where exactly the borders go for who is inside and outside this group of ruling elites is relative (some insiders are 'more inside' than others) and context dependent. The lack of clear borders between the two subsystems may account for much of the corruption and grey-zone governance.

A consequence of the unbound (informally constituted) jurisdiction is that the ruling elites are free to use either the normative or the prerogative state when approaching a given case. As we will see, it may be enough to make a telephone call to 'switch on' the exceptional subsystem in Russia. The key to the switch belongs to the ruling elites, who have access to clients within the legal system to serve their biddings. As the borders between the ordinary and political realms become internalized within the law enforcement structures, lower level clients may even switch on the exceptional subsystem themselves on behalf of their patrons. Because of the costs associated with all political interference, however, the actual use of the exceptional channel is much more limited in practice than what it *could* be (see Chapter 9). In practice, the prerogative state has neither the capacity nor the interest to interfere in every case. In the case of both Nazi Germany and Putin's Russia, the interference in practice took the form of somewhat predictable patterns (see Fraenkel 1941, 3).

Self-restraint in the dual state

Another characteristic of the dual state, sometimes omitted in the model's adaptation to Russia, is that the lack of interference by the ruling elites in the normative state's affairs is *self-imposed*. The regime needs not only a legal administration, but also a legal administration that is at least partly independent.[5] We cannot speak of a normative state, Fraenkel contends, if it does not continue to operate according to its own legal rules when not overridden. To retain and support this mode of operation is what strengthening the normative state is about.

In Germany, the prerogative state had *de jure* absolute power, but did not actually use it in the majority of cases (Fraenkel 1941, 57–8, 72). Issue areas like contract law, private property law, competition law, and labour law were in practice rarely touched by the prerogative state (ibid., 75–82). Albeit not without exceptions, these issue areas were largely kept isolated from political issues because of their importance for the economic development of the country. Indeed, the pockets of rational-legal governance were also institutionalized in the so-called economic estates (*Wirtschaftsstände*) that "deprived the state of its omnipotence" (ibid., 97). At the same time, both subsystems served as instruments to further the political project of the Third Reich. This is a key point for Fraenkel:

> *The limits of the Prerogative State are not imposed from the outside; they are imposed by the Prerogative State itself. These self-imposed restraints of the Prerogative State are of cardinal importance for the understanding of the Dual State. (Fraenkel 1941, 58)*

This is not to say, however, that the self-imposed restrictions are not contingent on external sources of motivations. In practice, all political actors are constrained by the complexities of incentives and norms in the elite group, society at large, or the international environment. From an instrumentalist perspective, however, these are not external impositions but incentives and factors influencing the choices of the actors. As discussed earlier in this book, political leaders may choose to empower courts for a number of reasons unrelated to having a soft heart. Many of the benefits of a rational-legal order are not derived from democratic legitimacy. Rather, the main source of benefits is Weberian and not Dahlian – rooted in the rational-legal principles of equality and impersonalism, not in involving the population in decision-making. Because of the limits to this legitimacy, Russia today cannot be considered a rational-legal order in full. Yet, the considerable element of rational-legal principles in its governance qualifies it as quasi-legal. The increased use of the legal system to accommodate everyday concerns is on the rise, and we saw in Chapter 2 tendencies of increasing trust in law enforcement agencies. This certainly grants the regime legitimacy. We should also note how the economic benefits of a rational-legal order are substantial, and the material wellbeing of the population of course a crucial aspect for securing legitimacy for most regimes. As noted in Chapter 1, the relative autonomy must be real, or at least appear to be real, in order to yield the favourable outcomes. Even if the arrangement is far from perfect, the relative isolation of the normative state from political intrigues makes it able to extract considerable legitimacy for the regime.

We may take selective law enforcement as an indication that political actors to some degree are restrained by empowered legal rules. At the same time, we may suspect that the normative state is functioning properly in so many cases because it is *allowed* to function properly. When the political leadership shows a sufficient determination and willingness to interfere in individual legal cases, it can easily make the normative state buckle. If everyone could penetrate the rational-legal logic, however, the rational-legal order would simply cease to be. On an individual level, the self-restraint may be explained in terms of the relative costs and benefits required to employ quasi-legal means. The relative empowerment of the normative state explains why a sounds legal basis is often favoured, and also why it is not necessary in all cases. Also, because the normative state is relatively strong, selective law enforcement does not always end up in formal sanctions (see Chapter 9). The important thing to note is that forcing matters through courts implies a significant cost to the insiders involved, much more so than initiating routine raids, pre-trial investigations, and administrative procedures. The central regime does not in general look favourably on coercion of high intensity or mass character.

The normative state as gatekeeper

In Chapter 5, I argue that politicians may depend on existing formal institutions in part to reflect and distort criticism by *instrumentalizing the ambiguity of overlapping formal and informal rules.* In addition to this ability, however, we should not forget the most straightforward reason to employ the state for particularistic interests. The state is after all a massive power-wielding apparatus, internally organized, fuelled with state money, and readily available. In other words, the law enforcement system is an organization with massive violent capacities, which makes it attractive for many purposes related to the use of force. While legal measures may seem soft compared to batons, low intensity coercion is ultimately founded on violence or the threat of such. Although it is low intensity, it is still coercion. The state apparatus is obviously an immensely powerful tool for those who control it. We should therefore not be surprised that the ruling elites delimit access to state power, nor should we be surprised that the very same state power is a popular tool for doing so. The state is an instrument, and since its powers are in short supply, the insiders guard it from freeriding.

Because of its relative significance (or insignificance) in political cases, the normative state may paradoxically work as a mechanism to *delimit and simultaneously support* exceptionalism. The reason for this apparent contradiction is the exclusive nature of exceptionalism itself. If the normative state had been too weak, the country would have been lawless - exceptionalism would be pervasive and in the final consequence become

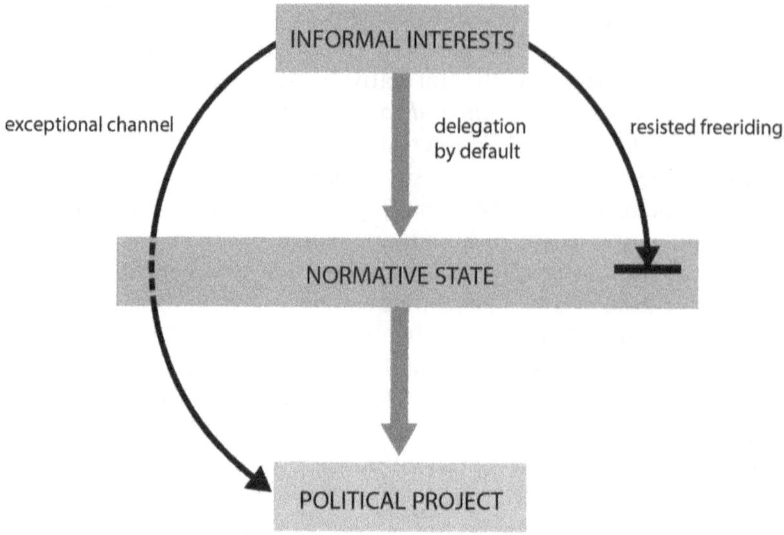

Figure 4.2 Organization of exceptionalism in Putinist Russia.

the norm. In today's Russia, as well as in other countries, the normative state is due to its relative empowerment able to withstand many attempts to influence its modus operandi (Figure 4.2).

The organization of exceptions *through* the state is an important aspect of how the politico-legal system of today's Russia works in practice. At the same time, it is exactly this resistance to interference that makes the exceptional channel exclusive. The normative state is to a degree able to resist localized or otherwise weak pressure placed on it. Precisely because of its relative empowerment, it limits freeriding in the exceptional lane and ensures that nobody gains more access than his or her position within the regime's informal structure would allow. As the severity of the repressive acts increase, so do the organizational and moral costs to push them through. The higher the cost of circumventing the normative state, the fewer will have the necessary prerogatives to do it (and tackle the consequences). In this fashion, the relative empowerment of the normative state serves to help the regime regulate the access to the exceptional system.

Pragmatic dualism – a cautious instrumental approach

Russia's quasi-legal order is not least a product of the unwillingness of the ruling elites to subordinate themselves to the constitution. The ruling elites are constantly exempting themselves from the validity of legal rules, and they circumvent and manipulate them for their own benefit. Nonetheless, it would be wrong to say that the informal and formal parts of the political system are simply in conflict. For the ruling elites, the state is not only a source of irritation and restrictions to dodge, but also their main power asset and source of legitimacy. Instead of seeing the contradictory rule sets as necessarily problematic from a practical governance perspective, I see them as parts of a dualistic political system that *works*. The political leadership retains and supports both pillars of governance since benefits may be reaped from both without completely satisfying either. By keeping the two relatively compartmentalized, the regime may seemingly cut down some of the costs associated with institutional hybridity.

This is not to say that either selective law enforcement or political dualism in general is a result of brilliant regime design. Indeed, the genesis of the current system tells a different story. As Solomon (2008b, 276) argues, "the court system was designed for a democratic political order in the making. That is, it is a judicial system meant to produce independent courts and impartial adjudication, and one invested it with responsibility for important decisions". Solomon (ibid., 262) claims that the courts "represent a legacy of incomplete, failed, or reversed democratization and [has] become an awkward institution in a competitive authoritarian environment". We may reasonably see the liberal foundation for the normative state to be a product of the international order after the end of the Cold War, and perhaps even as genuine attempts to create a new liberal Russia. In this respect, the legal situation reminds us of Russia after the 1864 reforms.

The quasi-legal order of today's Russia is built on top of an already existing institutional order dating back to the post Cold-War climate. The quasi-legal practices are largely the products of improvisation. Therefore, the dual state of contemporary Russia is not the result of an authoritarian masterplan. At the same time, it still carries out instrumental functions for its current masters. Even if the ruling elites did not create the rules of the game entirely by themselves, they are utilizing the enabling aspects of the inherited rules to considerable effects. The semi-autonomous legal order is *allowed* to retain its form because the benefits that the system provides the regime exceed the threat the autonomy poses. I contend that the balance between the two subsystems of the dual state is not a balance between a regime and the state as Sakwa (2011) suggests. Rather, it is a balance *within the regime* – a balance that *constitutes* it. In the words of Fraenkel (1941, 71) the two components "constitute an interdependent whole". For this reason, I suggest that the model of the dual state with benefits can be used in its original instrumentalist meaning when discussing contemporary Russia. Even if the normative state has a far greater impact on political life in Russia than it had in Nazi Germany, it has in either case been forced into an inescapable 'unholy alliance' (Hendley 2011).

Russian authoritarianism has become attached to the formal legal system like a parasite – borrowing both its muscle and its legal cover. The formal system naturally gets weaker, unable to take care of all of its core duties and suffering low support in the population. The quasi-legal order of today's Russia hinges on the relative weakness of the normative system – its penetrability. Yet, this parasite remains completely dependent on its host and cannot survive long without it. If a parasite does not kill its host, that is not a sign of the parasite's weakness. On the contrary, the parasite can continue to extract benefits from its host over the longer term. Sakwa (2011, vii) points out that neither subsystem "in present conditions can gain uncontested dominance over the other". Yet we should not interpret this as a balance between equals. While formal rules may partly restrict the political leaders' conduct, it is still the informal interests that call the shots.

In conclusion, today's Russia is not just hybrid, grey, and quasi, it is also a dual state in terms of its parallel logics. This duality takes the form of separate, yet interacting, impersonal and exceptional channels to get things done. In a way, selective law enforcement solves some of the problems that stem from the lack of formalized exceptional channels under a regime that insists on prerogative powers. By keeping the two relatively compartmentalized, the regime may seemingly cut down some of the costs associated with institutional hybridity.

Notes

1. The degree of legality attributed to this system was a major topic of debate within legal philosophy after the war. Most well known perhaps are the so-called Hart-Fuller debates that still resound in legal philosophy today. For a relatively recent collection of articles on the relevance of the debate in contemporary settings, see Cane (2010).
2. Whereas Fraenkel capitalizes the dual, as well as the normative and prerogative state, I will not.
3. Logic in a broad sense, since Fraenkel (1941, 48) sees the basis and operation of the prerogative state as fundamentally irrational and compares National Socialism to an inquisitorial church, "a theocracy without a god".
4. My use of the rule sets-terminology to Fraenkel's work seems largely consistent with Fraenkel's interpretation. Although Fraenkel conceptualized the prerogative state as *de jure* arbitrary, he contended it was *de facto* taking on (more or less) predictable patterns in the same way as the informal rules in my conceptualization.
5. Werner Best noted that "it is essential that many of the activities of the state should be carried out according to legal rules and that they should be calculable in advance" (Fraenkel 1941, 62). In the words of Hermann Goering (giving a lecture in 1934 before a group of attorneys and judges): "An arbitrary deviation from the law would constitute a violation of the judge's loyalty to the Leader" (in Fraenkel 1941, 74).

References

Cane, P. (ed.). 2010. *The Hart-Fuller Debate in the Twenty-First Century*. Oxford: Hart Publishing.

FraenkeL, E. 1941. *The Dual State. A Contribution to the Theory of Dictatorship*. New York: Oxford University Press.

Friedman, L. M. 1975. *The Legal System. A Social Science Perspective*. New York: Russell Sage.

Hale, H. E. 2015. *Patronal Politics. Eurasian Regime Dynamics in Comparative Perspective*. New York: Cambridge University Press.

Hendley, K. 2007. Putin and the Law. *In:* Herspring, D. R. (ed.). *Putin's Russia. Past Imperfect, Future Uncertain*. 3rd ed. Lanham: Rowman & Littlefield.

2009. 'Telephone Law' and the 'Rule of Law.' The Russian Case. *Hague Journal on the Rule of Law*, 1, 241–262.

2011. Varieties of Legal Dualism. Making Sense of the Role of Law in Contemporary Russia. *Wisconsin International Law Journal*, 29, 233–262

Knoops, G.-J. A. & Amsterdam, R. R. 2007. The Duality of State Cooperation within International and National Criminal Cases. *Fordham International Law Journal*, 30, 260–295.

Ledeneva, A. 2006. *How Russia Really Works. The Informal Practices That Shaped Post-Soviet Politics and Business*. Ithaca: Cornell University Press.

Pereira, A. W. 2008. Of Judges and Generals. *In:* Ginsburg, T. & Moustafa, T. (eds.) *Rule by Law. The Politics of Courts in Authoritarian Regimes*. New York: Cambridge University Press.

Robinson, N. 2012. Institutional Factors and Russian Political Parties. The Changing Needs of Regime Consolidation in a Neo-Patrimonial System. *East European Politics*, 28, 298–309.

2017. Russian Neo-patrimonialism and Putin's 'Cultural Turn'. *Europe-Asia Studies*, 69, 348–366.

Sakwa, R. 2011. *The Crisis of Russian Democracy. The Dual State, Factionalism and the Medvedev Succession*. Cambridge: Cambridge University Press.

Sharlet, R. 1977. Stalinism and Soviet Legal Culture. *In:* Tucker, R. C. (ed.). *Stalinism. Essays in Historical Interpretation*. New York: W. W. Norton & Company.

Smith, G. B. 2010. Legal Reform and the Dilemma of Rule of Law. *In:* White, S., Sakwa, R. & Hale, H. E. (eds.). *Developments in Russian Politics 7*. Houndmills: Palgrave Macmillan.

Solomon, P. H. J. 2008b. Judicial Power in Authoritarian States. The Russian Experience. *In:* Ginsburg, T. & Moustafa, T. (eds.). *Rule by Law. The Politics of Courts in Authoritarian Regimes*. New York: Cambridge University Press.

2015. Law and Courts in Authoritarian States. *In:* Wright J. D. (ed.). *International Encyclopaedia of the Social & Behavioral Sciences 2nd ed.*, vol. 13, 427–434.

Taylor, B. D. 2011. *State Building in Putin's Russia. Policing and Coercion after Communism*. Cambridge: Cambridge University Press.

Trochev, A. 2016. Legitimacy, Accountability and Discretion of the Russian Courts. *In:* Brusis, M., Ahrens, J., Wessel, M. S. (eds.) *Politics and Legitimacy in Post-Soviet Eurasia*. London: Palgrave Macmillan.

Whitmore, S. 2010. Parliamentary Oversight in Putin's Neo-Patrimonial State. Watchdogs or Showdogs? *Europe-Asia Studies*, 62, 999–1025.

Part II

Selective law enforcement in theory and practice

5 Selective law enforcement as a mechanism enforcing informal rules

From Part I of this book, it is evident that selective law enforcement is intrinsic to how the Russian politico-legal system works. So far, however, we have yet to analyse systematically the practice itself, and to create a comprehensive model of its components and its functioning. This will be the endeavour of the second part of the book. At first, it may seem futile. After all, selective law enforcement can be found in countless variations. It can be used to impede or block unwanted actions, such as the efforts of opposition parties or candidates to register for elections. Alternatively, selective law enforcement may take the form of aggressive legalistic attacks, be it selective investigations, administrative sanctions, or criminal proceedings. The pretext for the acts may be legally well founded, poorly founded or more or less unfounded, and the consequences for the victims may vary from long prison sentences to the minor irritations brought about by repeated state inspections or additional red tape. Correspondingly, selective law enforcement may scare journalists away from investigative journalism for good or it may have a softer impact – slowly draining their energy, motivation, and available resources. Whatever motivations may be behind the various legal acts are complex and diverse. In short, selective law enforcement is inherently chaotic, varied, and based on improvisation. No two cases are completely alike.

True as that may be, I will argue that selective law enforcement exists as a tangible object of research, that it takes on specific and observable patterns, and that it fits certain definitions that make the concept meaningful. There is a need for an academic concept that provides us with a language to discuss selective law enforcement in explicit terms and to uncover how it works. The next five chapters will contribute to this task.

The logics of rule enforcement

Selective law enforcement in many respects works just like other rule enforcement mechanisms, directed towards punishing or restricting actual and potential violators of rules. In the context investigated here, the politically motivated prosecution may enforce general obedience and suppress dissenting views. It seeks to keep political adversaries, civil society watchdogs, and other critics silent. By selective, but systematic and more or less predictable distribution of punishment, the practice also provides incentives for the rest of society to stay away from oppositional activities. The key message delivered by consistent politicized enforcement is that being in conflict with political authorities is a risky affair. In short, selective law enforcement reinforces existing political power relations by keeping insiders on the inside and outsiders out.

In the context of selective law enforcement, there are two main ways in which the directed appliance of violence may help to enforce rules. First, a punitive act may *deter* further non-compliance with any given rule. In the crude logics of rational choice theory, the punishment will "affect the calculus used by rational actors to assess their potential strategies and to select their rational choice of action" (Knight 1992, 17). In short, the punishment reinforces the belief that non-compliance will result in unpleasant consequences, and it thus makes the subjects more likely to comply. The punishment also reinforces the perception of threat for others that are (made) aware of the punishment – when they realize that violations are punished they have an incentive not to violate the rules themselves. Below, I discuss the implications and consequences of this mechanism in the case of quasi-legal repression at some length. Even if a rational choice perspective on punishment may be incomplete, it does serve as a useful point of departure for our purposes.

Second, impeding the ability to violate a rule can enforce the rule. Restricting entrance into a strictly forbidden area, for instance, is not just enforced by punishing trespassers, but also by setting up some sort of physical barriers. These preventive barriers help to keep persons outside, thus making sure that nobody will violate the rule of denied access. The physical restriction of imprisonment has a broader application as it blocks the subject's ability to commit a host of unwanted acts. As is the case with punishment, the preventive legal acts or sanctions may vary greatly in severity and be absolute or partial. Common to all forms of preventive acts is the ability to *constrain* potential non-compliers from committing unwanted acts, usually for a limited period of time (Friedman 1975, 67–75). While deterrence is dependent upon rational reasoning or psychological fear, acts of a preventative nature can be said to work in a more straightforward fashion.

Usually, preventive acts do not have the same broad impact as deterrence has. At the same time, prevention is a less complex mechanism and effective in its own way. In contrast with deterring punishment, someone whose non-compliance has simply been blocked need not *understand* the motivations behind law enforcement in order for the rule to be enforced. Furthermore, while deterrence is dependent upon providing incentives, a method that is known to be a gamble, preventive acts do not face these limits. The differences between these two aspects of rule enforcement carry implications for how selective law enforcement may be imposed effectively. Deterring and preventing constitute different strategies with different outcomes and scopes. Because general deterrence tends to have a broader impact, it is therefore less demanding on resources. In selective law enforcement, preventive acts carry the greatest significance when efficiently imposed to block the actions of consistent violators, those who will not be deterred. Keeping someone *preoccupied* works as a soft or partial prevention, restraining the target's ability to concentrate his efforts on unwanted acts. Preventive acts function only when a rule is prohibitive and not where it constitutes an imposition to perform a specific action. In this, they differ from deterrence, which in theory may impose incentives for any act: If you do *not* do it, then a sanction will occur.

In reality, many if not most legal sanctions have both punitive and restrictive elements. Imprisonment, for instance, impairs the prisoner's ability to commit serious violations. At the same time, it is traditionally also seen as a form of punishment, since the prospect of potential imprisonment is believed to shape the incentives of both former prisoners and the outside world for how to behave in the future. Similarly, a fine is both a punishment and a financial restriction, and an execution is certainly the ultimate preventive act against the person in question but also greatly deterring for others.

We need to approach punishment broadly in order to understand the impact of selective law enforcement upon society. The deterring effect is not dependent upon whether or not the punishment is officially recognized as such. The same holds true for restrictions. Repeated and prolonged court cases, for instance, may be interpreted as both punitive and restrictive even when they are won. Formally neutral acts, like 'routine' inspections, may have similar consequences. The litmus test of punishment is whether non-compliers are put in a (subjectively) worse situation than those who comply (Macrory 2008, 37). This insight is key to understanding the impact of selective law enforcement on society. Finally, to the degree that *investigative* acts are initiated selectively for ulterior purposes, they may also be encompassed by the term selective law enforcement. An example may be searches allegedly for unlicensed software but in reality more for internal documents and correspondence that can be useful in future suppression of legitimate activities.

Selective law enforcement's chain of purpose

Like all regulative rules, the informal rules enforced by selective law enforcement are composite. First, all regulative rules contain what Frederick Schauer (1991, 23) calls a *factual predicate*, a description of its scope.[1] The factual predicate defines the conditions to be met for sanctions to be imposed (or rewards given). The predicate may be translated into a 'if *p*' where *p* is a necessary and sufficient condition for punishment or reward. Second, the rule contains a *consequent*, 'then *q*', which specifies what will supposedly happen if *p* is fulfilled (ibid.). In deterrence-based enforcement, the rule is enforced by ensuring p indeed leads to q. In the case of preventive acts, the rule is enforced simply by making the predicate p difficult or impossible. In this understanding, the regulative rule thus includes a threat or warning that something might happen if the rule is violated (I will not discuss rewards). While the threat does not need to be explicit, it must be recognized for the rule to qualify as regulative. When we identify a regulative rule, we intuitively also accept that it has a consequent. A restaurant sign saying 'no dogs allowed' has no explicit consequent, yet most would understand the underlying rule, 'if you bring a dog, it will not be allowed into the restaurant' or 'if you bring a dog into the restaurant, you will be kicked out' (Schauer 1991).

Using the logic of deterrence, imposing punishment against noncompliers sustains the rule's integrity by reinforcing the link between predicate and consequent. In other words, punishment is primarily a means to an end, although the enforced rule is usually itself also a means to achieve some type of goal. Importantly, the punished must understand the significance of the punishment if they are to consider the rule. If those stopped from entering the restaurant do not understand that they are denied entry because of their dog(s), they might come back another day accompanied by the same dog(s) and expect to get in if they have upgraded their attire. For this reason, all rules that have ambitions to regulate behaviour beyond a single instance must be *promulgated* to have the desired deterring effect. In the above case, the sign 'no dogs allowed' does the trick. In the case of selective law enforcement, however, the main goal is not to enforce law. Legal rules are used as an instrument against a predefined target, and the legal steps are initiated based on external and legally irrelevant criteria. The doorkeeper of a bar may for instance deny entry to a person that fails to produce a valid ID, while the decision is actually motivated by racist discrimination. At this bar, the doorkeepers usually do not check IDs at all.

Selective law enforcement implies that the law enforcers in that instance do *not* act upon the legal rules that are instrumentalized. The doorkeeper is motivated by the informal rules as hinted at by the bar owners and influenced by its clientele; he or she uses the lack of ID as a pretext for racial profiling. At the same time, the pretext may fend off accusations of racism, which the bar owners fear may lead to all sorts of trouble. In such a case, the stated rule is purely pretextual; its purported enforcement takes no regard to the issue of ID. Had the person in question actually produced a valid ID, the doorkeeper may have simply changed the pretext and referred to the strict dress code. The motivations would remain the same and be unrelated to the pretextual rules utilized. Whether or not the guest complied with the instrumentalized rule is theoretically speaking *irrelevant* to the claim that it has been selectively enforced.

Political quasi-legal repression may take place according to a similar logic. After a series of peaceful but vocal street protests, a hypothetical mayor and an equally hypothetical political advisor may find the prolonged protests to be detrimental to their positions. They decide to contain the protests, but do not want to create a scandal. They know that an illegal crackdown with a strong hand may very well turn out to be counterproductive. They also know that it may hurt their popularity if they openly deny the official requests to arrange rallies. The political advisor makes a phone call to the local chief of police. During the ensuing days, several lead activists are detained and charged with taking bribes, using illegal substances, or distributing unlicensed software. The initiators of the investigation hope and expect that several other activist leaders will fear such legal scrutiny and stay home on the next day of the protests, finding that the risk is not worth the trouble. In this case, the concern of the police was not to enforce applicable laws, but rather to dig up any possible violation on the part of some predefined targets. This does not necessarily mean that the charges were entirely off the mark. The approach may or may not be built upon legally relevant information the police had already collected about their targets. The following week several of the leaders are absent, and the rank and file have been drastically reduced, perhaps due to information from activist websites spreading the word about the selective crackdown. In a relatively silent fashion, and with no obvious legal violations, the mechanism of selective law enforcement has reinforced the authoritarian rules of conduct. If the officials happen not to find anything useful, they may consider provoking a legal violation or simply fabricating some evidence, for instance by planting drugs on the victims. In any case, the relevant observers will know what likely caused the crackdown (see Chapter 4).

Above, I held punishment to be a means of enforcing a rule. By punishing criminals, for instance, the state strengthens the integrity of the Criminal Code. Selective law enforcement may at first glance seem to turn this logic upside down. In the above example, the legal rules become a means to the goal of punishing a predefined target and not the other way around. While it is true that a legal rule in selective law enforcement is a means to pursue punishment, this punishment again enforces *another*, informal, set of rules. This 'secondary' enforcement is the primary function of selective law enforcement. In selective law enforcement, legal rules are not to be confused with rules that are actually enforced. We can thus identify a chain of purpose: The legal rule is a means to punishment, which again is a means to sustaining the integrity of *informal* rules. To understand selective law enforcement as rule enforcement, we should not be distracted by the legal rules thrown at the scene to confuse us.

Legal acts are the tip of the iceberg

Punishment may deter in two main ways. First, it may deter the punished individual from pursuing further non-compliance, after the old principle 'once bitten, twice shy'. However, the target alone may not be the only one who is deterred by rule enforcement. We must also take into account the general deterrence – the so-called chilling effect. Not only may some of the detained activists in the above example fail to show up on the next rally for fear of further investigations or frame-ups, other activists and potential non-compliers understanding the political link will also contemplate the risks. Every time a target is punished, an unknown number of bystanders are considering the experience, and adjusting their future behaviour accordingly.

From a macro perspective on rule enforcement, then, the prosecution itself is predominantly a signal – it is a means rather than an end goal. While we can observe specific acts of selective law enforcement, we cannot easily estimate the impact of general deterrence and never count the number of statements and opinions that are never expressed publicly. Even the deterred individuals themselves are hardly able to recognize all the factors driving their decisions. The general danger associated with criticizing authorities leads journalists and others to self-censorship. I contend, however, that the term 'self-censorship' only clouds the repressive origin of the practice. What is self-censorship here but another word for successful enforcement of informal rules by means of deterrence? While it is well worth examining cases of individual prosecution, it should be underscored that most of the iceberg remains submerged and out of view.

Why informal rules must be promulgated

As already stressed, selective law enforcement is characterized by a link between the informal selection process and the formal legal procedures. Legal subjects may certainly misinterpret the political context, attributing a legal case with political meaning that the law enforcers never had in mind. Alternatively, prosecuted individuals may consciously lead others into believing in a political link that they have no belief in themselves. If the perception of a political link is established, the logic of informal rule enforcement will be partly valid even without the actual existence of ulterior motives on the officials' part. As Austin T. Turk (1976, 287) noted, "Law *believed* to be biased may be just as ineffective, or worse, as law that *is* biased".

According to Schauer (1991, 113), a subject of a rule can be said to *follow* the rule if and only if the rule constitutes a *reason for action*. If no consideration of the rule is involved in the subject's mind (the rule might for instance be unknown), the subject may of course happen to comply with it entirely by chance.[2] Similarly, if somebody does not comprehend the reason why punishment takes place, no mental link is established between precedent and consequent in the mind of the would-be-deterred. In this case no rule is enforced (except for prevention effects). The reason for prosecution must be known to the subjects, if they are to change behaviour in the way law enforcers seek (for the sake of argument, I will not discuss the possible effects upon unconscious behaviour).

Because of this important subjective aspect of rule enforcement, initiators of selective law enforcement must promulgate what trait or action they consider unwanted. Not only do they need to deliver this message to the law enforcers to be sure they take the necessary actions, but they also need to transmit the political message to the punished and others who might potentially be deterred. Importantly, it is the *perceived reason* for punishment that will determine rule enforcement, regardless of the intentions behind the prosecution. What may be perceived as a completely random display of force might certainly scare the targets but may not deter them.[3] Methodologically speaking, this is good news for a researcher. If insiders want to deter their critics, they necessarily need to leave some tracks that can be traced – indicators of selectivity.

Let us imagine another scenario of selective law enforcement to illustrate the point. The governor of the fictional region Primerskaya oblast is fed up with a journalist repeatedly looking into the regional leadership's shady involvement with the construction business. The governor fears for his reputation, but even more so he fears that sustained pressure may result in prosecution and his eventual downfall. As it happens, the accusations have more than a grain of truth to them, and even a governor is only above the law up to a point. The governor decides that action must be taken, yet subtly enough to not trigger scandal around the sensitive issues. The governor therefore arranges for the fire security agency to make a 'routine' inspection at the newspaper's premises. Knowing that the newspaper is located in an old building, he expects that no offices there will actually comply with the strict formal demands of fire security in Russia. The governor hopes that the agency can issue a fine to add pressure to the newspaper or shut it down to buy himself time. More than anything, however, he wants to signal that this line of investigation is unacceptable and needs to stop, and that he is willing to go to coercive measures to see it done.

When the agency has fulfilled its part of the deal, the future behaviour of the newspaper is entirely up to how its staff, editors, and/or owners perceive what has happened. If there is a misunderstanding about the governor's intentions or his role in initiating the fire security inspection, there will be minimal incentives for actors to change their attitudes regarding the regional government. Instead, the newspaper may address the fire security issue, perhaps by buying new extinguishers or installing fire doors. Ironically then, the formal rules are by mishap enforced instead of the informal. The governor's scheme fails. For the legal acts to deter future criticism of the regional government, therefore, the *de facto* reason for crackdown must be communicated. In the Russian case, both the editors and the population at large are already used to quasi-legal schemes and would most likely understand the rough meaning of the case anyway. Yet, if the newspaper for instance works on several contentious issues at the same time, it could be useful for the governor to signal which one he found unacceptable.

Selective law enforcement in terms of institutional interactions

We have seen how selective law enforcement may be described in terms of how it connects informal rules with legally imposed sanctions. In this conception, the practice is aimed at reinforcing the informal rules of political conduct by restraining or punishing those who challenge these rules. As noted in Part I of this book, there is a considerable literature discussing the interpretation, conceptualization, and systematization of our knowledge about how formal and 'other' institutions interact. The literature on *institutional interactions* also considers the hybridity and interactions between informal and formal elements. The hybridity of selective law enforcement, however, poses a problem to the existing typologies of institutional interaction and to the mainstream conceptualization of formal and informal institutions as being separate. In short, these conceptualizations or models seem unable to incorporate a notion of enforcing *informal* rules by means of *formal* enforcement procedures.

Kerstin Zimmer observed some of the same problems in her research on Ukraine. After criticizing normative concepts and existing typologies, she concludes that the boundaries between formal and informal rules in Ukraine are 'blurred' (Zimmer, 2008). This is reminiscent of how certain scholars have approached modern authoritarian regimes as existing in a 'grey-zone' between democracy and autocracy (Carothers 2002). This critique of existing dichotomies and typologies is meaningful and important. However, pointing to blurred boundaries does not provide us with any useful basis for building academic concepts for systematic inquiry. To conceptualize a complex phenomenon as essentially 'foggy' would make it impossible to break it down into its relevant components. By the same token, it would be meaningful and true to say that the Russian Internet is 'partially free.' An interactionist approach, however, would try to examine *how* it is free and *how* it is not free and look at how these two elements interrelate. Instead of jettisoning the dichotomy of formal and informal, I use it explicitly to highlight and disentangle the apparent dissonance it creates in analyses of Russia.

There are challenges associated with the use of a formal-informal dichotomy. Some scholars even reject it in full. Yaroslav Startsev (2005), for instance, argues that the formal-informal distinction is inherently biased and claims that the dichotomy presupposes the predominance of the formal. To describe a world of grey scales in terms of black and white arguably tends to lead us into residual categories with unclear meanings. Instead of explaining what a practice is, we may be tempted to call it quasi-formal for lack of better terms. In order to explore selective law enforcement as a phenomenon with a distinct hybrid character, however, the formal-informal dichotomy may still be useful. Properly used, quasi-formality may be more than a residual category. In positively defined terms, quasi-formality or quasi-legality may underscore rather than obscure the essence of what selective law enforcement is and how it works. At the same time, selective law enforcement is not easy to align with existent typologies of institutional interactions. In the following discussion, I will not offer conclusions about any preferred typology but instead provide a criticism of existing typologies with the peculiar practice of selective law enforcement in mind. For purposes of concept development, I also utilize the debate on institutional interaction to shed further light on the hybrid character of selective law enforcement.

Separate institutional chains and their interactions

In a simplified model of rule enforcement, violations of legal rules lead to formal sanctions, and non-compliance with informal rules correspondingly leads to informal sanctions. Agencies are authorized by the government to enforce legal rules, while society enforces informal ones. This model is arguably how we often think, and definitions that build on this understanding of separated institutional chains are many. Hans Joachim Lauth (2004a, 70) holds that while formal institutions "are guaranteed by state agencies and their violation is sanctioned by the state, most of the informal institutions are based solely on their existence and effectiveness". Another scholar defines informal institutions as those that are "not sanctioned or codified via legal recognition, legal enforcement, or official access to power/policymaking" (Grzymala-Busse 2004, 5). The enforcement of informal rules, then, may be seen as enforced "by means of sanctions such as expulsion from the community, ostracism by friends and neighbours, or loss of reputation" (Pejovich 1999, 166). In the interpretation of Gretchen Helmke and Steven Levitsky (2004, 727), informal rules are "shared rules, usually unwritten, that are created, communicated, and enforced outside of officially sanctioned channels". In a slightly different formulation, "state agencies and courts are not (officially) involved in the process" of enforcing informal rules (Stefes 2006, 18). Along these lines of thought, we may envision a model of two parallel rule sets with corresponding sanctioning mechanisms (Figure 5.1).

Even if scholars acknowledge the relative mismatch between the model and real life, the conceptual separation of informal and formal institutions is commonplace in scholarly literature. Considering how informality must necessarily be opposed to formality to make sense, this is hardly surprising. Selective law enforcement, however, challenges the model of separate formal and informal institutions because the concept also suggests that informal rules may be enforced by formal means. We may possibly salvage the conceptual integrity of a separation model by seeing the *initiation* of selective law enforcement as an informal sanction. Yet, a characterization that circumvents the hybridity so essential to the practice is in my view not satisfactory. In the case of selective law enforcement, the informal rules are certainly not "enforced outside of officially sanctioned channels" (Helmke and Levitsky 2004, 727). Likewise, state agencies

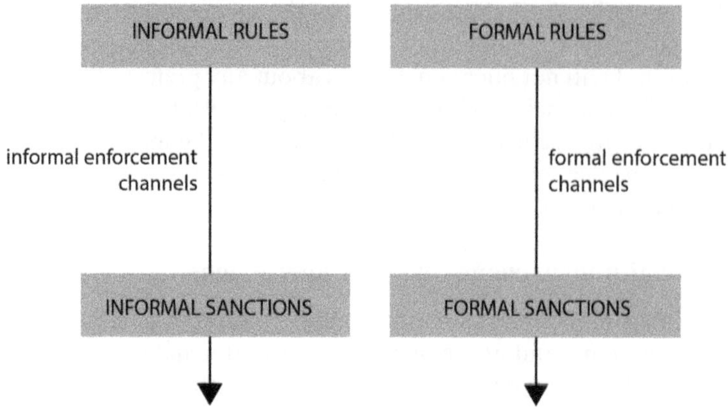

Figure 5.1 Separate institutional chains.

and courts are definitely "involved in the process" (Stefes 2006, 18) even though the rules are informal. In short, the mainstream model of separate institutional chains (Figure 5.1) cannot meaningfully explain this kind of hybrid practice.

The tight relationship between informal rules and formal institutions is widely acknowledged. While many definitions see informal and formal institutions as separate, scholars see them as interacting. Lauth (2004a, 73) even identifies informal political institutions by "their reference to binding decisions, guaranteed by the legally-constituted exclusive authority of the state". According to Lauth, this reference is exactly what separates informal political institutions from other informal phenomena. Following Guillermo O'Donnell's (1996) lead in engaging the topic of informal institutions, a number of works present models of institutional interaction on a similar platform. In these works, the informal institution types are, in one way or another, defined exactly by how they relate to formal institutions.

Like O'Donnell, Lauth primarily focuses on Latin America in his research. According to his typology of institutional interactions, the relationship between informal and formal institutions can be divided into the following categories: *complementary* – in which the institutions support each other; *substitutive* – in which the informal institution does what the formal fails to do; and *conflictive* – "when the two systems of rules are incompatible" (Lauth 2004b, 24). Based on her studies of Eastern Europe and Eurasia, Anna Grzymala-Busse (2004, 7) asserts a very similar categorization, discussing the different types of institutional interaction in terms of "substitution, undermining, and reinforcement". In a different article, however, Lauth adds a subcategory to his model of interactions that draws his observations closer to the topic of this book. Conflictive institutions, Lauth (2004a, 74) states, may either displace each other or the informal may penetrate the formal to the extent that the latter becomes 'occupied' and its functionality subverted. As I argue, the primary function of selective law enforcement is to undermine constitutional rights from within the legal system.

Victor Nee (1998) provides another typology from the perspective of institutional economics. Nee identifies three distinct types of informal norms – congruent, decoupled, and oppositional – based on how they relate to formal institutions. Like Lauth or Grzymala-Busse, Nee stresses the division between institutions in conflict or harmony with each other. The reference to decoupled norms, however, is a reintroduction of an idea earlier discussed by John Meyer and Brian Rowan (1977). Meyer and Rowan (1977, 345) found that formal institutions lend legitimacy to an organization because they are considered "proper, adequate, rational, and necessary". Yet, they also found that the activity of many organizations consistently deviated from the formal blueprint, to the degree that it seemed more or less independent from it. Formal rules are often created as vague or otherwise flexible, Meyer and Rowan observe, to provide legitimacy without restricting efficiency.

Helmke and Levitsky (2004) extend Lauth's and Grzymala-Busse's typologies. Building on the same logic, they restructure the typology to encompass four types of informal institutions along two defining dimensions (Table 5.1). The first dimension concerns the effectiveness of the formal institutions with which the informal ones interact. The second concerns whether the outcomes of the informal institutions are convergent or divergent with the formal. Three of the table fields are filled with institutional types we are now familiar with: complementary, substitutive, and competing (conflictive). In addition, Helmke and Levitsky (2004, 729) include in their four-field matrix the notion of *accommodating* informal institutions. These institutions "create incentives to behave in ways that alter the substantive effects of formal rules, but without directly violating them; they contradict the spirit, but not the letter, of the formal rules" (ibid.).

Helmke and Levitsky's discussion of accommodating institutions seems to build on the above-mentioned subtype that Lauth proposes and indicates that the authors do not neglect the widespread phenomenon of selective law enforcement. Yet, the matrix they present is by no means unproblematic from the perspective of selective law enforcement. Indeed, selective law enforcement highlights difficulties with regard to both the vertical and the horizontal axis of the model.

The distinction that makes up the vertical axis in Helmke and Levitsky is also implicated in the other typologies discussed, all of which operate with

Table 5.1 Typology of informal institutions in Helmke and Levitsky (2004, 728)

outcomes	*effective formal institutions*	*ineffective formal institutions*
convergent	complementary	substitutive
divergent	accommodating	competing

an idea that institutions may be in harmony or in conflict. While there is a degree of intuitiveness about such a distinction, it seems impossible to either foresee or measure any isolated *outcomes* of formal and informal institutions. In empirical studies, the impacts of theoretically separated formal and informal institutions seem impossible to disentangle. The problem of precisely identifying institutional causes for effects is obvious, but the trouble extends beyond this general problem.

The other key problem with the distinction stems from its institutional origins. As Douglas North (1990) observed, institutions are purposefully shaped within the existent opportunity structures; they are the creations of men and women operating in context. This fact means that legislators tailor new rules with the awareness of existing institutions and often in direct response to them. New rules may be created for the purpose of fighting old habits (informal institutions) or for complementing them. The *impact* of the rules, however, cannot be understood independently. This situation makes any notion of 'independent' institutional outcomes implausible. We may mend the problem of identifying causality by replacing 'outcomes' in the above typology with a notion that includes *intentions* of agents, such as 'intended outcomes' or 'institutional purposes.' Unless we choose to artificially isolate legal interpretation from its context, however, this conceptual adjustment will not resolve the deeper issue of institutional interdependence and contextuality.

The problem of measuring outcomes and intentions in empirical studies is obvious in the study of heavily corrupted and authoritarian regimes. As Keith Darden's (2001) study of Ukraine shows, anti-corruption laws were deliberately used for corrupt purposes, not only for individual benefit but also to keep the regime intact. Darden (2008, 41) maintains that "where graft is essential to the functioning of the state hierarchy … it is useful to think of hierarchy-reinforcing graft". Based on studies of Ukraine, Zimmer (2008, 268) contends that laws "are often purposefully designed in such a way, that informal patron-client relationship must be used in order to act successfully". This manipulation is not only a legacy of the past. While there are important elements of improvisation to the legal manipulation, the structural incentives for manipulation may also be part of active institution building and authoritarian regime design (see Chapter 7).

In many ways, this book adds to the circumstantial evidence in this regard, even if actual intentions behind law making will always be hard to prove. When the legislators belong to the same elite group as do the most powerful manipulators – and sometimes even are the same individuals – it would be counter-intuitive to interpret the intention behind laws to be in conflict with implementation practices. At the same time, it would be no more intuitive to conceptualize laws to be in harmony with their own abuse. In conclusion, the separation between convergent or divergent institutional outcomes, or even intended outcomes, is a less than optimal solution for our inquiry into the mechanics of selective law enforcements.

To make Helmke and Levitsky's vertical axis work properly after this critique, we can address the 'outcomes' of formal rules only in terms of their *formal purpose*. This formal purpose should not be addressed as the actual intentions of agents, but rather as a theoretical construct to denote a rational-legal 'promise' that a legal text supposedly gives its subjects. It is not impossible that Helmke and Levitsky (2004, 729) have something like this in mind when they hold practices that "contradict the spirit, but not the letter" to be examples of accommodating informal institutions. However, with the strong element of instrumentality in Russian legal culture in mind (Chapter 2), the 'spirit of the law' is not necessarily a fruitful point of departure for discussing selective law enforcement in Russia. To the degree legislators can imbue 'spirit' in a law, we would reasonably expect some degree of consistency between the legislators' motives and that spirit. Then again, we can only guess regarding their motives. If the motives of individuals are at best a challenging subject of research, then the motives behind group decisions are even worse. The only thing that remains certain is that these motives are diverse and complicated. As pointed out above, from the very creation of formal rules, the legislators take into account the existing world, including informal practices. The spirit of a law then, must basically equal its 'formal purpose' as laid out above.

The horizontal axis of Helmke and Levitsky's model separates informal institutions, depending on the effectiveness or ineffectiveness of the interacting formal institution. We also encounter challenges along this axis. As I will argue, selective law enforcement stands in a seemingly paradoxical relation to the formal legal system; it is at the same time dependent upon both the legal system's effectiveness *and* its weakness. The informal criteria that are enforced by means of selective law enforcement are in direct conflict with constitutional rights and thus the *formal purpose* of the legal system. To allow extralegal criteria to consistently influence law enforcement, the broader legal system must by definition be weak. Selective law enforcement also makes the legal system weaker by undermining it. It preys on the legal system's financial resources, and pervasive abuse also weakens its popular support. In turn, weak popular support hurts the ability of formal rules to be a regulative force in society.

Selective law enforcement, however, is also dependent on the continued existence of the legal system, included its allocated resources and its basis for legitimacy. Parasitic institutions are dependent upon the formal institutions they undermine. As in biology, no parasite can survive without a host, though the host can easily survive without the parasite. Lauth (2004a, 74) introduces the concept of *parasitic* institutions. According to him, parasitic informal institutions live at the expense of formal institutions by either "partially occupying or penetrating them". The more the legal system is abused, the less legitimacy it retains for rational-legal regulation and the less legitimacy it can lend back to selective law enforcement. With regard to physical resources, selective law enforcement is entirely dependent upon the state coercive apparatus. Because the scheme would be nothing without the muscles of the state, the parasite attaches itself to the formal institutions and preys upon its monopoly of legitimate violence.[4] The typology of Helmke and Levitsky does not account for such complex interactions.

Breaking the conceptual chains

We have seen how many definitions find common ground in a model in which formal and informal institutional 'chains' constituted by rules, enforcement channels, and sanctions are kept separated. We have also seen that an approach to selective law enforcement as the enforcement of informal rules by means of formally imposed punishment has certain advantages. Yet, this concept's bad fit with a traditional model of separated institutions is obvious. It is pertinent to ask, then, whether it is possible to break these institutional chains in order to reorganize them in a way that adequately addresses our subject of interest. As I argue below, the hybridity of the practice and the neopatrimonial setting again complicate our task considerably.

Stefan Voigt and Hella Engerer (2001) are among those who acknowledge the composite nature of institutions and the centrality of enforcement mechanisms to their functions. With background from law and economics, the two researchers define institutions as "commonly known rules to structure repetitive interaction situations plus an enforcement mechanism that ensures that non-compliance with the rule-component is sanctioned" (ibid., 132). In other words, they distinguish between two institutional components, namely rules and their enforcement. This is a useful point of departure for our purposes, as we have noted that it is exactly the rules and their means of enforcement that constitute the hybridity of selective law enforcement. A conceptual separation between the rule component and the enforcement component of an institution may therefore provide a more accurate model for our purposes than the above typologies.

According to Voigt and Engerer (2001, 132), "one can distinguish between rules whose non-compliance is sanctioned by representatives of the state and rules whose non-compliance is sanctioned by members of society". This premise again forms the basis to separate external institutions enforced by the state, and internal institutions enforced by society (ibid.). Voigt and Engerer (ibid., 133) also set up a typology of institution types based on categorizations along the lines of 'kind of rule' and 'kind of enforcement'.

In this typology (Table 5.2) Voigt and Engerer attach one specific type of rule to one specific type of enforcement. According to the resulting typology, the identification of one institutional component will therefore be sufficient to identify both the other component and the institution type. This bundling of the two institutional components 'rule' and 'enforcement' is unfortunate, as it largely ruins the point of addressing them separately in the first place. Moreover, their typology replicates the above identified problems of separated formal and informal institutions on a different level.

Table 5.2 Typology of institutions in Voigt and Engerer (2001, 133)

kind of rule	*kind of enforcement*	*type of institution*
convention	self-enforcing	type-1 internal
divergent	self-commitment of the actor	type-2 internal
customs	via informal societal control	type-3 internal
private rule	organized private enforcement	type-4 internal
state law	organized state enforcement	external

The separation of private rules – enforced by organized private enforcement on the one hand – and state law – enforced by organized state enforcement on the other – again provides a bad fit with the reality of selective law enforcement in Russia. We may possibly apply a distinction between just and corrupted legal acts to decide whether the rule enforced is a private rule or state law and whether the enforcement should be considered external or internal. Yet, we end up struggling with the same problems of discerning motivations and outcomes as identified above.

The problem of Voigt and Enger's typology originates in the authors' assumption of a clear separation between state and society. For this reason, the authors are not able to remove the fog surrounding hybrid institutions in neopatrimonial systems. In the case of selective law enforcement, the law enforcers are not acting purely on the behalf of the state (external sanction), but neither are they completely privatized for corrupt interests (internal sanction). Rather, the law enforcers attempt to combine the two rule sets in order to reach their informal goals *within* the formal framework. The coexistence of the two rule sets reflects the blur between the public and private sphere in Russian politics. *Both* formal and informal rules have a role to play in the enforcement mechanism itself, something not accounted for in the models discussed. It would be impossible to leave out this important fact in a concept of selective law enforcement.

As we have observed above, the neopatrimonial character of today's Russia makes the application of standard models of informal and formal institutional interactions problematic. Zimmer (2008) asserts that the Western separation between the public and private is normatively derived and as a research tool rigidly imposed on post-Soviet countries without regard for their social reality. Zimmer rejects much of the existing literature as ideologically biased and based on the erroneous assumption that neopatrimonial states can be seen as separate from their rulers. She contends that "informal rules and practices neither operate alongside nor in conflict with formal rules, and that they also do not replace the formal rules" (Zimmer 2008, 267). Instead, as we have seen, Zimmer asserts there is a "blurring of formal and informal rules" (ibid.). As noted, rules rarely develop in isolation from their environment. The interconnectedness of informal and formal rules is part of their functioning and their design. Notions of 'pure' formality are meaningless at least with regard to intentions.

We should also be aware of the trap of making formality a normative ideal in itself. As József Böröcz (2000, 352) puts it, a system of governance based on formality alone would be "just about the purest and most absurd" form of dystopia conceivable.

The literature thus approaches formal and informal institutions in a neopatrimonial setting either as separate or blurred. Selective law enforcement shows us that both perspectives are valuable, yet incomplete. My conclusive model integrates the two perspectives by explaining the apparent blur by means of institutional interaction. The separateness of the two is important, because the formal and the informal rules carry different functions to the mechanism in which formal rules are simply a pretext for the crackdown. In selective law enforcement, the formal rule stipulates 'if *p*, then *q*' yet we also see that 'if *r*, then *q*', where *p* is the formal predicate, *r* is the informal, and *q* is the expected consequence that gives the rules their integrity. In this model, the blurring of informal and formal rules is evident in the two rule sets sharing the same consequent(s). Because *q* is over-determined, it will ultimately be up to the prosecuted and observers to interpret the inspections with regard to *p*, with regard to *r*, or possibly with regard to both. While easy to keep separated on a theoretical level, an absolute distinction between formal and informal rules is sometimes harder to observe in actual cases. Questions regarding legality become fuzzy since the mixture of informal intentions and *de jure* legality is fundamentally non-transparent. By actively playing on the indeterminacy of these issues, selective law enforcement evades, complicates, and distorts attempts at objective identification.

As Guro Erdmann and Ulf Engel (2007, 105) note: "Under neopatrimonialism … formal structures and rules do exist, although in practice the separation of the private and the public sphere is not always observed". Indeed, Zimmer (2008) utilizes both the formal-informal and the public-private dichotomies in her own analysis. Rather than rejecting the conceptual pair as such, Zimmer presumably seeks to show how the interpenetration of the two makes a sharp distinction problematic and the relationship between them complex. Certainly, a distinction between formal and 'the other' has both a normative and a descriptive purpose. After all, there *is* a difference between formalized rules and informal rules of conduct, and in many cases the difference is intuitive and obvious. The constitution *is* a collection of formal rules, and the semi-institutionalized rates on kickbacks to state agencies certainly follow informal rules. This description holds true even if laws are designed in a process shaped by complex motivations, which may or may not involve positive expectations about their potential instrumentalization for extra-legal purposes.

Selective law enforcement as instrumentalized ambiguity

Based on the above discussion, I arrive at an illustrative model of selective law enforcement in which informal rules challenge the prerogative of laws to define what is punished within the formal enforcement channels.

It cannot be adequately conceptualized by a separate institutional chains model, but is rather characterized by the blur it creates between the formal and informal institutions. The blur does not occur at the level of the rule as such (formal and informal rules are distinguishable). Instead, the blur is evident in the over-determinacy on the level of the phenomenon. If we move up the chain from imposed sanctions to identify the reasons for the legal acts, we find that two different rule sets may possibly have influenced law enforcement.

Law enforcement officials and political insiders actively make use of this non-transparency. On the one hand, the crackdown against regime critics signals that the country is still governed by authoritarian leaders who insist on extra-constitutional prerogatives. At the same time, the practice suggests that the country is ruled at least *by reference to law*, a fact that the ruling elites can bring into play when they are pressed on the issues of quasi-legal repression.

A claim of selective law enforcement would necessarily stress the influence of informal rules, but initiators will be safeguarded by officially referring to the other, formal rule set. Figure 5.2 illustrates how selective law enforcement is an instrumentalization of the ambiguity created exactly by the problems identified in the above discussion of institutional interactions. In terms of our rule approach, we see a formal rule 'if *p*, then *q*', but also an informal rule 'if *r*, then *q*.' The two rules have the same consequent, making selective law enforcement non-transparent and leaving the question of what actually *caused* the law enforcement to be a matter of opinion and controversy.

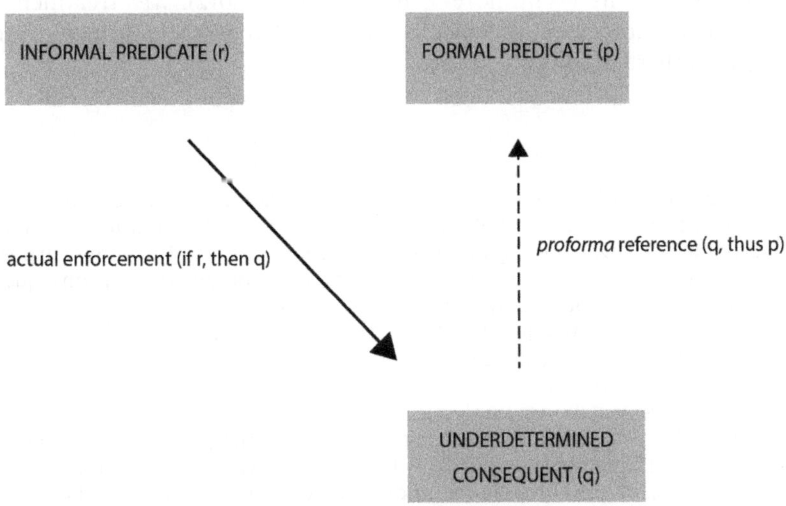

Figure 5.2 Hybrid model of selective law enforcement.

Critics of quasi-legal repression observe the outcome *q* and interpret it as an enforcement of an informal rule: 'if *r*, then *q*.' In other words, they believe *r* is what determined the decision to initiate a case. The authorities have already hinted that this assumption is a reasonable one (because they promulgate this rule) but will publicly brush off the accusations. To aid their argument, they will focus on the fact that there is a legal rule 'if *p*, then *q*' and that *q* is therefore the consequence of *p*. By utilizing this *discursive switch*, the authorities may move the discussion from one about political selection '*q*, thus *r*' to one about '*p* or not *p*.' This latter discussion, however, will largely be futile because the existence of *p* is a strictly legal question that cannot be decided outside a court of law. In this way, a spokesperson may deflect criticism without resorting to direct lies. In a sense, the deflection is nothing but a well-known conversational trick – dodging an unpleasant question by answering a completely different one. The answer is absurd in the sense that it does not address the question. Yet, this incongruity does seemingly not make it any less popular. As my analysis shows, we should keep separate the two issues of political selection and actual legal violations. Thus, the reference to legal violations cannot justify a political selection. In the same way, claims to political selection cannot justify legal violations.

In this way, we may conclude along the lines of Part I in this book. The interacting opposites and institutional hybridity is potentially beneficial if seen from an authoritarian governance perspective. As noted by Sakwa (2008, 879) "the contradictions themselves became a source of Putin's power" giving him the ability "to act in several different political and discursive spheres at the same time". Within the literature that employs neo-Weberian approaches to Putinist Russia, several scholars have reached similar conclusions (Whitmore 2010; Robinson 2012). My treatment of selective law enforcement as a mechanism to enforce informal rules is much in line with these findings.

Notes

1. I refer frequently to Schauer in my conceptualization of rules. I do not intend to contribute to any legal philosophical debates in my adaptation of Schauer but find his (1991) thorough conceptualization of rules useful for my purposes. In particular, I lean on his clear-cut separation of predicates and consequents and on his conceptualization of rules as separate from law.
2. Schauer (1991, 113) stipulates that "to be *guided* by a rule requires only that the agent take the existence of a rule as a not-necessarily-conclusive reason for action, but that to *follow* a rule requires both *being* guided by the rule and acting consistent with (complying with) its indications. Compliance with a rule is therefore different from following a rule precisely because of the way in which only the latter requires guidance by the rule. Conversely, non-compliance with a rule does not presuppose non-guidance, for non-compliance may be the conclusion of a reasoning process in which a guiding reason was outweighed by other guiding reasons".

3. This is why I favour speaking of selective rather than arbitrary law enforcement. 'Arbitrary' is often used in a contradictory fashion, in the meanings of both 'selective' and 'random or unpredictable.'
4. Vadim Kononenko (2011, 5) uses an almost diametrically opposite biologism to describe the relationship "between informal groups and formal institutions," calling it "a sort of symbiosis". The relationship that Kononenko sketches in that very same paragraph, however, is arguably parasitic. The state is "chronically weak and subordinate to the networks, yet it is kept afloat as a sort of institutional carcass that the networks need" (ibid.). Also Ledeneva (2013, 246) speaks of a "symbiotic relationship", reflecting the fact that the state is too weak to exist without informal practices to mend it effects, yet she also contends that the informal governance of Russia is detrimental to the official policies in the long term.

References

Böröcz, J. 2000. Informality Rules. *East European Politics and Societies,* 14, 348–380.

Carothers, T. 2002. The End of the Transition Paradigm. *Journal of Democracy,* 13, 5–21.

Darden, K. 2001. Blackmail as a Tool of State Domination. Ukraine under Kuchma. *East European Constitutional Review,* 10, 67–72.

2008. The Integrity of Corrupt States. Graft as an Informal State Institution. *Politics & Society,* 36, 35–59.

Erdmann, G. & EngeL, U. 2007. Neopatrimonialism Reconsidered. Critical Review and Elaboration of an Elusive Concept. *Commonwealth & Comparative Politics,* 45, 95–119.

Friedman, L. M. 1975. *The Legal System. A Social Science Perspective.* New York: Russell Sage.

Golding, M. P. 1975. *Philosophy of Law.* Englewood Cliffs: Prentice-Hall.

Grzymala-Busse, A. 2004. Informal Institutions and the Post-Communist State. *National Council for Eurasian and East-European Research.* Washington D.C.

Helmke, G. & Levitsky, S. 2004. Informal Institutions and Comparative Politics. A Research Agenda. *Perspectives on Politics,* 2, 725–740.

Jackson, R. H. 1940. The Federal Prosecutor. *Journal of the American Judicature Society* 24, 18–20.

Knight, J. 1992. *Institutions and Social Conflict.* Cambridge: Cambridge University Press.

Kononenko, V. 2011. Introduction. *In:* Kononenko, V. & Moshes, A. (eds.) *Russia as a Network State. What Works in Russia when State Institutions Do Not?* Houndmills: Palgrave MacMillan.

Lauth, H.-J. 2004a. Formal and Informal Institutions. On Structuring Their Mutual Co-Existence. *Romanian Journal of Political Sciences,* 2004, 68–89.

2004b. Informal Institutions and Political Transformation. Theoretical and Methodological Reflections. *Comparing Transformations. The Institutional Paradigm.* Uppsala: ECPR Joint Sessions of Workshops.

Ledeneva, A. 2013. *Can Russia Modernise? Sistema, Power Networks and Informal Governance.* Cambridge: Cambridge University Press.

Macrory, R. 2008. *Regulation, Enforcement and Governance in Environmental Law.* London: Cameron May.

Meyer, J. W. & Rowan, B. 1977. Institutionalized Organizations. Formal Structure as Myth and Ceremony. *The American Journal of Sociology,* 83, 340–363.

Nee, V. 1998. Norms and Networks in Economic and Organizational Performance. *American Economic Review,* 88, 85–9.

North, D. C. 1990. *Institutions, Institutional Change and Economic Performance.* Cambridge: Cambridge University Press.

O'Donnell, G. 1996. Another Institutionalization. Latin America and Elsewhere [working paper]. *Kellogg Institute.* Available at: https://pdfs.semanticscholar.org/e682/5bece7368441aec1c2bc9e0a7d00faefe24e.pdf [accessed 12.10.2018].

Pejovich, S. 1999. The Effects of the Interaction of Formal and Informal Institutions on Social Stability and Economic Development. *Journal of Markets and Morality,* 2, 164–181.

Sakwa, R. 2008. Putin's Leadership. Character and Consequences. *Europe-Asia Studies,* 60, 879–897.

Schauer, F. 1991. *Playing by the Rules. A Philosophical Examination of Rule-Based Decision-Making in Law and in Life.* Oxford: Clarendon Press.

Startsev, Y. 2005. 'Informal' Institutions and Practices. Objects to Explore and Methods to Use for Comparative Research. *Perspectives on European Politics and Society,* 6, 331–352.

Stefes, C. H. 2006. *Understanding Post-Soviet Transitions. Corruption, Collusion and Clientelism.* Houndmills: Palgrave Macmillan.

Turk, A. T. 1976. Law as a Weapon in Social Conflict. *Social Problems,* 23, 276–291.

Voigt, S. & Engerer, H. 2001. Institutions and Transition. Possible Policy Implications of the New Institutional Economics [working paper]. Available at SSRN: https://ssrn.com/abstract=294384 [accessed 12.10.2018].

Zimmer, K. 2008. Formal Institutions and Informal Politics in Ukraine. *In:* MEYER, G. (ed.). *Formal Institutions and Informal Politics in Central and Eastern Europe. Hungary, Poland, Russia and Ukraine.* 2nd revised and updated ed. Opladen: Barbara Budrich Publishers.

6 Three issue areas of controversy

In the previous chapter, I presented some of my main findings on what I call the analytical level of the concept. The next few chapters reduce the level of abstraction by presenting the examined legal context more directly and move to the operational level. Below I will initiate this discussion by presenting three legal issue areas with particular emphasis on cases of alleged abuse in the period between 2007 and 2011. The three legal issue areas, election registration procedures, anti-extremist legislation, and copyrights, all contained rules that served as popular pretexts for quasi-legal repression in this period. The legal issue areas have different characteristics, yet similar outcomes, and are thus particularly useful for the further examination of law in selective law enforcement. The review is mostly concerned with the immediate and time specific context of the examined crackdowns. Before I launch the review of the three legal issue areas, I will briefly introduce the political context of the period in question.

A peephole into quasi-legal governance

Following the so-called colour revolutions in Georgia, Ukraine, and Kyrgyzstan, a period of intensified crackdowns took place against non-systemic opposition in Russia, particularly between 2005-2007. The focus was directed not least against civil society actors who cooperated with partners abroad, especially on topics such as democratization or human rights. Simultaneously, the authorities suppressed the emerging protest movement associated with the coalition and later political party The Other Russia (*Drugaya Rossiya*) through various means. According to Robert Horvath's (2013) in-depth analysis of this wave of crackdowns, the measures amounted to a 'counter-revolution' to meet the tangible, albeit possibly exaggerated, domestic threat of a colour revolution.

Some years later, the election protests of late 2011 and mid 2012 spurred another Kremlin offensive against critics and activists. A number of protesters faced controversial trials, first in St. Petersburg ('the case of the twelve') and the next year in Moscow ('the Bolotnaya trials'). The well-known corruption hunter and opposition leader Aleksey Navalny was charged with embezzlement and has since been detained on a routine basis for various protest related activities. The period of increased political tension also saw a significant increase in the use of anti-extremist legislation against non-violent activists (Sova 2013). Other controversial cases from this period include those against members of the Punk group Pussy Riot, the activist Yevgeny Vitishko, the film maker Oleg Sentsov, as well as many others. Notably, the period also saw a considerable purge of regime insiders by means of selective law enforcement, amongst which the case against former Minster of Economics, Aleksey Ulyukayev, is perhaps the most well known. A number of new legal initiatives, including bans on 'homosexual propaganda'[1] and the branding of NGOs funded from the West as 'foreign agents'[2] put renewed international focus on the deterioration of civil and human rights in Russia, as did amendments to anti-terror legislation ('the Yarovaya package') giving law enforcement agencies sweeping powers. Finally, Putin's third term saw considerable efforts to strengthen the authorities' control over domestic media, not least including the online world (Soldatov and Borogan 2015; Pallin 2017).

An important part of the presented research focuses on the interim years between these two waves of crackdowns, roughly corresponding to Dmitry Medvedev's term as president but also including the events of 2007 and excluding the major protests in late 2011. In part of this period, the country was busy coping with a financial crisis, and because of Medvedev's relatively liberal rhetoric and modernization slogans, some expressed hopes for a modest loosening of the screws on civil society and oppositional activities. While the Sergey Magnitsky affair from 2008 became well known internationally, the period should have been relatively quiet for Russian liberal critics in general, or so it might have looked from the outside. Instead, things were not so quiet on the inside. In these years, new amendments and additions to the federal law on extremist activities gave authoritarian leaders in the regions new tools to fight old adversaries. The offensive included the establishment of the so-called E-centre (*Tsentr E*), a controversial new anti-extremist unit, within the Ministry of Interior. The regime also tightened election laws in several ways, and selective registration denials abounded in federal, regional, and local elections. The systematic suppression of Other Russia and the Dissenters' Marches continued, as did everyday repression of local and regional critics, not least by quasi-legal means. For the most part, my interviewees interpreted the quasi-legal attacks in this period not as part of any large-scale federal initiatives, but rather as initiatives by regional elites to hit back at their personal critics and rivals (see Chapter 8).

As does formal legislation, also the informal rules regulating selective crackdown change with political circumstances. The borders of what is permissible to say, write, and do is constantly changing. For instance did the 'moral turn' since 2012 and the situation in Ukraine since 2014 move the borders for what the regime considered to be acceptable public behaviour. The prosecution of Yury Dmitriyev and Kirill Serebrennikov may indicate that new fronts are being opened on the cultural and historical domains. The core rules of authoritarianism remain the same, however, and much of the underlying logics play out today as they did a decade ago. As a political tool, selective law enforcement works to keep the insiders in and the outsiders out. There are things you cannot do and words you should not utter, and quasi-legal and systematic repression makes sure society knows where the *real* borders for constitutional freedoms are.

An analysis by Gel'man (2015) highlights how selective law enforcement remains relevant under hardened authoritarianism. The post 2012 wave of repression took a complex legal form, including both repressive legislation and selective law enforcement of various brands. As has been the case since the 1970s, however, Russian kept the numbers of crackdowns relatively low, favouring precision and selectivity before mass repression. While selective law enforcement over time may change gradually, it will retain many of its key features. I intend my following analysis, therefore, to be relevant for the interaction of law, power and political dissent throughout the whole period of Putinism. Even if my fieldwork research merely samples a few years of quasi-legal practices, this sample constitutes a peephole to a phenomenon of considerable durability.

Selections before elections: Double standards in implementing registration demands

For a considerable part of the political opposition in Russia, elections have been something to watch from the sidelines. Prior to elections, the election committees and courts have determined who could stand for elections and who could not. Most committee chairs and judges responsible for legal review would insist that they have simply been applying the law. Many among the opposition, however, have experienced registration procedures as a legal minefield designed to eliminate unwanted candidates and monopolize the contest for political power. The enforcement, they claim, is consistently selective. By influencing the enforcement patterns directly and indirectly, the ruling elites have been able to filter out many unwanted candidates before Election Day. With one viable contester after the other removed from the race, the elections themselves may be far less competitive than was the preceding fight for registration. As a result, the quasi-legal practices deprived many voters of their favoured candidates – resulting in a dramatic reduction in democratic output. The candidates who were able to avoid these mines emerged with a considerable advantage.

Building primarily on material from local and regional elections in Perm and Vladimir in 2011, this section will discuss the legal framework and enforcement practices related to the registration of candidates to stand for elections and the denials of such registration. In both Perm and Vladimir, the elections were marked by serious controversies after election committees denied several viable opposition candidates registration. After the elections in Perm, a prominent member of Russia's Central Election Committee said he was alarmed by "possible double standards" in the implementation of election registration procedures in the region (Polina 2011a). Remove "possible" from his statement, and most interviewees in this study would probably agree with him.

The formal framework

At the time of inquiry, the legal framework regulating Russian elections was a very heterogeneous affair. Not only did it differ throughout the Federation, but it was also constantly amended on both the federal and the regional level. While one could otherwise suspect constant amendments to be the result of a fluctuating political landscape, the amendments started to escalate only after United Russia achieved its dominant position in Russian legislatures (since about 2003 (see Lyubarev 2011b)). In Vladimir, the legislature amended the local Election Code 20 times in the course of one legislative period (Lyubarev 2011a, 416). In Perm kray, it amended the relevant regional laws 16 times during 2010 and 2011 alone.[3] Even the federal framework law (Federal Law No. 67-FZ of 12 June 2002) that is intended to provide the main guidelines for federal and regional elections was amended several times every year in a period when United Russia enjoyed an absolute majority in the State Duma (Lyubarev 2011a, 425). Frequent changes lead to uncertainty, as every subsequent election had a different legal basis than the previous one. Moreover, the legislatures adopted many changes immediately prior to the elections, giving candidates scant time for preparation (Lyubarev 2011a).

According to Russian law, regional electoral legislation should not contradict the federal 'framework law.' One may therefore reasonably expect that changes in federal law would trigger waves of regional amendments throughout the Russian Federation in order to adapt and bring regional legislation into accordance with the new federal requirements. That would however be an insufficient explanation for regional amendments. According to Lyubarev, most amendments were not intended to clarify the situation or bring the legislation up to date. On the contrary, they bore witness to "the creative spirit of regional legislators" (Lyubarev 2011a, 425).

According to Andrei Buzin's (2007) study of regional election laws from this period, regional legislatures tended to adopt the most restrictive standards allowed by the federal framework. Buzin, who has intimate knowledge of Russian elections, concluded that the amendments in sum made the legislation more vulnerable to extralegal pressure. The regional chapter of Golos (2011b) was of the opinion that the regional amendments to laws in the Vladimir region were detrimental to everyone but United Russia. In short, in the period examined the legal minefield has not been cleared, but rather made ever harder to cross.

Perceptions of selectivity

Most of my interviewees in this field were either experts on elections and election law, or saw themselves as victims of selective registration denials. Common to both groups was a striking lack of satisfaction with Russian election laws. From the stories they tell of legal abuse, however, we can clearly see that Russian election law cannot be understood separately from its enforcement practice. A political scientist and campaign councillor in Perm summed up the situation in these terms:

> *[The main problem] is the implementation, of course. But in reality, it is both this and that because the law provides basis for this implementation. In reality, the law is contradictory and contains too many restrictions. Therefore, everything actually depends on the discretion of those implementing the rule.*

Against the opposition, the interviewees claimed, election committees took great care to identify even the most marginal mistakes. Another political advisor I interviewed had a chat with a colleague who reportedly "worked against" one of the candidates:

> *She told me openly that it had been hard to block [the candidate]. They called on some special lawyer from Moscow and searched for every possibility, worked tightly with the election committee to dig up a sufficient basis to block him from the elections. And dig it up they did.*

If the candidates were favoured by the current authorities, however, even outright falsification of registration documentation could easily pass, at least according to the claims of some interviewees. As the above-mentioned advisor recalled, the election committee had brushed off his own request to engage graphologists to examine more closely the signatures of another candidate, "even though a blind man could see that these signatures were just fake".

The above-mentioned advisor summarized the situation in terms several other interviewees would probably agree with:

> *The thing is that the law [enforcement] is selective … The [election] committee gets an instruction: "We don't need this guy, use whatever means it takes to get him removed," and everything is switched on. Or the committee on the contrary gets the instruction: "This is our guy so please don't touch him." … It is simple selectivity. The rigidity of the law will only be applied on occasions when it is necessary to block the road.*

Notably, the complaints of denied candidates greatly resemble the opinions of Russian experts. This similarity holds true not only for interviewed local experts, all of whom may possibly have had stakes in the regional political games, but also for internationally known Russian researchers such as Arkady Lyubarev, Andrey Buzin, and Grigory Golosov. Lyubarev (2007, 27), for instance, notes that the abuse of registration procedures often leads to "a selection of candidates and parties, not allowing those with good chances for victory to stand for elections". He holds this problem to be a major drawback for political competition in Russia and even calls it the "main inadequacy of Russian elections" (ibid.). Golosov (2011, 627) notes how the deliberate disqualification of "viable challengers" from elections has become widespread throughout the country. Scholars from outside Russia make similar conclusions (White 2011; Ross 2011). The election monitoring reports from Golos (2011c), confirm the tendency of an increasing politicization of administrative procedures prior to elections in this period.

In contrast with the other fields examined in this chapter, readily available data exists on registration denials relative to party affiliation. In the 27 regional elections that took place in 2011, 0.46% of United Russia members nominated on party lists were denied registration. For the other Duma parties, the numbers were significantly higher, ranging from 1.67% to 3.60%. For two of the larger extra-parliamentary parties (Right Cause and Patriots of Russia), it was higher still, at 7.80% and 9.42% respectively. In the case of the Yabloko party, comparable in size to these two at the time, and a well known platform for liberal opposition, 41.70% of its candidates on the party lists were blocked off. In single-mandate districts, the percentages of denied candidates equalled 0.36% for United Russia, about ten times higher for other parliamentary parties (3.50% - 4.76%), and between 50% and 70% for the above-mentioned extra-parliamentary parties (Ross 2014, 156–157). In single-mandate districts, candidates from these extra-parliamentary parties were thus roughly 200 times more likely to be denied registration than candidates representing the party of power. The data cannot tell us anything about the particular reasons for the denials. Also, we cannot consider a candidate's partly affiliation to be an entirely *informal* criterion for crackdowns, not least since the registration requirements are not identical for parliamentary and extra-parliamentary parties. Yet, the data provide interesting background material and confirm highly notable enforcement patterns.

Common controversies

Even though the legal framework is heterogeneous in time and space, it is possible to identify some categories of common registration controversies in these years. Most often, the registration denials found their formal basis in one or more of the following broad categories: (1) the committees' hired expertise found too large a percentage of the collected signatures invalid; (2) the candidates' registration documents contained errors or contradictions; or (3) the candidate had allegedly violated certain Russian laws in the pre-election campaign.

The requirement to collect signatures has possibly been the most controversial feature of Russian election law, and for good reason. Before each election, independent candidates (*samovydvizhentsy*) or parties not currently represented in the State Duma had to amass signatures to document their support among the electorate. The number of signatures to be collected depended on the size of the constituency, and thus ranged from a handful in a small electoral district to the two million signatures needed to register as an independent candidate for president of the Russian Federation. If more than a certain percentage (also varying) of the signatures were be deemed invalid (*nedeystvitel'nyye*) or inauthentic (*nedostovernyye*) by expert evaluation, election committees could refuse that candidate or party list the right to run in the elections.[4]

Regardless of the indisputable importance of signatures in the registration of *samovydvizhentsy* or smaller parties, federal legislation lacked specifications for how the signatures were to be verified. The procedures, then, were often a subject of controversy. At the end of the day, the legal actors were left with wide discretion in deciding whether a candidate's signatures should be considered valid or not (Buzin and Lyubarev 2008). The level of discretion granted the committees, and their simultaneous fixation on detail in verifying the signatures can be illustrated by a case from the Perm elections. Among the signatures collected to document support among the electorate (for an incumbent), the experts found one signature which they insisted had been written with the letter 'п' (p), not 'ы' (y) as in the person's actual name. Little did it help that the signer publicly verified that it was indeed his signature (Golos 2011c, 103). In Vladimir, the party list of Yabloko was first registered by the committee but later lost the registration in court. The reason was blots or corrections in signatures that according to Golos (2011b) were irrelevant in determining their authenticity.

More often, the committees focused on alleged inconsistencies in the personal data that are to accompany the signatures (see Buzin 2006; 2007; Buzin and Lyubarev 2008). In Perm, for instance, many signatures were found invalid because of incorrect home addresses. A few years earlier, the region of Perm *oblast* had merged with Komi-Permyak *okrug* into Perm *kray*, a new federal entity. Perm oblast was thus officially no longer a Russian region, and could correspondingly not be a valid address. As if this rule stickling was not enough, it corresponded with the fact that most passports still had the old name listed as home region. This effectively produced a catch-22 situation. It was therefore impossible for signers to provide information that would correspond with both their passports and with the official registers (Golos 2011c, 103). In several controversial cases, signers were alleged to have given incorrect residential addresses. In particular, this was common when street names contained abbreviations or were known under two different names, something which is not unusual in Russia (Buzin 2006).

Russian law at the time stipulated that *all* signatures collected on incorrect forms were to be deemed invalid. In many cases in which the percentage of invalid signatures seemed extraordinarily high, the dispute was not actually about the individual signatures but about the sheets on which the signatures were collected. Alfred Khaybrakhmanov, for instance, had to cancel his plans for re-election as city deputy in Perm. Officially, he was denied the opportunity to fight for another period on the grounds that the signature sheets for his candidacy had printed the text “year of birth (if 18—day and month of birth)” as header of the column where the signer should write down his or her age. In recent amendments to the regional law, the header had been specified to be “year of birth (if age of 18 *on the day of election—in addition* day and month of birth)”. Since the extra seven words in the column header were not written on the signature collection sheets, all of the signatures were found invalid, and Khaybrakhmanov was denied registration although nobody who had actually signed the list were below the age of 19. This fact was deemed irrelevant by the Sverdlovsk District Court in Perm, that maintained that it would be wrong to show flexibility in the enforcement of such a clearly-stated requirement, as this would “violate the principle of equality before the law of all the candidates, the principle of equal suffrage and [the right] for citizens to exercise their eligibility”.[5] In this way, the legal instrumentalism of contemporary Russia seemed able to combine a remarkable formalism with aloof references to higher principles of law.

Signature collection was not the only headache for politicians seeking to get their candidacy registered. Another frequent basis for denials was the alleged irregularities in the documents provided for the committees. All candidates had to submit registration documents, and this pretext could also be used to reject candidates nominated by parliamentary parties. Federal law does not specify the exact demands for documentation, so once again a considerable amount of discretion remains with local actors. The case of one of my interviewees may illustrate the point. After 12 years as a city deputy, she was suddenly requested by the election committee to produce her marks from high school, a document she had not seen in 30 years. In other cases, the stated basis for denial concerned inadequate documentation or lack of correspondence between the information given and the documentation provided. In yet other cases, the documents were simply found invalid. In Perm, for instance, one candidate who planned to run for the Communist Party (CPRF) had his registration denied due to an allegedly invalid passport, but won back the registration in court (Golos 2011c, 106). The same thing happened to a political veteran running for the party Just Russia (*Spravedlivaya Rossiya*) in Vladimir. Problems with passports were a common basis for denials in Russia in these years. Typical foundations included incidental remarks in the passport (by state officials) or failure to provide a copy of the empty pages.[6]

Finally, a third category of cases was constituted by cases where the candidate had allegedly violated certain laws during the election campaign. At first glance, this commonly applied basis for refusing registration may perhaps seem more substantial than the others. Among the violations that constitute valid basis for denials are abuse of office, using money from sources other than the election fund, and violating intellectual property rights or conducting ‘extremist activities’ during the election campaign. As has become common knowledge thanks to the Navalny case, registration can also be denied based on previous sentences. The well-known opposition candidate had his registration for Presidential Elections 2018 denied on grounds of a previous convictions, even though the European Court of Human Rights had found the trials in question flawed.

The rule against financing election campaigns from sources other than the election fund is reportedly routinely violated, but only cracked down upon on occasion. In these few selected cases, however, it is sometimes interpreted in an incredibly strict and formalistic manner.[7] To deny candidates or parties on grounds of extremist charges have been relatively rare. In one case from the examined period, Yaroslav Nemchaninov got some attention when he was accused of having incited hatred against a supposed "social group" – which consisted of "deputies of the State Duma, excluding the CPRF [Communist Party] faction" (Golos 2011b, 10). It was more common to be denied registration due to copyright infringements, yet also these case are rare compared to the number of candidates denied due to various documentation issues (Golos 2011b; 2011c).

The devil in the details

The interviewed candidates from Perm and Vladimir agreed in one respect: the legal framework was incredibly demanding on technical details.

> *It is very strict, very formalized ... If you want to remove somebody, find a comma - no problem. Some bagatelle, trifle or imprecision ... Any tiny non-correspondence and it will mean removal from the elections.*

In the words of another interviewee:

> *The legislation is used in such a way that it is possible to find violations absolutely everywhere, but only on some occasions and only with some candidates will they [actually identify them].*

In some respects, the detailed demands of Russian election law are not so unique. After all, modern bureaucracies everywhere tend to create masses of rules and standards. Commonly, however, those who fail to meet administrative standards will simply face the irritation of additional paperwork. At times, they could be subjected to a fine or an administrative fee. In the cases reviewed here, in contrast, the principle of proportional punishment seems completely neglected, as legal actors used administrative infringements to deprive the candidates of their constitutional right to stand for elections. As Lyubarev pointed out, "all important laws concerning registration should have only this goal: to filter out unserious candidates, but let those pass who have or can get real support from the electorate".[8] The official purpose of registration requirements is to filter out completely unserious candidates. Denying registration because of minor technicalities has little or no connection to this purpose. But then again, the interviewees did not see this as the real reason why they were denied.

This relentless formalism was also evident in the fact that signatures were almost exclusively rejected for being invalid (*nedeystvitel'nyye*) and very seldom for being inauthentic (*nedostovernyye*), that is, written by another person (see Lyubarev 2007). This was also true with regard to federal elections. When Mikhail Kasyanov failed to register as a candidate for the presidential elections in 2008, for instance, 80 147 of the signatures controlled were found invalid, but only 213 unauthentic (Buzin and Lyubarev 2008, 81). When Grigory Yavlinsky was unable to register as presidential candidate four years later, 25.66% of the signatures controlled were found invalid, but almost all of them because they had been delivered to the Central Election Committee (CEC) in the form of photocopies. In other words, the rejections were based not on claims of foul play, but of sloppy handiwork.

This formalism with regard to minor infringements has greatly frustrated critics. As a Yabloko politician commented:

> *Of course there might be mistakes. But this is not a crime, not a falsification … Even if there is an error in the [reported] passport number, this does not mean that the person is non-existent. It just means that the passport data have been written incorrectly.*

Frequent denials for invalid or inauthentic signatures, have repeatedly caused citizens to depose or testify before committees and/or courts to confirm that their support and signatures are real. Often, however, committees and/or courts tend to rely on expert evaluations despite witness statements (Eshanu 2011b). When formalism takes priority in this way, the signature collection in practice becomes less a way to document public support, and more a procedure to show organizational prowess. According to a member of United Russia and a regional CEC, the party's organizational skills are exactly why United Russia stands out in registration processes. United Russia's low number of registration denials, he maintained, was due not least to the high quality of hired professional lawyers. From this perspective, he added, "signatures are money". Many observers, however, would find the crackdown on these alleged technical violations a strange priority in a country ridden with much graver election violations and even blunt falsifications (Myagkov et al. 2009; Skovoroda and Lankina 2017). They make more sense, if interpreted as selective law enforcement.

An insider's perspective

When I interviewed a CEC member and asked him about selective registration denials, he made a common discursive switch. Instead of answering the question, he assured me that the committee he worked for had only rejected those who were actually violating the law:

> *Every time we have had scandals, I have looked at the basis for denials. The law has been applied in a clean way, legal and correct … The reasons [for denials] have been mistakes done by the collectors and the candidates' lawyers.*

The election committee did not deny any candidate without a legal basis, the CEC member explained. The committee was in fact so soft-hearted that its members on several occasions had given candidates and party lists particularly *light* treatment. Recently, he claimed, the committee had let through candidates from CPRF on pure goodwill. Earlier, the Union of Right Forces (*Soyuz pravykh sil*) had also been allowed to run under the governor's protection despite grave violations of the election law. "We have in [our region] no instances when the law has been applied unrightfully", the CEC member concluded, "[but] I can find instances where the law has not been applied – when more [candidates] could have been refused".

In single-mandate districts, popular in regional elections at the time, only a handful of candidates are eligible, and the local committees must vote over the registration of each of them. The registration process is binary in that it has only two possible outcomes. Selective non-enforcement therefore becomes an active decision in the same way as selective enforcement. From this perspective, the above-mentioned CEC member was in practice reformulating the pig Napoleon's decree in George Orwell's classic novel *Animal Farm*: All animals are equal (none is *unequal*), but some animals are more equal than others. The politician from United Russia stressed that party membership was not necessarily decisive for selective law enforcement or non-enforcement: "We are not always independent from politics, but dependent on politics in ways not favourable to United Russia". In fact, the only case of selective law enforcement (in his definition) he could think of was against a United Russia candidate. Incidentally, Lyubarev mentioned this same case as the only recent example he could recall when a United Russia candidate had been deregistered in a controversial manner.[9]

Preliminary conclusions

While practices such as bribes or ballot stuffing on Election Day still take place in Russia and elsewhere, electoral manipulation has in modern states become increasingly legal or quasi-legal (Gandhi & Lust-Okar 2009). Not only may changes in the electoral system have dramatic consequences for how the votes cast translate into delegate seats, but also the *supply* side of elections may be altered, with important impacts. In several African countries, for instance, incumbent legislatures have included nationality clauses in the election laws in attempts to block specific opposition candidates (Schedler 2002, 42).

My findings sketch out the workings of a less direct way of manipulating which parties or candidates end up on the ballot. Unlike, for instance, the above-mentioned nationality clauses in African countries, selective law enforcement is not openly restrictive against any particular candidates. Instead, selective denial of a candidate or party registration in Russia is based on a technically demanding environment for *all* candidates, including regime insiders who stand for elections.[10] The interviewed candidates complained first and foremost about double standards in the implementation of registration requirements, and were united in their belief that the motives for denials were overwhelmingly political.

While unable to verify these accusations about ulterior motives in individual cases, this analysis documents serious dysfunctions in Russian electoral law that make it prone for abuse. The combination of vague and frequently changing laws, mixed with a lot of strict requirements, formalistic enforcement, and harsh punishments, created a legal environment in which no one was entirely safe from denials without leaning on patronal structures and informal support from *within* the system. Because the ruling elites had both formal and informal influence over administrative and legal actors, they could rely on this formally apolitical administrative framework to work as a *de facto* political filter.[11] Selection prior to elections in this way reduces the need to employ more direct and illegal means on Election Day in order to ensure victory at the polls. At its full potential, it can even make other means of manipulation superfluous. In many districts, the ultimate consequence is that the people are deprived of their right to vote for their favoured candidate. Especially in single-mandate districts, alternatives are often scarce.

Extremism or criticism: Controversies of anti-extremist legislation and enforcement

Moving from electoral politics to the legal issue of anti-extremism makes for a radical change of political setting. Anti-extremism is a politicized legal field overtly intended to curb the harmful by-products of free speech, delimiting constitutional freedoms to maintain the social order. In the field of Russian anti-extremism, however, two practices distorted this logic. First, the legislation was enforced excessively against elements of little or no relevance to the stated purpose, predominantly to boost agencies' performance ratings and satisfy quota fulfilments. Second, law enforcers employed the legislation selectively against various groups seen as harmful to the regime rather than the state or the population. Among them, political activists constitute a considerable group. This second case study will focus on the legal field of anti-extremism, with particular focus on claims of selective law enforcement in the period 2007 to 2011 and their legalistic underpinnings.

Confronted with considerable problems of anti-constitutional and violent groups of both nationalistic and extreme Islamist character, the Russian authorities have under the leadership of Putin and Medvedev channelled considerable amounts of money and prestige into fighting political and religious extremism. The measures against extremism, however, quickly assumed a character whereby freedom of speech was arguably excessively compromised. In several cases, law enforcers seemed to confuse the security of the state with the survival of the political regime. Moreover, taking advantage of the situation, some Russian state actors saw opportunities for ensuring their own welfare rather than that of the Russian state and society. The examined practices illustrate not only how Russia's authoritarian system works, but also how state actors can instrumentalize the law's weaknesses for their own purposes. They also remind us how absurd the outcomes can get when formalistic law enforcement is not anchored in common sense.

According to Sova (2008b), the trend of using anti-extremism for targeting political opposition and regime critics was evident earlier, but grew considerably stronger from about 2005. It should be noted, however, that controversial prosecution of regime critics involves a low number of cases compared, for instance, to the systematic persecution of religious minorities based on the same legal framework.[12] Of course, this fact does not make prosecution of politically critical actors any less real. In the period under scrutiny, controversial enforcement of anti-extremist legislation against critical voices was a persistent problem. Since 2012, the persecution of political dissent by this and related means has continued and expanded, underpinned by new regulations of the Internet and the so-called Yarovaya-package of 2016.

To some extent, the Russian authorities have been addressing the issue of violent nationalist groups in both word and deed. In 2002, a uniform legal framework "On Combating Extremist Activities" (114-FZ of 25 July 2002) was adopted to encourage prosecution. This new law may not have changed much, legally speaking, yet it had a significant political impact and facilitated increased law enforcement activity and anti-extremist prosecution (Levinson 2003). While the legal analyst Brian D. Gross (2003, 732) welcomed the initiative of creating a separate legal framework, he also feared that the law would be open to abuse, especially on the local level "where enforcement tends to be arbitrary and self-serving". In his evaluation of the law, Gross (2003, 759) specifically discussed the possibility of using the law as a tool for cracking down on political opponents. The main issue in this regard was the list that defines extremist activities. As Gross (2003, 723) indicated, it could be considered "rather vague and unpredictable". For the next 15 years, and probably well into the future, the critical reception of new anti-extremist legislation in Russia came to echo this early analysis.

The law "On Combating Extremist Activities" underwent significant amendments just before the examined period. In 2006, The Duma passed a law (148-FZ of 27 July 2006) to further expand the definition of extremist activities. Perhaps realizing the poor quality of the changes, however, the Duma cancelled many of them the next year. The key legal documents of relevance to the period of inquiry is therefore the amendments of 2007 (211-FZ of 24 July 2007), as well as the original text from 2002. Worried civil society actors subjected these amendments to heavy criticism. Sova (2008a) however, maintains that many of the 2007 amendments were for the better, at least from a technical point of view. Not only were many uncertainties from 2006 removed before they came into use, but the changes also attempted to address a need to deal with the ideological and political motivation behind, for instance, neo-Nazi attacks on anti-fascists or ideologically motivated killings of gay men – actions that previously had fallen outside the concept of racial or religious hatred. It established 'extremist-oriented crimes' as "any crimes motivated by political, ideological, racial, ethnic or religious hatred or animosity, or by hatred or animosity towards any social group". This formulation is now included in several articles of the Criminal Code. While legislators have repeatedly changed the definition of extremist activity, the vagueness seems to have survived all the amendments.[13] In concrete allegations of selective law enforcement in 2007-2011, the content of the term 'social group' became a particularly hot topic, which I will address in the following.

Anti-extremism simultaneously deals with major crimes, minor administrative infringements, and offenses mentioned in neither the Criminal Code nor the Administrative Code. All of these offenses have been subsumed under a rather lengthy 'definition', or rather list, of extremist activities. While the law on extremist activities by itself provided grounds for sanctions against organizations (including media outlets), individuals can only be legally sanctioned for violations of specific articles contained in the Criminal or Administrative Codes of the Russian Federation, many of which were changed by the amendments mentioned above. For our purposes, the most relevant formulations in the Criminal Code can be found in Article 280 (Public Appeals for the Performance of Extremist Activity), Article 282 (Incitement to Hatred or Enmity, as well as Abasement of Human Dignity), Article 282-1 (Organizing an Extremist Community), and Article 282-2 (Participation an Extremist Community).

In 2008, a special anti-extremist department, frequently referred to as the E-Centre, was created under the Ministry of the Interior. Its formal purpose was to intensify and coordinate the enforcement of various extremist-related crimes. As will be seen in a later chapter, this agency also played a role in several selective law enforcement schemes, even if its exact function remains hard to pinpoint without more structured analysis.

Selective enforcement of anti-extremist legislation may be divided into two subtypes. In some cases where it was used against regime critics, the political content was more or less overt, even if formulated in legalistic terms. In other cases, the interviewees claimed that technical issues were pushed to fore as pretext for ulterior motivations. We will deal with the two types separately, starting with the former.

Prosecution through vagueness

The opaque character of Russian anti-extremist legislation has resulted in a large volume of cases hardly in line with any normal conception of the term 'extremism.' Echoing the infamous Soviet political laws, the anti-extremist legislation "makes a perfect instrument for prosecution of political opponents or other groups that stand out from the mainstream" (Sova 2016). The interviewees consistently reproduced the idea that 'extremism' was a highly flexible tool in the hands of political authorities. Many of them stressed how one could stretch the law to encompass every political statement:

> *Now I am sitting here with you, and they can issue a warning that we are extremists. That is, [the definition] is so broad, that anything can count as extremism ... Look, we have tested it ourselves, it is really like that – every action can according to this law count as extremism.*

> *If you here [in Russia] criticise the authorities today, you are an extremist. That is the approach. They try to present every publication critical to the authorities as extremist.*

> *Earlier when someone was not pleasing* (ne ugoden), *they [law enforcers] tossed some narcotics into his pocket. Now it is very easy simply to charge him with extremism ... The law in its current form lets [the law enforcers] punish not only extremists but also those who are not pleasing the authorities* (vlast').

The case against human rights activist Vadim Karastelev may serve to illustrate how controversial enforcement can follow from a vague definition of extremist activities. In this case, a special slogan used in one demonstration became central in the accusations of extremist activities. The banner said, "Freedom is not granted, it is taken", a reference to Maksim Gorky's words "rights are not granted, they are taken" from the 1901 drama *Meshchane*, sometimes translated as *The Philistines* in English. According to the expertise that the court used as foundation for their ruling, this text implied the following proposition:

> *A human being has individual and unalienable natural rights – the freedom or right to think, express himself, live and so on. Thus, one cannot wait for these rights to be given man from somebody "above", but one need to take them with force, use them without preliminary permission. (in Florin 2009)*[14]

The experts found the slogan to have an 'extremist character' and to serve the purpose of Russia's enemies. Their statement even referred to the Dulles's Plan, widely known to be a false conspiracy theory. The Russian Ombudsman on human rights subjected the court decision to heavy criticism in his annual report: "If this slogan is extremist ... so is the Russian Constitution". He considered the expert conclusions to be "endlessly far from the truth" and made the original Gorky quote the epithet of his annual report (ibid.).

In the caseload presented by Sova from this period, we see a significant number of overtly political interpretations of the term 'any social group' (*kakaya-libo sotsial'naya gruppa*) between 2007 and 2011, as well as later. The legal term figures in Article 29 in the Russian Constitution, protecting minority rights, and the concept of political, ideological, or social hatred is included in several articles in the Criminal Code, including Article 63, which lists hate motive as an aggravating circumstance for any crime under Russian Law. However, it was not until 2007, when the concept of hate crimes became "completely absorbed" by the anti-extremist legislation, that the term became a favourite tool for prosecuting regime critics (Sova 2008b). The notorious Article 282 of the Criminal Code has an especially prominent role in this process.

In the period of inquiry, Article 282 applied to:

> *Actions aimed at the incitement of hatred or enmity, as well as abasement of dignity of a person or a group of persons on the basis of sex, race, nationality, language, origin, attitude to religion, as well as affiliation to any social group, if these acts have been committed in public or with the use of mass media.*

It should be noted that Article 282 did not address 'political' or 'ideological' hatred directly. The term 'social group' however, has proven extraordinarily flexible when anyone has wanted to infuse it with a political meaning.

The period from 2007 saw what could be called a creative urge to test what could be achieved by using this term. In 2009, for instance, in one case the law enforcers claimed that an individual had incited hatred towards the social group of 'owners of domestic motor transport' (Sova 2010). In 2012, a similar case appeared with reference to the social group of 'men' (Sova 2013). Two years earlier, Roman Zamurayev was memorably accused of inciting hatred against "people who had not joined the organization *Armiya voli naroda*" (Army of the People's Will) (Sova 2010b). In this latter interpretation, the 'social group' included almost every human being on earth and turned the idea of protecting minorities on its head. More important, however, was the persistent push of law enforcement officials to establish a political interpretation of the term 'social group' to shield the political authorities and themselves from criticism. According to Sova, the cases in which Article 282 was used to protect professional groups with close connections to the regime constituted a "vast majority" of the cases that invoked this term in these years (Sova 2011). In contrast, only a few attempts were made to apply the article to protect sexual minorities. These attempts repeatedly failed on the grounds that sexual minorities were not found to constitute 'social groups' (ibid.).

The broad and varying interpretations of Article 282 was made possible at least partly by the fact that both the terms 'hatred' and 'social group' were poorly defined in Russian law. In addition, the 2007 amendments to extremist legislation included a technically minor, yet greatly consequential, move to disconnect the formation of 'incitement to hatred' from that of 'violence or threat of violence.' As completely nonviolent actions could also be seen as inciting hatred, it then became hard to distinguish ordinary criticism from hate speech – legally speaking. According to Verkhovsky, the director of the Sova Center, the only strictly legal interpretation possible is that virtually *all* political agitation is extremism, "because incitement to social discord is the general agenda of any political movement".[15] It seems that well-connected political forces took advantage of the blurred legal lines to push their own agenda, often by punishing critics of the regional government or law enforcement.

In a plenary session resolution in 2011, the Supreme Court addressed the problem of political abuse. According to this resolution:

> *Criticism in mass media of state servants (professional politicians) or their actions and views should not in all circumstances in itself be counted as actions directed against the dignity of an individual or a group of people. In relation to these people, the limit of what is acceptable criticism should be broader than that concerning private persons.*

The resolution went on to underscore the point that law enforcement should take into account the motivation of the individuals who have been spreading the extremist material. To convict someone of violations under Article 282, the court maintained, is was not sufficient that a crime had been committed *in* hatred but that the action was intended to *incite* hatred. The resolution also stressed that fact based political and scientific discussions should not be considered a violation of Article 282. Actual law enforcement practices following the resolution, however, suggests that resolutions like this may have limited impact in Russian context. A Sova report from the same year observed that the "prosecutors and judges are so far simply ignoring [the 2011 resolution]" (Sova 2011). In May 2012, a court closed one case and concluded that "there is no consensus whether the police comprise a particular social group". Yet, the tide did not turn. On the contrary, the cases based on Article 282 only increased, including cases the Sova experts found inappropriate. As one of their reports concluded, the courts have in general displayed little eagerness to curb the general problems of underdetermined laws on the one hand, and their selective application on the other (Sova 2015).

Formalism and counter-intuitive 'anti-extremism': Prosecution through strictness

Some parts of the defining list of extremist activities were fairly clear and semantically consistent. Yet, Russian law enforcement agencies also used these legal provisions in a controversial manner. Indeed, a formalistic *lack* of flexibility in these cases seems to back up controversial rulings. According to Sova reports, imitated anti-extremism based on formalistic interpretation and a wish to fulfil enforcement quotas was widespread. Monitoring agencies have for instance issued thousands of warnings to schools and libraries – for not blocking access to banned Internet sites[16] and for distributing extremist literature,[17] respectively (Sova 2010b; 2013). In 2009, a state agency issued a formal warning to a Moscow newspaper for mass distribution of extremist content. The case is a good example of how a formalistic application of anti-extremist legislation may be used against liberal critics. To understand the dynamics, however, more detailed legal background is necessary.

Amongst offenses deemed extremist by law, are actions described in the Administrative Code's articles on "demonstration or dissemination of Nazi symbols" (Article 20.3) and "mass dissemination of extremist materials" (Article 20.29). A common criticism raised against these formulations was that they paid no attention to the context in which Nazi symbols or extremist materials were used. For instance, practically all screenings of documentaries about Nazi Germany could by a strict interpretation be considered a public demonstration of Nazi symbols, regardless of how negative an attitude they displayed towards Nazism.

The responsibility to ensure that the Russian media complied with law belonged at the time with the monitoring agency Roskomnadzor.[18] If Roskomnadzor identified extremist content in a publication or broadcast, the monitoring agency had the mandate to issue a formal warning, in theory to make the media outlet refrain from extremist activities in the future. Sova lists a range of cases in which they find Roskomnadzor's warnings to have been unfounded, although not necessarily selectively initiated on political grounds. According to their analysis, 15 out of 33 warnings issued in 2009 were inappropriate or unfounded (Sova 2010). In 2010, the figure was 10 out of 28 (Sova 2011). Such a formal warning is in itself inconsequential, but a repeated violation within a year provides grounds for liquidation proceedings in court. Thus, formal warnings functioned as a good way to beef up case numbers without creating scandals (in practice, the first formal warning is rarely followed by a second). At the same time, formal warnings are a useful tool for exerting pressure.

In 2009, Roskomnadzor issued a formal warning to a Russian federal newspaper. The formal reason for the warning was an article that quoted and published visual material from the webpage of Russkiy obraz, a group of ultra-nationalists.[19] According to a journalist of the newspaper, the article in question intended to show the readers the real nastiness of this (legal) nationalist group – a group which was seemingly involved in the murder of human rights lawyer Stanislav Markelov and the journalist Anastasiya Baburova. Roskomnadzor, however, found the newspaper article to "incite social, racial, national and religious discord (*rozn'*)" as well as "propagandizing and publicly demonstrating Nazi attributes or symbols".[20] As a newspaper representative said:

> *You can call anyone an extremist ... The news about our warning gave the fascists a good laugh. They laughed hard on the right-wing websites, these people that are always writing commentaries about how we are an anti-fascist newspaper.*

Another interviewed journalist found the case depressing. As he put it: "You cannot fight extremism by punishing those who are trying to fight extremism".

Also on this issue, the Supreme Court (2010, Article 23) made an effort to change abusive practices of a simplistic, formalistic, and counter-intuitive nature. In a plenary resolution, it stressed that mass media quotes should not be taken out of context when considering their legality. In 2011, the director of Roskomnadzor, Sergey Sitnikov, also expressed a need to eliminate contradictions in the legislation on what should be consider propagation of Nazi symbols, a statement that at the time created some hopes for improvements (Sova 2012). The attempts to change the counter-intuitive practices, however, suffered the same fate as many other positive initiatives before the 2011/2012 protests, and largely came to naught (Sova 2013).

Preliminary conclusions

This analysis of anti-extremist legislation and its enforcement has pointed to several plausible answers as to why anti-extremism has become a rather popular tool of selective law enforcement in Russia. The material indicates that new amendments to the legislation served to create legal uncertainties that law enforcement officials and their patrons quickly exploited. Selective law enforcement of this legal issue area seems to take place in two distinctly different ways. First, the discretion provided by vague formulations can encourage politically skewed law enforcement. Second, we have once again seen how strict rules, if enforced relentlessly, may serve to support what would normally be considered against the spirit of the laws. In the legal issue area of anti-extremism, this sort of formalism does, however, seem to be a much less prominent problem for critics than the vague formulations.

When a legal rule, like Article 282 for instance, is *overtly* oriented towards delimiting civil freedoms, it is not self-evident whether a politically skewed use should count as selective law enforcement as such. While the legal term 'social hatred' is very unclear indeed, one cannot say that it is a catch-all in the same sense as the minefield of bureaucratic demands we saw in the case of election registration. In contrast with the notion that everyone may be framed guilty, many critics of anti-extremist legislation have proposed that the legal formulations have been so broad that every form of *criticism* could be encompassed under the term. The difference not only concerns whether *all* are under the threat of legal sanctions, but also relates to the degree of *agreement* between formal and informal predicates (see previous chapter). This difference is purely relational and cannot be understood by looking at the formal or informal components separately. When overtly political laws such as the ones on extremism are overextended, self-perceived targets and other critics of selective law enforcement roughly agree with the legal documents with regard to what action caused a reaction. Not only is the legal issue area highly politicized to begin with, but we may also find it less easy to separate the distinct meaning of vague legal rules from informal rules that are also fluid by definition. The interviewees' conceptualization of said law enforcement also reflects this. Typically, a critic may claim that the regime uses anti-extremist law as an instrument to target critics of the regime rather than to fight *real* extremism. This assertion is in essence not only a claim of political selection, but also a statement that disputes the law enforcers' interpretation of what can be considered extremism. Thus, the contention is also over the meaning of poorly defined terms.

At the same time, this form of law enforcement may still fall under the definition of selective law enforcement. It is clearly politically biased, and the law enforcers' purported 'interpretation' of formal rules seem in these cases guided by informal interests. We may suspect that the targets for prosecution are often predetermined, and that the law itself is merely an instrument to get the job done. While the interviewees in many cases did not challenge the official reasons for crackdown (they may agree on what statements triggered a response), they still insist that the motives were extra-legal and not prescribed by law. Finally, we might suspect the enforcement of Article 282 may be selective due to the fact that other and more relevant cases are consistently neglected.

Raids on pretext of copyrights enforcement

The third and final legal issue I will consider in this chapter is the legislation surrounding intellectual property rights and copyrights on computer software in particular. The practice of using, buying, and selling pirated software, movies, and music is known to be rampant in Russia. In the period of inquiry, piracy products were distributed openly on the Internet, by street vendors, and even in shops. As in most parts of the world, the majority of citizens had no reason to worry that the violation of software copyrights might suddenly result in legal sanctions. Violations were simply too common and the millions of offenders effectively crowded out each other.

While the task of policing may seem overwhelming, officially Russia is not blind to the problem of copyright violations. It was under Putin's second term that Russian authorities started to take the issue more seriously, partly due to considerable pressure from international actors. After a few years of increasing state attention, stakeholders' reports (BSA 2004-2012) indicated impressive results, though certainly from a poor starting point. In the entire period investigated, reported enforcement of copyrights went up, and the relative amount of pirated software went down. At the same time, there have also been accusations of selective law enforcement against critics of the government and candidates of the opposition. Copyright legislation is therefore the third legal issue area I will examine in this chapter. As will be evident, the analysis sheds light on yet more aspects of selective law enforcement and variations on how it may be employed for political purposes.

The legal framework and its enforcement

According to the annual Global Software Piracy Reports of the Business Software Alliance (BSA) the Russian legislation seems to be solid in the period of inquiry (BSA 2004-2017). Klein Preston, an expert on the topic, asserted in 2008 that "Russian law on copyrights provides a more than adequate legal framework for protecting intellectual property rights … and has created an atmosphere of legal predictability" (in Smith 2010, 141). Although homemade copies were still distributed openly, the statistics indicate a largely successful enforcement of copyrights in Russia in the examined years. In this period, the percentage of pirated software went down every year despite challenging economic conditions. In 2006 the estimated share of unlicensed software on the software market was 87% of total worth. Five years later, it was down to 63%. In the years 2007 and 2008 Russia could boast the greatest improvements in the share of licenced software of all the 110 countries included in the BSA reports (BSA 2009b).

In a 2010 press release, Georg Herrnleben, the regional leader of BSA, praised the Russian government.[21] Herrnleben evaluated Russia's efforts as "highly effective", not least considering the uneasy world economy (BSA 2010b). Two years later, the BSA (2012b) still evaluated Russian efforts positively and accredited the success to both the legislation itself and its effective implementation.

For the purposes of this book, the most relevant legal text within the legal issue area is Article 146 of the Criminal Code (Violation of Copyright and Neighbouring Rights). The Duma laid down the basic outline of the article in 2003 and defined the scope of possible punishment for the illegal acquisition, use, and sale of illegal software. Article 146 contained a set of aggravating circumstances, including "repeated violations or violations by a group of persons in a preliminary collusion or by an organized group", and since 2003 allowed for a punishment of up to five years of incarceration for the most serious cases.

Most of the controversial crackdowns based on Article 146 took place in the years directly following the amendments of early spring of 2007 (42-FZ of 9 April 2007). By these amendments, wilful possession and use of software was considered a criminal offense if the total worth of the software exceeded 50 000 roubles. In addition, the amendments increased the maximum punishment for aggravated crimes from a five year sentence to a six year sentence. While this latter change at first glance may seem relatively inconsequential, it does have important ramifications. After the changes, an aggravated violation of software regulations was now considered a 'grave' (*tyazhkiy*) crime according to Article 15 of the Criminal Code – more or less the Russian equivalent to a felony.

> *The mere planning of a grave crime shall be punishable (Art. 30 of the Code); heavy fines (those exceeding EUR 15,000) may be imposed on an offender who commits a grave crime (Art. 46). ... A person who committed a grave crime may be brought to justice for such an offence at any point within ten years from the date of wrongdoing (Art. 78). A convicted grave crime offender shall endure a sentence in a penal colony (Art. 58). A release on parole shall be a complicated and long-lasting procedure in the case of committing a grave crime (Art. 79). Finally, a person who was given a sentence shall only have the right to cancellation of a criminal record six years after his (her) release from custody (Art. 95). (Golovanov 2007)*

In other words, the changes turned copyright violations into very serious crimes, out of touch with the actual behaviour of Russian end-users and their real expectations regarding the law's enforcement. The changes effectively altered the dynamics of how the law was used.

Controversial enforcement

In the spring of 2007, just a month or so after the new changes to the Criminal Code came into force, a conflict escalated in and around Samara, in which unlicensed software suddenly became a hot topic. A Council of Europe summit was to be held in Samara-Tolyatti on May 17-18, and Angela Merkel and other top-level international actors had announced their attendance. To benefit from the international attention regarding the event, the protest movement associated with The Other Russia umbrella decided to hold the annual 'Dissenters' March' on the same date as the said summit. The authorities had sanctioned the meeting, yet chose to suppress it with a large-scale campaign involving mass arrests, intimidation, and harassment of local organizers, as well as other means. Shortly before the rally was supposed to take place, a special police department conducted several controversial raids in the city – allegedly in search of unlicensed software. The inspectors seized a number of computers from the purported suspects and initiated criminal proceedings for alleged violations of Article 146. Not only are there strong reasons to believe that the raids were politically motivated. It also seems that the cases completely lacked a legal foundation. The 'tip' that purportedly made the investigators conduct the raids came from a dubious source. As the legal proceedings continued, it also became apparent that the investigators (alternatively their hired expertise on software issues) seemed to fabricate evidence. The prosecution eventually crumbled, and the state was later required to pay compensation to the subjects of prosecution for unlawful actions. At the same time, the targeted organizations, news outlets, and individuals had a difficult time preparing for the upcoming rally, which was presumably the result the law enforcers had hoped for.

In the same year and on the same pretext, a number of well-known targets experienced similar raids in Nizhniy Novgorod. Newspapers and human rights organizations were targeted, and once again the prosecutor's office initiated criminal procedures against one editor. In these cases, the interviewees also shared the view that ulterior motives guided the legal processes and that fighting software piracy simply served as a handy pretext. Another controversial took place the same year and on the same pretext was the raid against an organization in Tula that supported the presidential candidacy of Mikhail Kasyanov (who was denied registration), and there were also a few isolated cases in Moscow, St. Petersburg and Siberia. In addition, my material includes an interview I did with an activist from Southern Russia who experienced similar trouble in 2009 and 2010. Taken together, these cases account for the most blatant cases of political abuse of this kind in Russia in the relevant timeframe. In comparison with the other two reviewed issue areas in this chapter, this makes the selective enforcement of copyright law relatively infrequent.

Common to most cases of politicized copyrights enforcement, and in clear contrast with the other two legal issue areas, was the participation of private and international actors in the controversial prosecution. Not only the Russian state but also international firms and copyright holders have intensified their fight against software piracy in Russia. As for the mentioned cases, Microsoft was involved in several of them. Some observers interpreted this circumstance as important. "Our law enforcement finally realized that computers are very important for their opponents", said Vladimir Pribylovsky at the Panorama Information and Expert Group in Moscow, "and they have decided to take away these tools by doing something close to the West's agenda" (Finn 2007). In Pribylovsky's interpretation, the cooperation of law enforcers with private partners made it more difficult for international actors (particularly in the U.S.) to criticize the selective crackdown. Only after the *New York Times* highlighted the issue did a Russian interest group representing the victims of selective law enforcement manage to meet with Microsoft. As a result, the software giant halted its support for selective law enforcement and instead took some initiatives to counteract it (Levy 2010a; 2010b).

Before we continue the analysis of the above cases, it should be mentioned that selective and political use of intellectual property rights at the time not only concerned raids against critical organizations, but also deregistration of candidates for Russian elections. As mentioned earlier, a candidate standing for election can according to Russian election law request an opponent to be disqualified on the grounds that he or she violated intellectual property rights during the election campaign. A number of controversial cases have appeared on this pretext. Similar to other quasi-legal tools for depriving candidates of the right to stand for elections, the approach involves a combination of creativity, extreme formalism, and completely disproportionate punishment.

In Perm, for instance, the central opposition figure Konstantin Okunev had his registration withdrawn after he had used photos of a public monument in his campaign material, without the necessary permissions (Polina 2011b). A local source claimed that at least one candidate from United Russia had done the same thing, but that the case against him was dismissed.

A third path to selective law enforcement

Despite the positive remarks of BSA, the support and respect for copyrights in Russia remained underwhelming between 2007 and 2011. One interview suggested that the pervasive non-compliance with this law had made it a popular tool "to calm down ... the more intelligent part of the population". Considering the massive non-compliance at the societal level, the odds of striking gold on randomized raids for pirated software were presumably good. According to a representative of one of the above-mentioned newspapers, "of course" it did not have all the software in use licensed at the time of the crackdown.

> *[One of the officials] told me personally that almost 99 per cent of [the city's] newspapers have licensed software. Of course I knew that this was untrue because it is not possible for a regional newspaper to have the money for licensed software – it is a very expensive thing. So of course I was supposed to be ashamed ...but I just looked at him and said, "Oh please don't tell me this lie because it is just ridiculous."*

Referencing the insights from election law and the law on extremist activities, the reality of selective copyright enforcement indicates how a law need not be vague or otherwise weak in order to be effective as a repressive tool. Because non-compliance with the legislation was so common in this case, even a crystal clear law had the potential to be used selectively and with expected success against a large segment of the population. Several interviewees claimed that 'everyone' used pirated software in Russia. While international actors and stakeholders may support a high degree of criminalization, other may see the harsh punishment and the extensive mandate of investigators as draconian and as an invitation to quasi-legal schemes and extortion. Furthermore, it is not always easy for end-users to know at all times whether the software being utilized is indeed genuine, or simply skilfully crafted to look like the real thing.

The fact that interviewees brought up these issues, however, does not imply that the targets of selective enforcement were actually guilty of any violations. Most of the interviewees in fact stressed that their software was indeed licensed. In at least some of the cases, the later development of the cases indicated that they were right. In one case against a newspaper editor, a second expert analysis (on the initiative of the defence) revealed that somebody had installed the pirated software *after* the day of confiscation, a discovery that won the case and embarrassed the prosecution. In a case against an NGO leader in the same city, the law enforcers accused her of using a pirated version of Garant. According to the accused party, however, the law enforcers had not even bothered to remove the USB stick they had used to install the pirated software before taking photos of the computer screen as evidence: The message 'a new USB device has been detected' still showed in the corner of the screen. Since the investigators according to standard procedure can pick and choose experts to conduct the technical examination for piracy software, the 'neutral' expertise provide poor guarantees against the fabrication of evidence. In these examined cases, lack of evidence did not stop raids from taking place or criminal cases from being initiated, at least in some situations.

The popularity of this suppressive 'technology' around 2007-2008 can seemingly be explained by two main factors. First, the law enforcers enjoyed a broad mandate to act on weak or non-existing suspicions. As one official put it, "any person with a sense of justice" could file a request to conduct a search. This individual would according to law be safeguarded from legal repercussions unless the accusations could be proven to be deliberate lies. In the case of the above editor, the investigators formally acted upon a suspicion filed by a person completely unknown to him. When the tipster was later called in for interrogations, he claimed to have read about the newspaper using unlicensed software on a website, but could not remember which one. Considering the widespread use of quasi-formal schemes in Russian law enforcement, the Russian police can easily produce tipsters of whatever kind. When they raided a news agency next door to the newspaper, however, the police reportedly had no permit at all. Instead, they improvised on the spot, and acquired a backdated document later, the news agency leader explains.

The second factor to explain why this practice became so popular is the immediate and crippling effect of hardware confiscation. The method left the targets no time to react or defend themselves before they had already come in harm's way. The political context of the raids suggests that they were timed to coincide with particular events. Furthermore, ongoing criminal investigations are often accompanied by travel bans, and excuses can be made to hold computers for prolonged periods. In addition, raids can be an efficient way to gather intelligence on troublemakers. Even if the search and subsequent expert examination revealed no actual violations, the law enforcement officials' efforts may have serious consequences for the targets.

As was the case with anti-extremism, we can see how increased legal attention towards a legitimate problem can create new opportunities for actors who want to pursue their informal interests. In both cases, we see how federal authorities poured resources into the legal system to fight a general problem, and the subsequent instrumentalization by elite groups for extra-legal purposes. As was the case with anti-extremism, legitimate state building and intensified abusive practices coexisted simultaneously, reproducing the logic of the dual state within these limited fields (see Chapter 4). The two legal issue areas are very dissimilar, however, since anti-extremist laws openly address political views while laws on software piracy are more technical of nature.

In addition, the examined abuse of Article 146 seems to be primarily a tactic to cripple the short-term and medium-term capacity of the targets through confiscations, travel restrictions, and criminal investigations. Formally, at least, more severe punishment was rare in the examined caseload. At the same time, we cannot rule out that the massive non-compliance with copyrights law in Russian society also contributed to the decision to utilize this particular tool in selective law enforcement. Because the level of compliance is so low, the prosecutors had a statistically good chance of acquiring substantial evidence upon which they could build more solid legal cases and thus hope for more severe punishment to be imposed. In addition, we cannot tell what would have happened if the law enforcement agencies had fabricated evidence with more skill and care.

Notes

1. Ryazan oblast already introduced a law against "homosexual propaganda" in 2006, but regional bans became more frequent in the spring and summer of 2012. The Federal Law 135-FZ was passed on this issue in June 2013. See also Wilkinson (2014).
2. Federal Law 121-FZ of 20 June 2012*: On Amendments to Legislative Acts of the Russian Federation regarding the Regulation of the Activities of Non-profit Organisations Performing the Functions of a Foreign Agent.*
3. According to a list posted on Perm Central Election Committee's webpages at the time, but later removed.
4. Signatures are a common feature in Russian law, essential also to the registration of parties and the initiation of referendums. For the legal specifics for Perm kray and Vladimir oblast, see *Perm Kray Law No. 766-PK* and *Vladimir Oblast Law No. 10-OZ.* On invalid signatures, see Article 32 and 33, respectively.
5. Sverdlovsk District Court, Perm. Delo No. 2 -2696/2011 goda. "O priznanii nezakonnym resheniya territorial'noy izbiratelnoy kommissii", 14.02.2011.
6. Arkady Lyubarev. Author's interview, 2.6.2011, Moscow.
7. Arkady Lyubarev. Author's interview, 2.6.2011, Moscow.
8. Author's interview, 2.6.2011, Moscow.
9. Author's interview, 2.6.2011, Moscow.
10. Yet the candidates or party lists do not face identical regulations, as the parties with representatives in the State Duma have enjoyed important privileges with regard to registration demands.
11. The regime's control over the committees is rather straightforward. The central election committee in Perm, for instance, had for the most part been set up by the governor and the incumbent legislature, with the leader nominated by the Federal CEC in Moscow. Also various less formal methods allowed the incumbents and administration to fill the committees with loyal members (Buzin 2007; Popova 2012). On the short biographies of the members presented on the Perm CEC webpage in 2011, four of the committee members were listed with explicit reference to the ruling party (author's field notes). There is also general consensus among observers that non-partisan committee members were also dependent upon incumbents and regional administration, not least for structural reasons (Buzin 2007; Golosov 2011; White 2011). Even the CEC member interviewed admitted that the committees' set-up was "politics, purely politics". While the Duma parties were represented with one candidate each, even a united opposition of three votes would hardly have made a difference

among the committees' 14 participants when it came to a vote on registration. Golos (2011a) in Vladimir has complained that the TECs tend to be the products of CEC lobbyists representing the interests of the ruling party, and Lyudmila Eshanu (2011a) claims that rapid reshuffling of the territorial election committees (TECs) just before the elections had already become a "tradition".

12. The groups that have been hit most severely include various non-violent Muslim religious organizations and not least Jehovah's Witnesses. See Sova reports on at http://www.sova-center.ru (Russian) or http://www.sova-center.ru/en/ (English).
13. In addition to their reports on enforcement, the Sova Center also provides sound analysis of the amendments in their legal, social, and political context. Further documents are available on Sova's webpages at http://www.sova-center.ru (Russian) or http://www.sova-center.ru/en/ (English).
14. The external specialists have clearly copied the entry in the *Encyclopedic Dictionary of Winged Words and Expressions* (Serov 2003) word for word.
15. Author's interview, 12.11.2010, Moscow.
16. Schools were required to block all *potential* access to all extremist websites, regardless of whether they were actually visited using school computers. Schools are dependent upon state provided filtering software that often did not adequately block access to these sites.
17. Libraries were caught in a catch-22. They were prohibited from providing access to 'extremist literature', such as *Mein Kampf,* yet by the laws regulating libraries were not allowed to remove them from their collections. After a cooperation project with Sova amongst others, the Russian Library Association (RBA) provided its members with special instructions on how to best cope with the contradictions in organizing their activities. For details, see Zaytsev (2010), also available at http://www.sova-center.ru/racism-xenophobia/docs/2010/06/d19095/ [accessed 06.12.2017].
18. Roskomnadzor was up to 2008 organized as part of the agency Rossvyazokhrankulturu.
19. Nikita Tikhonov, the editor of the Russkiy obraz' journal, was in 2011 sentenced to life imprisonment for these murders.
20. Official warning from Roskomnadzor to the newspaper (author's archives).
21. Eastern and Central Europe, the Middle East, and Africa are together considered one region in the BSA organization chart.

References

BSA (Business Software Alliance). 2004-2017. Global Software Piracy Study (annual). Available at: http://www.bsa.org/studies/ [accessed 06.12.2017].

2009b. Rossiya demonstriruyet znachitel'nyy progress v snizhenii urovnya komp'yuternogo piratstva. *BSA News Release*, 14.05.2009.

2010b. Uroven' komp'yuternogo piratstva v Rossii skorashchayetsya na fone mirovogo krizisa. *BSA News Release*, 12.05.2010.

2012b. V 2011 godu rossiyskie piraty ustanovili nelegal'nogo programmnogo obespecheniya na summu boleye 3 milliardov dollarov. *BSA News Release*, 15.05.2012.

Buzin, A. 2006. *Administrativnyye izbiratel'nyye tekhonologii.: Moskovskaya praktika.* Moscow: Panorama.

2007. *Administrativnyye izbiratel'nyye tekhnologii i bor'ba s nimi.* Moscow: Panorama.

Buzin, A. & Lyubarev, A. 2008. *Prestupleniye bez nakazaniya. Adminsitrativnyye tekhnologii federal'nykh vyborov 2007-2008 goda.* Moscow: Nikkolo M.

Eshanu, L. 2011a. Opyat' polittekhnologi? *GOLOS Novosti, Vladimirskaya Oblast*, 07.10.2011.

2011b. Zhdëm resheniya Konstitutsionnogo suda. *GOLOS Novosti, Vladimirskaya Oblast*, 22.11.2011.

Finn, P. 2007. Russia Casts a Selective Net in Piracy Crackdown. *The Washington Post*, 14.11.2007. Available at: http://washingtonpost.com/wp-dyn/content/article/2007/11/13/AR2007111302070.html [accessed 06.12.2017].

Florin, D. 2009. Ekspertiza sochla opasnymi lozungi protivnikov 'komendantskogo chasa' v Novorossiyske. *Kavkazskiy Uzel*, 09.07.2009. Available at: https://www.kavkaz-uzel.eu/articles/156415 [accessed 09.01.2018].

Gandhi, J. & Lust-Okar, E. 2009. Elections under Authoritarianism. *Annual Review of Political Science,* 12, 403–422.

Gel'man, V. 2015. The Politics of Fear. How the Russian Regime Confronts Its Opponents. *Russian Politics and Law,* 53, 6–26.

Golos. 2011a. Pervoye zayavleniye Vladimirskogo 'GOLOSa'. *GOLOS Report* 13.02.2011.

2011b. Vtoroye zayavleniye assosiatsii 'GOLOS' po rezultatam dolgosrochnogo nablyudeniya goda izbiratel'nykh vyborov, naznachennykh na 13 marta 2011 g. (etap agitatsionnoy kampanii). *GOLOS Report*. Moscow: GOLOS

2011c. Vybory v Rossii 13 marta 2011 goda. Analiticheskiy doklad. *GOLOS Report*. Moscow: GOLOS.

Golosov, G. V. 2011. The Regional Roots of Electoral Authoritarianism in Russia. *Europe-Asia Studies,* 63, 623–639.

Golovanov, D. 2007. Violation of Intellectual Property is Now a Grave Crime. *IRIS Legal Observations of the European Audiovisual Observatory*.

Gross, J. B. 2003. Russia's War on Political and Religious Extremism. An Appraisal of the Law 'On Counteracting Extremist Activity'. *Brigham Young University Review*, 717–760.

Horvath, R. 2013. *Putin's Preventive Counter-Revolution. Post-Soviet Authoritarianism And the Spectre of Velvet Revolution*. Oxon: Routledge.

Levinson, L. 2003. S ekstremizmom budut borot'sya po-stalinistski. *Rossiyskiy byulleten' po pravam cheloveka,* 16.

Levy, C. J. 2010a. Microsoft Changes Policy Over Russian Crackdown. *New York Times*, 13.09.2010. Available at: http://www.nytimes.com/2010/09/14/world/europe/14raid.html [accessed 06.12.2017].

2010b. Russia Uses Microsoft to Suppress Dissent. *New York Times*, 11.09.2010. Available at: http://www.nytimes.com/2010/09/12/world/europe/12raids.html [accessed 06.12.2017].

Lukin, V. 2010. Doklad Polnomochennogo po pravam cheloveka v Rossiyskoy Federatsii za 2009 god. *Rossiyskaya Gazeta*. 28.05.2010. Available at: https://www.rg.ru/2010/05/28/doklad-lukin-dok.html [accessed 09.01.2018]

Lyubarev, A. 2007. Prepyatsviya dlya svobodnoy konkurentsii na vyborakh. Zakonodatel'stvo i pravoprimenitel'naya praktika *Rossiyskoye elektoral'noye obozreniye*, 20–8.

2011a. Electoral Legislation in Russian Regions. *Europe-Asia Studies,* 63, 415–427.

2011b. Khronologiya izmeneny rossiyskogo izbiratel'nogo zakonodatel'stva, 1988-2011. *Tsentr Geliks Report*.

Myagkov, M., Ordeshook, P. C. & Shakin, D. 2009. *The Forensics of Election Fraud. Russia and Ukraine*. Cambridge: Cambridge University Press.

Polina, D. 2011a. Chlen TsIK RF Yevgeny Kolyushin ne isklyuchayet, chto na vyborakh v gordumu primenyayutsya dvoyniye standarty. *Kommersant*, 17.02.2011. Available at: http://www.kommersant.ru/doc/1587178/ [accessed 06.12.2017].

2011b. Verkhovnyy sud otklonil zhalobu Konstantina Okuneva. *Kommersant (Perm)*, 24.11.2011. Available at: http://kommersant.ru/doc/1822940 [accessed 06.12.2017].

Popova, M. 2012. *Politicized Justice in Emerging Democracies. A Study of Courts in Russia and Ukraine*. Cambridge: Cambridge University Press.

2017. Putin-Style 'Rule of Law' & the Prospects for Change. *Dædalus*, 146, 64–75.

Radio Svoboda, R. 2011. V Samare zhurnalist otsudil u minfina 450 tysyach rubley. *Svoboda.org,* 02.02.2011. Available at: http://www.svoboda.org/content/news/2295676.html [accessed 06.12.2017].

Ross, C. 2011. Regional Elections and Electoral Authoritarianism in Russia. *Europe-Asia Studies,* 63, 641–661.

2014. Regional Elections and Electoral Malpractice in Russia. The Manipulation of Electoral Rules, Voters, and Votes. *Region*, 3, 147–172.

Schedler, A. 2002. Elections without Democracy. The Menu of Manipulation. *Journal of Democracy,* 13, 36–50.

Serov, V. 2003. Entsiklopedicheskiy slovar' krylatykh slov i vyrazheniy.

Skovoroda, R. & Lankina, T. 2017. Fabricating votes for Putin. New tests of fraud and electoral manipulations from Russia. *Post-Soviet Affairs*, 33, 100–123.

Smith, G. B. 2010. Legal Reform and the Dilemma of Rule of Law. *In:* White, S., Sakwa, R. & Hale, H. E. (eds.). *Developments in Russian Politics 7*. Houndmills: Palgrave Macmillan.

Soldatov, A. & Borogan, I. 2015. *The Red Web. The Struggle between Russia's Digital Dictators and the New Online Revolutionaries*. New York: Public Affairs.

Sova. 2008a. Anti-Extremist Legislation, its Use and Misuse. *SOVA Report*. Available at: http://www.sova-center.ru/en/xenophobia/reports-analyses/2008/07/d13739/ [accessed 06.12.2017].

2008b. Overview of the Amendments Introduced in the Anti-extremist Legislation in 2007. *SOVA Report*. Available at: http://www.sova-center.ru/en/xenophobia/reports-analyses/2008/03/d12841/ [accessed 06.12.2017].

2009-2017. Inappropriate Enforcement of Anti-Extremist Legislation in Russia (annual). *SOVA Report*. Avalable at: http://www.sova-center.ru/en/misuse/reports-analyses/ [accessed 06.12.2017].

2010b. Inappropriate Enforcement of Anti-Extremist Legislation in Russia in a First Half of 2010 [sic]. *SOVA Report*. Available online at: http://www.sova-center.ru/en/misuse/reports-analyses/2010/10/d19880/[accessed 06.12.2017].

Supreme Court Of The Russian Federation. 2010. Postanovleniye plenuma Verkhovnogo suda Rossiyskoy Federatsii No. 16 ot 15.06.2010. O Praktike primeneniya sudami Zakona Rossiyskoy Federatsii "O sredstvakh massovoy informatsii".

2011. Postanovleniye plenuma Verkhovnogo suda Rossiyskoy Federatsii, No. 11 ot 28.06.2011. O sudebnoy praktike po ugolovnym delam o prestupleniyakh ekstremistskoy napravlennosti.

Sverdlovsk District Court In Perm, 2011. Delo No. 2 -2696/2011 goda. O priznanii nezakonnym resheniya territorial'noy izbiratel'noy kommissii, 14.02.2011.

White, S. 2011. Elections Russian-Style. *Europe-Asia Studies,* 63, 531–556.

Wilkinson, C. 2014. Putting 'Traditional Values into Practice'. The Rise and Contestation of Anti-Homopropaganda Laws in Russia. *Journal of Human Rights*, 13, 363–379.

Zaytsev, V.N. 2010. Instruktsiya o rabote s izdaniyami, vklyuchennymi v 'Federal'nyy spisok ekstremistskikh materialov', *Informatsionnyy byulleten'* RBA, 55, 30–2.

7 A legal minefield

The role of laws in selective law enforcement

I have underscored the point that formal rules in selective law enforcement primarily function as a pretext for enforcing the informal rules of political conduct. A consequence is that selective law enforcement is really not law enforcement at all – no laws are enforced. We have also seen that Russians in general do not emphasize the role of laws in repression, but rather stress its subordination to the personal interests of the powerful. Proverbs, native vocabulary, and the interviewees' stories all reflect the laws' irrelevance when confronted with powerful interests. While laws do not serve as the law enforcers' reason for action, however, the phrasing of laws still have an important part to play in selective law enforcement. The previous chapter provided some answers to why different legal issue areas have become favoured tools for selective law enforcement. In this chapter, I will increase the level of abstraction and synthesize some of the findings to explore how the phrasing of law is put to use in quasi-legal repression. As will be clear, the metaphor of law as a minefield is not entirely off the mark (Riabchuk 2004). Towards the end of the chapter, I will also provide some tentative conclusions on whether it would be plausible that weak laws are being legislated on purpose.

Before I launch my discussion of how prohibitive laws may encourage selective law enforcement, the role of 'secondary rules' should be mentioned. Various rules that delimit jurisdiction and set out procedures are important for selective law enforcement on several levels. On a fundamental level, the empowerment of rules and legal actors to implement them is at the core of the rational-legal mode of organization on which selective law enforcement is parasitic. Just as it is impossible to envision a legal system without jurisdiction, it is also impossible to imagine selective law enforcement without it. The institutionalization of checks and balances between the executive branch and the judicial branch is also crucial to how discretionary rules turn out in actual enforcement practices. In addition, jurisdictional rules shape selective law enforcement in a more direct fashion. Extending a law enforcement agency's mandate to conduct surveillance or make inspections, for instance, may have a direct impact on how this agency is utilized in quasi-legal schemes. We have seen how the mandate to conduct searches based on thin evidence has been important to selective raids formally initiated on suspicions of pirated software.

Why the choice of pretext matters

This study does not deal with jurisdictional questions at great length. Whereas the secondary rules are not a core aspect of my conceptualization of selective law enforcement, the *formal predicates* of prohibitive rules play a central role – namely the role of *pretext*. Even though selective law enforcement is theoretically speaking not law enforcement at all, the choice of a particular legal pretext bears significance for at least four reasons:

- **Popular support may be a relevant aspect of selective law enforcement**

The choice of legal issue area may have relevance for the economic funding and popular support of the repression. As argued throughout this book, we should not overestimate the level of popular approval the 'legal veneer' may lend selective law enforcement. This fact is abundantly true in Russia where trust in both law and its enforcers is extraordinarily low in the sense that the population *expects* politicized justice. That said, we cannot rule out that instrumentalization of formal rules on *some* occasions may resound positively with *some* parts of the population.

There are presumably two minimum prerequisites for selective law enforcement to gain popular approval. First, the legal charges must have some degree of credibility. Second, the legal violations should resound with societal norms. In Russia, where law suffers from considerable disrespect and thus has a limited degree of normative authority in itself, we can expect that the violation itself must be in direct conflict with established norms for the violation to lead to social condemnation. For this reason, prosecuting politicians for large-scale embezzlement will have a greater chance of mobilizing society's support than accusing them of copyright violations. Notably, these two requirements are the very same that would make for an effective smear campaign. We may therefore ask whether it is the legal veneer or rather the enforcement of societal norms that produces popular support. If the prosecution of Khodorkovsky attained a certain level of popular support, it was not necessarily because he was believed guilty as charged, but because many thought he *deserved* punishment, morally speaking.

A third factor influencing the popular support of selective law enforcement relates to how popular acceptance for legal acts may be manipulated through the framing of an issue. The Putinist campaign against extremism provides a good example of a propagandized campaign in part intended to mobilize popular approval for repressive purposes. During most of his years as president, Putin spent considerable time promising to fight the threat of extremism, and Medvedev also stressed this topic in his interim years. The clustering of extremism with other political issues such as political dissent, foreign interference, and political instability presumably made it easier for the government to prosecute political dissenters as extremists (Horvath 2013). The legal stigmatization of 'foreign agents' from 2012 has served to strengthen this conceptual bundling in official rhetoric, framing the relevant actors as inherently dubious and questioning their patriotic values.

The degree to which an authoritarian regime can legitimize political repression in the eyes of the public simply by wrapping it in legal claims remains limited. As E.P. Thompson (1975, 262–3) postulated, "The essential precondition for the effectiveness of law, in its function as ideology, is that it shall display an independence from gross manipulation, and seem to be just". If this precondition is too seriously undermined, legal façades "will mask nothing, legitimize nothing" (ibid.). The obvious use of legal tools for repressive purposes will, over time, undermine any attempts to convince the general public that today's Russia is ruled by law and not men: observers "will not be mystified by the first man who puts on a wig" (ibid., 262). With regard to anti-extremist legislation, Sova (2011) reports that its continued abuse has led to an "ultimate loss of public confidence" in its enforcement.

Officially propagated state campaigns may also generate a sort of pressure that can influence selective law enforcement indirectly. Many resources and much prestige may be invested in such campaigns, something that will also produce administrative pressure to produce statistics to justify the efforts. In the previous chapter, I mentioned for instance how law enforcers have rushed into inappropriate and unnecessary acts against targets such as schools and libraries. Sova (2012) links this action to "beefing up the numbers of anti-extremist activity". One of the interviewees noted how this might have affected law enforcement with political motives:

> *For the people in power* (dlya vlastey) *it is very important to charge civil activists precisely for extremism. A verdict of extremism is very important for them because the E-department is measured by the number of cases it produces within the frames of extremist legislation. They don't want to catch real criminals, as this is very difficult. However, we are always nearby.*

- **The pretext may influence legal behaviour**

Selective law enforcement may also retain a modicum of *actual* law enforcement – if not by intention then in practical consequences. So far, I have argued that neither patrons nor legal actors intend selective law enforcement to enforce formal rules – when enforcing laws selectively, they do not seek to strengthen the integrity of the law nor delimit its violations. Furthermore, I have stressed that at the end of the day it is the *perception* of predicates that decides how people will react to a punitive act. For this reason, I have suggested, selective law enforcement is really not law enforcement at all. In practice, however, even actors who claim to be prosecuted for entirely political purposes may still choose to respond to the legal issues. The interview material suggests that some targets *do* follow the law more carefully after they have experienced a crackdown, at least when the laws are internally coherent. While one of the above quoted editors found it unrealistic for a regional newspaper to use licensed software, she also pointed out that the newspaper nevertheless did acquire all the necessary licenses after the crackdown. As will be discussed in the next chapter, the case is not unique.

With this in mind, one may argue that the enforcement is somewhat effective and possibly legitimate after all. In my opinion, however, neither claim is credible. First, we should examine the effectiveness and legitimacy of enforcing formal rules in relation to the overall tasks of law enforcement. With regard to the above example, punishing minor end-users may be less than effective when considering the well-known leniency towards distribution of the very same pirated software literally around the corner. Second, and more importantly, we should not confuse the separate issues of legal violations and political selectivity. Even if a given organization 'deserves' the law enforcers' attention from a legal point of view, and even if such attention will increase the level of legal compliance in the future, these facts do not legitimize *political selection*. The modicum of actual enforcement of formal rules does not change the defining characteristic of selective law enforcement: legal procedures have been initiated based on informal criteria.

- **Laws define the scope for *de jure* punishment**

The choice of pretext is also important because it defines the scope of possible *de jure* punishment. This element of a rule, the *consequent* in the terminology from Chapter 5, presumably influences how a certain law is used in selective law enforcement. To get a well-known political activist behind bars in order to scare the politically active public, the initiators of selective law enforcement would need a different scope of *de jure* punishment and a different pretext than if they only wanted to impede the efficiency of an organization temporarily without creating a great scandal. An equally harsh punishment for every form of non-compliance would also remove the incentive for petty violators not to radicalize and increase the severity of their infringements. In this way, the functional aspect of the proportional punishment principle is also valid for the enforcement of informal rules.

- **The laws constitute the backdrop for informal influence**

Finally, and most central to my below analysis, the way in which laws are phrased may be important because some formulations invite informal influence into the legal system. Therefore, not all laws carry the same potential for selective law enforcement. A law that is coherent, clear, and not overly strict, as well as routinely enforced and only occasionally violated, can be manipulated only with difficulty. If such a law is to be utilized in selective law enforcement, law enforcers must base their actions either on both real and substantial violations or alternatively on fabrications – at least if they are to push a case all the way to (and through) a court of law. As the analysis in the previous chapter suggested, certain types of laws are better tools for quasi-legal repression than others. Laws that contain vague formulations or bureaucratic demands that nobody adheres is commonly utilized for this purpose. Alternatively, as we saw in the case of copyright law, a lack of the law's alignment with social norms may serve a useful tool as well.

As will be discussed at length below, these various sources of incoherent laws contribute to a legal situation in which legal actors are granted wide discretion to make decisions based on legally irrelevant criteria. Instead of legislating laws that openly discriminate against liberal and leftist opposition, the skilled manipulator can use the potential inherent in what we would normally see as weak laws – laws that for instance are excessively vague. In this way, incoherent laws can decrease the need for manipulation beyond the initiation of a case – and increase the chances of an informal violation ending up in a formal setting. Quasi-legal schemes thus put dysfunctions into active use.

Catch-all perceptions

Most of the interviewees gladly told me about what laws they have been accused of violating. Many claimed that their cases were riddled with procedural errors or even that law enforcers had fabricated evidence against them. Some admitted that they did indeed infringe on the law, while others rejected this. All the prosecuted individuals, however, had in common a dismissive attitude to the legal pretext. They did not in any way feel that they have infringed upon any rule of normative significance. In the previous chapter, we saw that the interviewees frequently argued that the laws used against them could be used against whomever the authorities pleased. Some also suggested that the laws are legislated for the particular purpose of selective enforcement against people such as themselves.

I have noted how Russians' colloquial phrases reflect a full subordination of law to power, leaving little room for complexities. According to the framing of selective law enforcement I sketch out above, the law may indeed seem irrelevant. If laws may be used against more or less everyone, these laws will have little impact upon actual behaviour. The reason is simply that no adjustment of behaviour would be meaningful if the targets could not escape the trap anyway. From this perspective, the ways in which the predicate of a given legal rule is formulated may at first glance seem irrelevant to the practice of selective law enforcement. Yet, we may also turn this argument on its head. The formulation of the given laws is the key to *opening up* the legal system for informal influence. Thus, it is the weakness of laws that make them so useful for repressive purposes. In other words, a law may be important by virtue of its weakness. What the regime insiders would need for the purpose of quasi-legal repression would be a law that does not stand in the way between the informal initiative and the harmful consequence to the target. They would want a law that bends easily to give access to the coercive power associated with it.

The proposition that Russia has a legislative framework where every critical voice may be found guilty of non-compliance in some way or another is a crucial aspect of my interviewees' stories of selective law enforcement. In the following sections, I will refer to this idea about the legal environment as *catch-all* perceptions or *catch-all* theory. I will deal with the catch-all theory in four ways.

First, I will explore the legal foundations for the catch-all perceptions. Legal incoherence may be constituted in different ways which all can potentially contribute to selective law enforcement. As will be seen, these different *sources of incoherence* give the laws a broad field of possible application.

Second, I will show why these sources of incoherence in themselves do not provide a sufficient explanation of how laws connect to actual quasi-legal practices. The argument is that while incoherence gives laws a broad field of possible application, so do also other discretionary laws – including those that in positive terms are called flexible. I will argue that the essence of legal discretion concerns *delegation* of power and that the outcome of discretionary laws is entirely dependent upon the mechanisms that influence this delegation of power. In other words, the idea of catch-all and hence the contribution of laws to selective law enforcement can only be understood in cultural and political contexts. This is not to suggest that the phenomenon is unique to Russia, but merely that catch-all perceptions are not entirely a product of the written laws as such.

Third, I will explore and extend a concept used by Ledeneva to address legal incoherence in the specific Russian context. I will also discuss the possibilities for incoherent laws in this context to be legislated for the particular purpose of selective law enforcement. Finally, I will subject the catch-all theory to a number of objections and point out some weaknesses in the interviewees' claims. As will be clear, we should not accept the pointed formulations at face value, yet neither should we dismiss them as irrelevant.

A typology of incoherence

Lon Fuller (1958/1977, 33–9) famously showed his readers eight ways in which a law can *fail* to be law. The dull King Rex in Fuller's allegory has a sincere wish to attain a status in the history books as a 'great lawgiver.' Despite relentless efforts, however, Rex simply fails. Subjected to one meaningless law after another, the king's subjects fail to see their purpose and find no incentives to act upon them. Fuller's point was that law has an 'inner morality', a set of traits necessary for law to succeed in being law.

I have no intentions to participate actively in the voluminous and still ongoing debate that Fuller's perspectives have raised on the inherent morality of law.[1] Rather, I use the below list as an illustrative example of what Jeremy Waldron (2008, 1145) calls 'legal principles' – and then especially 'formal principles' – "principles about the form the legal norms should take". In a non-essentialist meaning, these principles are not highly controversial as rules of thumb, albeit all of them may be subjected to exceptions if we look hard enough (see Marmor 2003). Fuller formulates the principles in the negative, summarized in a list of "eight distinct routes to disaster":

> *The first and most obvious lies in the failure to achieve rules at all, so that every issue must be decided on an ad hoc basis. The other routes are: (2) a failure to publicize, or at least to make available to the affected party, the rules he is expected to observe; (3) the abuse of retroactive legislation, which not only cannot itself guide action, but undercuts the integrity of rules prospective in effect, since it puts them under the threat of retrospective chance; (4) a failure to make rules understandable; (5) the enactment of contradictory rules or (6) rules that require conduct beyond the power of the affected party; (7) introducing such frequent changes in the rules that the subject cannot orient his action by them; and, finally (8) a failure of congruence between the rules as announced and their actual administration. (Fuller 1958/1977, 39)*

While no real legislation would fail so utterly to regulate human conduct as did the laws in Fuller's allegory, some laws do, if seen through critical lenses, come remarkably close. Russian laws that are utilized in selective law enforcement have been criticized as being difficult to understand, excessively burdensome, contradictory, too frequently changing, close to impossible to comply with, and marked by inconsistent and arbitrary enforcement. Rather than simply dismiss all Russians as legal nihilists, we should also look at how the legislators are contributing to the uncertain legal situation by acting partly as King Rex did. In the following sections, I will outline some of the key ways in which Russian legislators create what may seem to be ineffective legislation.

- **Rubber formulations**

Clarity is often reported to be lacking in Russian legislation. Laws that have been termed opaque, vague, or ambiguous also seem particularly popular in quasi-legal schemes.[2] We may call the controversial passages *rubber formulations,* as their main quality for the purposes of selective prosecution is that they can be stretched to encompass a large number of cases. The political use of legal vagaries is a well known practice from the historical and contemporary experiences in many countries. Soviet authorities were notorious for repression though opaque rules, often of political nature.[3]

With regard to anti-extremism today, vagueness constitutes the most important foundation for selective law enforcement, not least in relation to the term 'social group'. Aleksandr Verkhovsky, director of the Sova Center, suggests that the law on extremism offers no legal guidance on how to enforce it: "It is very easy to accuse practically anybody of extremism. Of course it is used selectively – how can it not be used selectively?"[4] Verkhovsky's position is not unfounded and certainly not unique – similar views are common among my interviewees. It should be noted that while some vague laws may be overextensions of their mainstream interpretations, rubber formulations may also provide legal pretexts in cases in which there is no agreement between formal and informal predicates.

- **The regulative minefield**

Another good place for the regime to seek suitable legal pretext for quasi-legal crackdowns is the infamous Russian bureaucracy. Bureaucratic overregulation has long been a major problem in Russia, cutting into the power of the sovereign and keeping the population hostage to extortionist schemes (Karklins 2005). We remember the words of Pobedonostsev quoted in Chapter 2. More than a century later, Vladimir Pastukhov (2002, 68) found the Russian bureaucracy still reminiscent of that of the pre-industrial era: "A machine which is irrational and not subject to genuine control". In the case of selective law enforcement, however, it is not the bureaucratic actors themselves who are the main extortionists. Rather, they partake in the fight against political dissent on behalf of their patrons.

Ordering a legal subject to cross a legal minefield without making mistakes is in effect close to demanding the impossible. As Fuller (1958/1977, 37) puts it: "To command what cannot be done is not to make law; it is to unmake law, for a command that cannot be obeyed serves no end but confusion, fear and chaos". Surely, there are no laws in Russia similar to his caricature legislation in which citizens summoned to the throne were given ten seconds to report (Fuller ibid., 36). The number of legal traps, however, compensates for such requirements. To quote Jackson (1940, 19) again: "With the law books filled with a great assortment of crimes, a prosecutor stands a fair chance of finding at least a technical violation of some act on the part of almost everyone". The above review of election registration enforcement is full of examples of how a legal minefield may work in practice. With help from the best lawyers, the most experienced of politicians may *possibly* manage to get through the minefield unharmed, but this manoeuvre surely cannot be a meaningful requirement for participating in political elections in a democracy.

- **Sleeping statutes**

Sleeping statutes are incoherent in a way that differs starkly from the rubber formulations. In fact, sleeping statutes may be both clear and coherent *internally*. They are also different from the regulative minefield discussed above, since it would not necessarily be so difficult to comply with a sleeping statute. To the degree that we can speak of incoherence in the sleeping statutes, it lies with their lack of touch with the real attitudes, expectations and behaviour in society. When a law is generally not enforced and is ignored by many or most legal subjects, its sudden enforcement can provide a handy pretext in quasi-formal schemes.

Violations of sleeping statutes may in theory lead to severe repercussions, as in the case of the Russian law on intellectual property rights. Even if the law has been increasingly enforced, the majority of violators have no reason to expect their infringements to have legal consequences. Few thus experience the sleeping statute as a major constraint. Instead, there is a mutual understanding between the law enforcers and the population that the law will be left sleeping or only enforced in grave cases. Such deliberately lax enforcement is sometimes referred to as *gedogen* after the (previous) Dutch policy on light narcotics.[5] When the otherwise unenforced law is suddenly selectively and harshly enforced, it comes as a surprise attack. We have seen that international observers are very satisfied with the Russian progress in enforcing copyrights. One may argue that it does not, then, fit the notion of a sleeping statute. Considering the massive numbers of minor end-users who infringe on this law, however, the chance of being randomly caught is miniscule.

- **Contradictory rules**

Legal subjects may from time to time encounter legal situations in which the law requires and prohibits the same conduct at the same time, both 'φ' and 'not φ.' As Fuller (1958/1977, 65) points out, a *requirement* to do both 'φ' and 'not φ' simultaneously is not a contradiction in *logical* terms. While it is not logically contradictory to demand something and then impose a punishment for the very same act, however, such laws will surely be both mean and unfair. If two contradicting rules would also lead to equal sanctions, they will also lack any ability to guide behaviour and effectively ruin the legal subjects' possibility to stay on the virtuous path of law. This latter attribute is why contradictory rules are useful in quasi-legal schemes.

Rasma Karklins (2005, 22) has claimed that exploiting contradictory rules was "a common tactic" in Russian business, but today many of the more blunt legal contradictions have been removed. From my presentation of politically motivated law enforcement, we remember a peculiar situation arising from the signature verification process in Perm. When signers in Perm had to state their registered place of residence in the 2011 elections, many residents found themselves trapped in a situation in which two authoritative documents (passport and official name of the region) provided different answers to whether they officially lived in Perm oblast or Perm kray. Because there were no established standards in written law to sort out the issue, the controllers could find any answer to be wrong. This trap of binary and mutually exclusive interpretations is not an inherent contradiction in the law itself, but rather is based on contradictory interpretations. Yet, the outcome is reminiscent of a catch-22.

- **Lack of promulgation or frequent changes**

If we stick with Schauer's (1991) terminology, a subject may 'happen to comply' with a rule he or she does not know about, but cannot be *guided* by this rule, and thus not *follow* it. Therefore, while provisions unknown to the public may guide law enforcers, they cannot guide the conduct of legal subjects. It is unlikely any ordinary citizen or even expert knows all legal rules in detail, but we usually depend on the information being available when sought after. When rules are not promulgated, we have no certainty that we are complying with them. Whereas not as pervasive as they were in Soviet times, secret laws and decrees do exist in contemporary Russia, and they could in theory provide a powerful political tool. In practice, however, such laws are not seen as a big problem within the Russian human rights community today and certainly not with regard to the examined legal issue areas.

Closely associated with the lack of promulgation, and far more relevant to the examined cases, is the practice of amending rules so frequently that the legal subjects cannot react to the changes. The obvious example from the material presented above is the incredibly frequent amendments to Russian election legislation. According to my interviewees, Russian legislators often introduce amendments just before elections, or when key opposition deputies are away on summer holidays or otherwise unaware. The idea is to amend the requirements so close to the election campaign that the opposition has no time to prepare properly and will fail to recognize all the subtleties of the new amendments until it is too late.

Legal discretion and the delegation of power

Rules can never be equal to their justification. A rule is by definition an abstraction that sacrifices case specific circumstances to more easily comparable criteria (see Schauer 1991). A legal formalist may argue that, for the benefits of an impersonal mode of governance, a few unfair or even absurd rulings may be justifiable. In Schauer's (ibid., 228) words, "it is exactly a rule's rigidity, even in the face of applications that would ill serve its purpose, that renders it a rule". Within this conception, we would normally expect legislators to delegate authority to the rules by making them coherent. By doing so, the rule makers would entrench some generalizations of today to make these generalizations valid in the world of tomorrow (ibid.). Only to the degree that the rules are clear will the legal actors understand what the rules (or rather the legislators) require of them.

Even so, it is not rigidity but flexibility that has become the mantra of modern law. As one scholar puts it, "foregoing maximum clarity is a sign of compromise and pluralism" (Marmor 2003, 27). In this way, laws in modern societies are increasingly rules of thumb. In many cases, it makes sense for legislators to leave further specification of broad laws to the experts in specialized departments. Leaving room for interpretation not only makes room for the more specialized legal actors to decide on how the can function well. It also makes it easier for said actors to adapt their practice if the law's implementation reveals unintended consequences. To safeguard flexibility for dealing with yet unspecified threats to the state, legal systems also tend to include rather lofty references to vital interests. Political leaders do not want rigid rules to stand in the way when real threats are to be dealt with. In other words, the open-ended character of the Russian law on extremism is not unique. Even the European Convention of Human Rights endorses the principle that security can trump individual rights. As formulated in the Convention's Article 2.10, some restrictions to civil and human rights are legitimate in the interests of "national security, territorial integrity of public safety, for the prevention of disorder or crime, for the protection of health or morals, for the protection of the reputation or the rights of others, for preventing the disclosure of information received in confidence, or for maintaining the authority and impartiality of the judiciary". Most find security too important to leave it to law alone.

Discretionary rules are good because they allow legal actors to consider the context. We may hope, therefore, that legal actors will use this discretion to interpret the 'purpose' or 'spirit' of the law. In this way, "open flexible rules are arguably fairer, less harsh, more in tune with the sense of justice" (Friedman 1975, 35). At the same time, we have seen how in certain contexts any such hopes would be in vain. How then should we interpret the Russian catch-all theory? Why does discretionary justice turn out to be so radically different in different settings?

Following Schauer (1991), legislating is normally a process done to entrench generalizations and to *empower* them so they will have real influence on decision-making elsewhere and in the future. However, if these generalizations are very broad or otherwise unclear, they are not really much empowered because their ability to curb the discretion of the legal actor will be minimal. By legislating a discretionary law, therefore, the legislators delegate less power to the rules and more power to the legal actors; the legislators in effect grant the implementers *de facto* legislating power. In the words of Andrei Marmor (2003, 14), "the question is basically one of institutional choice". Notably, this is exactly why the Russian tsars advocated for a strong formalism in the first place: to avoid discretion and the resulting usurpation of the power of the legislator-autocrat.

If we see flexible rules as necessary, then legal systems "must somehow keep discretionary rules in proper bounds" (Friedman 1975, 35). In other words, legislators grant the legal actors discretion by legislating flexible laws, but they are also responsible for controlling and delimiting this very discretion. Influences that limit the actual discretion may be many, but the power to define what is proper (in Friedman's terms) does not transcend the power relations in a society. When the rules leave discretion with legal actors who are vulnerable to outside pressure, the outcome of this discretion will largely depend on the political context. For these reasons, it would be naïve to trust a claim that discretionary rules necessarily take heed of our 'sense of justice.' Instead, discretionary rules pave the way for extra-legal influences, and they do this for better or for worse. Put differently, the discretionary law will never be better than the legal actors responsible for implementing it, the legal and political systems they are acting within, and the tradition in which they are partaking. Political and social tendencies may play into the actual enforcement, and so may also personal or group interests. In an environment with strong traditions of patronalism and instrumentalism, incoherent formal rules can turn out to be especially troublesome for those who challenge the people in power.

Catch-all in the Russian context

The above analysis indicates that catch-all perceptions are at least partly justified. It also suggests, however, that the weakness of laws is not a sufficient explanation by itself. If weak laws open the way for injustice and manipulation, so may also other laws in other societies where some room of manoeuvring is seen as a common good. Why then, do these laws turn out to yield so different outcomes in different contexts? Why is vagueness sometimes good and sometimes bad for legal output? Two characteristics of the Russian legal and political system, I argue, are especially relevant to explain this.

First, the legal actors are highly dependent on the power networks in charge of the country and we may therefore suspect that they interpret rules according to the interests of the political regime. The top-down dimension of legal nihilism in Russia will lubricate the willingness of regime insiders to instrumentalize the discretionary laws for their own purposes and the willingness of legal actors to participate in the scheme. The authoritarian and patronal incentive structures will presumably reinforce this tendency. Second, the population in general shows a dismissive attitude to law and legal institutions they do not trust. Many rely on informal practices to survive in the grey-zones of the Russian economy and to deal with the state. The element of legal nihilism in society influences the role of laws in selective law enforcement because nihilism lubricates its catch-all properties 'from below'. As we recall from Chapter 5, it was not least the pervasive level of corruption that enabled President Kuchma in Ukraine to use threats of selective law enforcement to keep his subordinates in line (Darden 2001). Dazzled by the apparent cynicism and unfairness of the above cases, we should not forget how societal attitudes to law can also influence quasi-legal repression.

We cannot understand the role of law without considering the legal culture in the population at large. The election committee member from United Russia, for instance, lamented how horribly bad the opposition, especially the local communists, filled out their registration documents: "What the communists do with their documentation show two things. First, they spit on the preparation of documents, on quality. The question is what are they hoping for? [They hope] for a scandal or for administrative resources!" The United Russia politician sorts election candidates into three categories. First, you can be an *yedinoross* (a member of United Russia). Second, you can be on the governor's black list. Third, you can be a nobody. Every candidate wants to run for elections under the flag of United Russia, the party member claims, but "it is better to be in the black list of the governor than a nobody". Also Verkhovsky notes that claiming to be politically persecuted has become a viable strategy for individuals that are charged with extremist activities and also among those who in reality have little to complain about.[6] When I discussed selective law enforcement with a representative for the Lawyers for Civil Society organization, she was quick to complain about how the opposition networks lack legal compliance:

> *From my point of view, it is easy to follow legislation ... My colleagues whom you mentioned don't like to follow the law, but rather to tell me or other lawyers that it is impossible ... If our oppositional groups and organizations were ready to follow the law, they would not have any problems. But unfortunately, they do not ... And every time they think that [their problems] is because of their political orientation.*

There is probably a grain of truth in these statements, even though they seem excessively harsh in light of most of the cases I have examined for this book.

One scholar who tries to deal with the interactions between the particular post-Soviet Russian environment and incoherent formal rules is Alena Ledeneva. Ledeneva (esp. 2006, 10–27) considers how the legal texts and path dependencies interact to form opportunity structures upon which actors form their strategies and practices. In her view, we cannot see the legal dysfunctions independent of Russian historical trajectories and legal culture. In other words, she does not challenge the potential of the laws to regulate behaviour as such, but points to its shortages in the Soviet and Russian experience and how these shortages are reproduced.

According to my interviewees, the Russian laws utilized in selective law enforcement contain certain properties that make everyone vulnerable for prosecution. Ledeneva observes the same phenomenon in her research on Russian informal practices: "The incoherence of formal rules compels almost all Russians, willingly or unwillingly, to violate them" (Ledeneva 2006, 13). In order to structure social life, the citizens develop informal practices to compensate for legal dysfunctions. In the very next sentence, however, Ledeneva shifts her focus to see the legal dysfunctions as products of the economic and social context: "Anybody can be framed and found guilty of some violation of the formal rules because the economy operates in such a way that everyone is bound to disregard at least some of these rules".

In other words, the laws may not be exceptionally well written, but they are particularly dysfunctional because they are not in line with the society they are expected to regulate (see Barsukova and Ledeneva 2018). Ledeneva makes no attempt to hide her disregard for post-Soviet lawmaking but underscores that it is the *totality* of the legal situation rather than independent laws that reproduces the informal practices. When corruption pervades a system, even anti-corruption laws may be easily adapted for corrupt purposes.

> *Because of the pervasiveness of rule violation, punishment is bound to occur selectively on the basis of criteria developed outside the legal domain [...] 'Unwritten rules' compensate for defects in the rules of the game and form the basis for selective punishment. The violation of unwritten rules can result in the enforcement of written ones, which paradoxically makes it just as, if not more, important to observe the unwritten rules as the unwritten ones. (Ledeneva 2006, 13)*

In this way, we can see how weak laws work in the specific Russian context and identify a link between catch-all (as produced by both incoherent laws and path dependencies) and the influence of informal criteria in selective law enforcement. The result is a situation where the individual is extremely vulnerable to the system: "While everybody is under the threat of punishment, the actual punishment is 'suspended' but can be enforced at any time" (ibid.). Because the state has neither the capacity to nor an interest in punishing everyone, punishment "becomes a resource in short supply" (ibid.). Ledeneva seems to argue that the influence of extra-legal criteria is not only a possible consequence of the legal vacuum but indeed entailed by it.

The idea of suspended punishment is in many ways reminiscent of *kompromat*, the gathering of compromising material for purposes of direct or (more often) indirect blackmailing. In both cases, the individuals are kept under constant pressure, what is sometimes called 'on the hook' (*na kryuchke*) in Russia. In the case of suspended punishment, however, the collection of compromising material is downplayed. As the argument goes, because rule violations are everywhere (at least according to a strict interpretation), the manipulators do not need to search extensively to find them. The regime insiders have no need for massive surveillance to find a legal basis for prosecution if the legislation itself is really catch-all. As we have seen by now, the legal system and its mismatch with society produce a 'pool' of formal pretexts. It is this pool that constitutes the source of catch-all legality in the Russian context – a pool consisting not only of laws but also of a legal system unable to curb grave manipulation and a political system where informal patronage is the fundamental form of organization.

While the above-mentioned legal vacuum created by pervasive rule violations may possibly encourage the penetration of extra-legal rules into the legal domain, it does not in itself provide a sufficient explanation as to why this happens. Indeed, we may reasonably claim that no modern state has ever had the capacity to punish everyone guilty of infringements. Due to a lack of resources and imperfect knowledge, punishment is therefore a resource in short supply everywhere. Law enforcement agencies are hardly able to catch every criminal or regulate every exchange, and pervasive non-compliance is common worldwide in fields like software licensing. Yet, the degree and character of extra-legal influence vary across time and space.

There is more than one way for the regulators to solve the issue of distributing punishment. Legitimately it might be solved by establishing a transparent policy of priorities, like selectively investigating the potentially gravest violations before minor infringements within the same field. To effectively combat software piracy or narcotics criminality, smart law enforcers will prioritize catching the big fish or limiting supply rather than arresting private end-users. If we presuppose that law enforcers are rational (and impartial), they will seek the best overall accomplishment of their tasks within the frames of their limited resources. Second, the limited 'supply' of punishment may give room for the norms and values of the legal actors, which in general would be expected to reflect that of the population as a whole. In this form of discrimination, there are in general no immediate material benefits involved for the prosecutors, even if they may be privileged by the given norms. A typical example would be systemic racism through systematic, but not necessarily conscious, prosecutorial bias. Third, the mechanism of suspended punishment may lead to selective law enforcement. As stressed earlier, the actual outcomes of legal discretion are highly contingent upon political context and legal culture, something my study serves to illustrate.

Weak laws on purpose?

With the assistance of Ledeneva's idea of 'suspended punishment', I explored above how incoherent laws in Russia might stimulate the creation of legal vacuums that may open a door for selective law enforcement. The institutional insufficiencies, it may seem, have certain 'enabling aspects' that actors can exploit (Ledeneva 2006). This is why the law not only does not hinder informal practices to take root, but indeed creates the framework for them (Barsukova and Ledeneva 2018). This line of thought has at least one implication worthy of separate attention: those who are able to fill the legal vacuum may have an interest in creating it in the first place. In other words, because authoritarian leaders are in a position to benefit from the non-transparency and incoherency in legislation, they also have incentives to contribute to its reproduction. In this sense, weak laws may be useful in quasi-formal governance.

The interviewees predominantly find regime insiders to be behind the initiation of their cases. Not seldom do they blame individuals closely associated with legislators. In other words, it seems the very same group of people that write the laws, are also encouraging these laws to be manipulated. At least since 2007, as we saw in Chapter 3, Putin's super-elite has been controlling the State Duma and most regional legislatures through the party United Russia. Many of the laws and provisions I reviewed previously were legislated at a time when this party enjoyed about two-thirds of the seats. From this position, and despite the processes of hearings, reviews, and sharp criticism of draft laws, Russian legislators kept acting like the dull King Rex in Fuller's allegory, not least with regard to laws on extremism and elections. It is pertinent to ask why.

While we cannot definitively determine the intentions of lawmakers, we can assess incentives and legal output. We know from experience that Russian legislators are not reluctant to use legislating power for furthering private or group interests. The interview material shows, moreover, that many believe that laws indeed are purposefully legislated to be incoherent. We have also seen that election law amendments often give scant time for preparation, suggesting that they are not intended to change behaviour but to deny candidates. Within the field of election law, we know of various ways to tweak the system in the incumbents' favour through gerrymandering or nationality clauses. These practices commonly uses law to regulate the playing field directly. In the case of selective law enforcement, the legislators instead allocate power to legal actors. As Wilson (2005, 84) notes: "the authorities have a vested interest in *not* cleaning the system up. As long as all are guilty to an extent, the state decides who is punished". In our conceptual framework, however, we would say that the ruling elites decide who is punished, while the state does *not*, because the latter by definition is debilitated by the legislation of weak rules. Thus we may suspect that the laws are created for the purpose of cracking down in periods of increased political tensions. It appears the laws and their abuse may paradoxically be aimed at the same target.

Several experts on post-Soviet legality seem to have thought along the same lines, though the length and complexity of such arguments is lacking, and evidence remains circumstantial:

> *Formal rules [in Ukraine] are often purposefully designed in such a way, that informal patron-client relations must be used in order to act successfully and that all actors are rendered potentially vulnerable. The legal framework creates uncertainty and can simultaneously be used as an instrument to exercise control and power. (Zimmer 2008, 268)*

Hendley (2010, 6) notes how Soviet law was often drafted in a purposefully vague manner with the goal of preserving maximum enforcement flexibility for the state. Robertson (2011, 193) holds that the amendments to NGO legislation in 2006 were intended to create "a legislative framework that can be used selectively". Also Ledeneva suggests on occasion that incoherence in fact may be the legislators' ulterior purpose and not necessarily a work accident:

> *The government could set up selectively targeted but accountable tax policies to regain the profits that were made by the oligarchs in the 1990s. But this would 'liberate' the oligarchs, enable them to play further with such clearly set formal constraints, and deprive the state of informal means of control. Reserving informal leverage against oligarchs in order to make them stay in line is an effective tool and an essential feature of political power in Russia. (Ledeneva 2006, 194)*

Ledeneva thus strongly suggests that the political regime refrains from legislating better laws because they want to retain their informal means of control. The weak formal institutions and their manipulation, Gel'man (2004, 2016) concludes, are not a legacy of the past but a result of political institution building. From this perspective, this use of quasi-legality to an extensive degree violates Waldron's formal principles of legality, exemplified in Fuller's list. In sharp contrast to Fuller's King Rex, however, Putin's use of incoherent laws has had some success. For purposes of regime consolidation and repressing dissenting voices, the selective enforcement of incoherent laws has been a very useful tool.

Fuller's point of departure was that the law is *necessarily* intended to guide human conduct. I build upon rather than challenge this basic premise. What other purposes may rules possibly have if they do not fall within this general purpose? Fuller did not, however, account for the possibility of the law promoting the ability to shape human behaviour in a different fashion. More than anything, selective law enforcement is a mechanism of rule enforcement and is thus aimed at guiding human conduct. While the mechanism of selective law enforcement utilizes law, it does so in a very different way from what Fuller considered. In our case, goals are achieved through a domination of the whole system, including legislators, law enforcers, purportedly neutral expertise, and partly the judicial branch. For this reason, there is no need to draw the rules for exercising power clearly on the legislative level. Even though the laws are unclear, they can be used to carry out an important instrumental function in the political system. As we have seen, incoherent rules may assist the repression of diverging views and the reproduction of the regime. Obviously, the incoherent rules do not achieve this *by themselves*, isolated from the political context. They only guide human conduct when supported by informal institutions. In themselves, we might contend, they are not much more than hollow shells. But then again, no laws work independently of their implementation.

What selective law enforcement lacks in clarity and structure, it gains in applicability. Selective law enforcement can promote interests and enforce rules where democratic or constitutional constraints hinder these interests to be pursued by means of ordinary law enforcement. In fact, had these rules been perfect laws in a Fullerian sense, they would have been all but defunct for what we now speculate is their designated purpose. The Fullerian model not only assumes that law *must* guide behaviour in order to be a law, but also that law must do this in a special *way*. In other words, it does not take into account a political system in which laws may work in a completely different fashion and be legislated with quasi-legality in mind. Yet all laws are legislated in a particular context, and their meaning cannot be grasped outside it.

On the validity of catch-all claims

Above, I have discussed the catch-all theory in a broader perspective of legal discretion. So far, I have largely accepted the foundation of this discussion, namely the catch-all theory itself. In this section, I will adjust the perspective somewhat by subjecting the catch-all theory to some validity tests. While a notion of catch-all may be useful, not least in discussions like the one above, it should be used with care and benefits from being employed in a moderated version.

Mariya Rozalskaya is correct when observing that many Russians are "likely to note that in our country this concept [extremism] is 'elastic' and that 'virtually everyone can be labelled as extremist" (Sova 2011). Rozalskaya is also correct, however, when she adds that this is not an "entirely accurate https://www.sova-center.ru/en/misuse/reports-analyses/2011/04/d21360/" description of reality. Many critics that promote such a view lack "sufficient command of the necessary facts or legal issues to be able to expand on their statement" (ibid.). My analysis indicates that several Russian laws have properties that make them valued tools for selective law enforcement. Yet it would be a simplification to accept that everybody may be found guilty according to Russian law. Perhaps the strongest argument against the belief that everyone may be found guilty of legal violations is that many indeed are *not* found guilty in courts, even when powerful interests seem to be pushing the case against them. While investigations have been *initiated* on a great variety of pretexts that may give us the impression of catch-all legislation, the cases are filtered through a system of legal actors who do not always support the accusations. Prosecutors may refuse to run cases handed to them, and judges may turn down many selectively initiated cases on the grounds that nothing illegal has in fact been done, or alternatively return them for further investigations or otherwise let them die silently.

Within the interview material, there is a frequently appearing inconsistency. While many of the interviewees make claims supportive of the catch-all theory, several of them simultaneously exempt themselves from its validity; they themselves are *not* guilty. The interviewees that blame the law simultaneously lament the various illegal elements *within* the legal cases. I have already mentioned cases of planted evidence in Samara. Another illustrative case is the speculative trial against an anti-fascist activist in a small city a few years later. For his alleged leading role in the storming of a local administration building, the young man was charged with aggravated hooliganism motivated by hatred. He rejected the charges, however, and claimed that the prosecution used small time criminals to produce false witnesses in court:

> *The police did not put them in prison, but used them for their own ends. Usually, they go to the court to give [false] explanations. These guys have taken part in many court cases earlier … When the court case began I had the first opportunity to speak with these guys. After three questions it was obvious that they worked for the police and had never even been in [the city].*

Less serious violations on the part of law enforcement officials seem to be very frequent in the examined cases, at least if we are to believe the interviewees. Procedural errors are a big problem in the execution of justice in Russia's legal system, and it does not seem less prominent in selective law enforcement. Many cases that are filed by individuals on quasi-legal pretexts, moreover, have been subsequently rejected by the Procuracy or courts as legally unfounded. Likewise, legal experts are not always impressed by the legal veneer: "You don't have to be a lawyer to understand the absurdity of these claims", writes Buzin commenting on a case from the Moscow region: "But being a lawyer I will say that this is, I beg your pardon, judicial drivel (*bred*)" (Buzin, undated). We have seen the Russian ombudsperson and even the Supreme Court voicing similar opinions.

The legality of cases is often up in the air as the secondary rules and judicial practice are also subjected to interpretation. Far-fetched 'interpretations' of vague formulations, formalistic enforcement, disproportional punishment, dubious expert analysis, and raids based on poor foundations are all elements whose legality is not always easy to determine. The great advantage of selective law enforcement as an instrument of repression, writes Riabchuk (2009, 269), is that it allows for "persecuting political opponents with clearly non-political charges, in full conformity with the letter of a law" (also see Barsukova and Ledeneva 2018, 488). My own research indicates that the legal procedures are ridden with violations big and small. If the laws had indeed been so incoherent that they would make everyone guilty of violating them, conscious manipulation and fabrications would be superfluous.

If we turn to the reactions of the prosecuted targets, we can also observe a phenomenon that forces us to adjust the catch-all theory. As indicated in the beginning of this chapter, some targets of selective law enforcement adjust their legal behaviour in order to 'remove the pretext.' This behaviour would be irrational if the targets fully believed in the catch-all theory. If there is an indefinite number of pretexts in the pool, it would make no sense to remove one or two of them.

In conclusion, Russian law is in this sense *not* a tool of universal application from which no political activist can escape, even in an environment that in many ways seems to encourage particularistic use of laws. In many cases, at least, the legal filters are too strong (or not weak *enough*), and at the very least the success of the cases is contingent on how much political power is put behind them. Russia is not a lawless society, only one in which the law is frequently manipulated. Also, Russia is not a repressive machine whose only interest is to please its leader. The police, the bureaucracy, different special agencies, the secret services, the Procuracy, and the courts in many cases do not act in unison, even when a case is selectively initiated by powerful forces. Rather, they operate in a complex social reality and are, like other human beings, subject to impulses and capable of independent thought.

At the same time, the incoherent laws *do* seem to play an important role in how the political authorities and law enforcement agencies suppress critical voices. Many of the controversial cases are founded precisely on the most criticized legal formulations and often shortly after new amendments provided the opportunities. While we should be aware of the limitations, there are several reasons to take a moderated catch-all theory seriously.

First, in order to be a meaningful concept, catch-all should of course not be understood literally. Catch-all does not refer to *all* legal subjects as such, but rather to an unreasonably high proportion of them, the exact numbers being less interesting for my purposes. A second observation that makes a notion of catch-all relevant is that, while a selectively initiated case against a regime critic will not always get that individual convicted, the legislation seems to provide sufficient grounds to *initiate* legal action. As will be elaborated on in Chapter 9, the interview material suggests that even when no punishment is officially recognized as taking place, legal acts have preventive and punitive qualities in themselves. To a considerable extent, therefore, law enforcement agencies can enforce the agenda of the political regime without extensive support from the judiciary. At the very least, incoherent laws seem to be a sufficient pretext to engage in quasi-legal harassment. Third, the catch-all theory is possibly more relevant to targets who lack the resources and capabilities to defend themselves adequately. Because a well-organized defence can mobilize public support and draw on informal networks in addition to providing legal assistance, it would be reasonable to suspect that speculative accusations will have a lower chance of success in these cases. We can only suspect that targets with less to put up against selective charges will buckle to unfair proceedings and court rulings more quickly.

Finally, we should note that the hypothetical question of whether everyone *may* be found guilty according to Russian law cannot be answered; we can only see that not everyone is in practice. If the laws had indeed been used to its full potential, the prosecutors would have had a better chance of imposing a formal punishment. In reality, however, the effect is often limited by the prosecutors' failure to prepare a solid case. A previous study of selective law enforcement indicates that incompetence in preparing cases has been an important factor in why human rights NGOs often win their cases in spite of political pressures (Bækken 2009). In the mentioned study, the lack of ability and experience of state actors to frame a case upon NGO legislation became starkly evident when contrasted to the skill and professionalism of civil society lawyers specialized in exactly this legal field (ibid.).

Summarized, we can conclude that selective law enforcement in practice is connected to incoherent laws, but also dependent upon a particular legal culture and political environment. The combination of these key factors create a situation where selective legal acts can be employed relatively easy and without too great political risk. When the ruling elites initiate a case selectively and exempted normal procedures, this does not retain the normative legal system completely subjugated or meaningless. Yet, the interaction of cultural, political and legal factors render all targets of quasi-legal repression highly vulnerable.

Notes

1. The publication of Fuller's *The Morality of Law* in 1958 came to be a subject of hefty debates, especially the one in retrospect known as the Hart-Fuller debates. See Fuller (1958), Hart (1958) for the original contributions and Cane (2010) for a recent collection of articles on the debates. For a criticism of Lon Fuller's more controversial claims on the tight relation between morality and law, see for instance Kramer (1998) or D'Amato (1981). For an integrating perspective, see Waldron (2008).
2. Marmor (2003) underscores that vagueness should not be confused with ambiguity, the latter being a more technical deficiency in legislation such as those raised by homonyms. The reviewed literature and informants do, however, not consequently discern between the two terms.
3. The Soviet experience indeed made the term 'rubber article' (*rezinovaya stat'ya*) popular in Russian colloquial language.
4. Author's interview, 12.11.2010.
5. '*Gedogen*' is Dutch and roughly translates as 'tolerate', 'permit', or 'condone' (www.wiktionary.org), though some claim it does not translate into English at all. As opposed to toleration, *gedogen* is an active government policy to deal with behavior that is legally forbidden yet culturally acceptable.
6. Author's interview, 12.11.2010, Moscow.

References

Barsukova, S. & Ledeneva, A. 2018. Concluding remarks to Volume 2. Are Some Countries More Informal than Others? The Case of Russia. *In:* Ledeneva. A (ed.) *The Global Encyclopaedia of Informality. Understanding Social and Cultural Complexity. Volume 2*. London: UCL Press.

Buzin, A. undated. *Vyrozhdeniye vysshego vyrazheniya*. Available at http://www.votas.ru/shchelkovo.html [accessed 18.09 2018].

Bækken, H. 2009. Selective Law Enforcement against Russian NGOs. Pursuing Informal Interests through Formal Means. *NUPI report*. Oslo: Norwegian Institute of International Affairs.

Cane, P. (ed.). 2010. *The Hart-Fuller Debate in the Twenty-First Century*. Oxford: Hart Publishing.

D'amato, A. 1981. Lon Fuller and Substantive Natural Law. *American Journal of Jurisprudence*, 26, 202–218.

Darden, K. 2001. Blackmail as a Tool of State Domination. Ukraine under Kuchma. *East European Constitutional Review,* 10, 67–72.

Friedman, L. M. 1975. *The Legal System. A Social Science Perspective*. New York: Russell Sage.

Fuller, L. L. 1958. Positivism and Fidelity to Law. A Reply to Professor Hart. *Harvard law Review,* 71, 630–672.

1958/1977. *The Morality of Law (revised edition)*. New Haven: Yale University Press.

Gel'man, V. 2004. The Unrule of Law in the Making. The Politics of Informal Institution Building in Russia. *Europe-Asia Studies,* 56, 1021–1040.

2016. The Vicious Circle of Post-Soviet Neopatrimonialism in Russia. *Post-Soviet Affairs*, 32, 455–473.

Hart, H. L. A. 1958. Positivism and the Separation of Law and Morals. *Harvard Law Review,* 71, 593–629.

Horvath, R. 2013. *Putin's Preventive Counter-Revolution. Post-Soviet Authoritarianism And the Spectre of Velvet Revolution*. Oxon: Routledge.

Jackson, R. H. 1940. The Federal Prosecutor. *Journal of the American Judicature Society* 24, 18–20.

Karklins, R. 2005. *The System Made Me Do It. Corruption in Post-Communist Societies*. New York: M. E. Sharpe.

Kramer, M. 1998. Scrupulousness Without Scruples. A Critique of Lon Fuller and His Defenders. *Oxford Journal of Legal Studies,* 18, 235–263.

Ledeneva, A. 2006. *How Russia Really Works. The Informal Practices That Shaped Post-Soviet Politics and Business*. Ithaca: Cornell University Press.

Marmor, A. 2003. The Rule of Law and Its Limits. *USC Law and Public Policy Research Paper*, 3.

Pastukhov, V. 2002. Law under Administrative Pressure in Post-Soviet Russia. *East European Constitutional Review,* 11, 66–74.

Riabchuk, M. 2004. From 'Dysfunctional' to 'Blackmail' State. Paradoxes of the Post-Soviet Transition. *The 38th Annual Shevchenko Lecture*. University of Alberta.

2009. Dubious Strength of a 'Weak State': The Post-Soviet Ukraine in the Nineties. In Maćków, J. (ed.) *Autoritarismus in Mittel- und Osteuropa*. Weisbaden: VS Verlag für Sozialwissenchaften.

Robertson, G. B. 2011. *The Politics of Protest in Hybrid Regimes. Managing Dissent in Post-Communist Russia*. Cambridge: Cambridge University Press.

Schauer, F. 1991. *Playing by the Rules. A Philosophical Examination of Rule-Based Decision-Making in Law and in Life*. Oxford: Clarendon Press.

Sova. 2011. Inappropriate Enforcement of Anti-Extremist Legislation in Russia in 2012. *SOVA Report*. Available at: http://www.sova-center.ru/en/misuse/reports-analyses/2011/04/d21360/ [accessed 06.12.2017].

Thompson, E. P. 1975. *Whigs and Hunters. The Origins of the Black Act*. New York: Pantheon Books.

Waldron, J. 2008. Positivism and Legality. Hart's Equivocal Response to Fuller. *New York University Law Review,* 83, 1135–1169.

Wilson, A. 2005. *Virtual Politics. Faking Democracy in the Post-Soviet World.* New Haven: Yale University Press.

Zimmer, K. 2008. Formal Institutions and Informal Politics in Ukraine. *In:* Meyer, G. (ed.). *Formal Institutions and Informal Politics in Central and Eastern Europe. Hungary, Poland, Russia and Ukraine*. 2nd revised and updated ed. Opladen: Barbara Budrich Publishers.

8 Perceptions about political interference

The idea of selective law enforcement as a complex mechanism of rule enforcement presupposes a set of conceptual components introduced in the introductory chapter. In the following, I will examine those conceptual components that relate to the informal workings of selective law enforcement. In the second part of the chapter, I will also look more closely at how and why the interviewees come to interpret the cases as political. These indicators of selectivity are necessary for actors to interpret legal acts as being informally motivated. In this way, they tell us how the political regime may transmit its informal rules to actors within society.

The chapter is almost in its entirety based on interviews. On some issues, the perceptions of actors who see themselves as subjected to selective law enforcement are crucial to the functioning of the mechanism itself. Perceptions of informal criteria, for instance, directly influence how actors act upon the legal problems. Information as to why the interviewees come to believe in these criteria, moreover, tells us something about how informal rules are transmitted and reproduced in society. How the interviewees experience this politicized law enforcement is part of what selective law enforcement is and how it works. On other issues, the perceptions themselves are not of crucial impact with regard to how the mechanism functions. Here, our interest therefore lies not with these perceptions, as was the case in the above examples. Rather, we seek empirical data about informal political games to which my methodological approach has no *direct* access. Questions of this type include who the initiators of selective law enforcement are, what their motives are, and how they communicate their wishes to the legal actors who act upon them. The answers my methodology can produce on these issues are second-hand. Considering the interviewees' field of work and their experience with selective law enforcement, we should approach their statements on these topics as those of experts, albeit clearly biased ones, considering their personal or professional stakes in the cases.

As will be seen, the research presented on the informal components in many ways stirs up more questions than the explorative research design is able to address adequately. Yet the data is sufficient to sketch out the great variation within the conceptual components of selective law enforcement, and it suggests how further research can address the variation. For the sake of textual fluency and the considerable interconnection between various components, I address some elements outside of their designated subsection.

The informal criteria

The words, faces, and voices of my interviewees indicated bitterness, frustration, and sometimes contempt for the individuals responsible for their problems. Yet, their narratives were strikingly matter-of-fact. Often, the interviewees rationalized the legal actions against them as dictated by the logics of power and by reference to the personal character of Russian politics. They did not depict their adversaries as much as demons, but as *cynics* within a corrupt system. Selective law enforcement is in this view the product of instrumentalism, pragmatism, and ideological nihilism. The successful manipulator is the one who is willing and able to instrumentalize both formal institutions and informal networks. In other words, the interviewees tended to see selective law enforcement through the lenses of instrumental rationality.

If I were to articulate one core rule that guides selective law enforcement in Russian politics as interpreted by my interviewees, it would be something like this: If you threaten the interests of powerful groups or individuals – by criticizing or otherwise drawing negative attention to them – you stand a high risk of experiencing quasi-legal trouble. According to the interviewees, problems occur for those who are "not agreeing", "not pleasing", "unwanted", "who speak their mind", or are "critical to the authorities". One interviewee gathers that the main principle is always the same: "to pressure those who think and speak differently".

There are certain costs in terms of time and resources to arrange a selective legal crackdown. Although Putin's regime as a hybrid political system may be particularly vulnerable to political dissent, we would expect intervention to take place only when it is assumed to be worth the price. The more visible, personal, and well documented the criticism is, the more likely it is that the ruling elites will pick it up as a considerable threat, and the greater is the risk of reprisals. One activist explained how his NGO had been working consistently and purposefully against the interests of the regional authorities for years.

> *[The regional authorities] want to create a good image for themselves. We talk about the ugly stuff that is going on, and this contradicts what they are saying in the mass media. Because we also point to facts, laws, experts, and so on, they don't like it at all. If we just shouted "Aaaah, everything is bad here," they would hardly pay it any attention. But when we come up with facts, take them to court, write letters, meet journalists – they don't like it. This has gone on for more than ten years, so now they simply hate us. If somebody put a gun in their hands, they would shoot us immediately.*

Some of the prosecuted interviewees saw their cases primarily in terms of a long-lasting bad relationship with the authorities. Others saw the prosecution primarily as triggered by a specific act or acts that preceded the legal crackdown. Typically, this trigger could be the publishing of a critical report, conducting a journalistic investigation, or organizing a particular event. In one case that concerned supposed tax arrears of a human rights NGO, for instance, one of the organization's lawyers interpreted the legal claims as a direct response to the organization's initiative to bring a high-ranking police officer to justice: "This was the main and obvious reason, there can be no other reasons". She explained that the NGO repeatedly put forward such cases against the regular police, but that they first experienced trouble when they touched one of its leaders. In a third set of cases, the selective law enforcement took the form of pre-emptive actions aimed at impeding planned events, such as meetings, conferences, rallies, and similar activities.

While we may categorize the informal criteria for prosecution in the way I did above, they often appeared more mixed in real conflicts. Frequently, the legal crackdown was part of a dynamic conflict that had lasted for some time. Commonly, for instance, a sour, long-term relationship culminated over specific issues or actions. In more than one case, the pressure emerging from these dynamics was sustained through election campaigns, in which the political leadership was particularly sensitive to criticism. In one examined case, the trouble started with repeated conflicts at work in which the interviewee attained some experience with the legal system. Then the issues escalated after he became involved in a property dispute and went even further as he decided to run for office with the opposition in the local elections. As he summed up, referring to the local power networks: "My activity was too high for them". As the situation developed, he came to fear for his life. In order to protect himself, he started to send letters of caution to various state agencies, including FSB. As it seems, the letters unleashed a chain of legal charges, starting with accusations of planned terrorist bombings of the local court. The subject of these claims states that the court chair personally filed 38 accusations against him in the following months.

The complexity and time span of legal cases allow for considerable improvisation in the duration of the process. Actors on both sides have time to adapt to changing circumstances and engage in informal bargaining. The motives for initiating a case are not necessarily the same as the motives for sustaining it over time. While selective law enforcement is *phased* in the meaning that a selection by definition precedes the first legal acts, this does not imply that the informal influence is limited to the initial selection only. On the contrary, there are obvious reasons to suspect that informal interests will continue to interfere in cases where they are stakeholders.

In addition, in the few cases in which we would possibly have expected informal criteria to be more clear-cut, the improvisation upon changing circumstances makes the informal criteria more complex and context bound. The raids that took place in one large Russian city in 2007 may serve as examples.

Circumstantial evidence and the timing certainly indicate that the raids were related to the suppression of the so-called Dissenters' March, a planned opposition rally that was set to coincide with a major EU-Russia Summit in the region. The rally was officially sanctioned, but its potential for mass mobilization was suppressed by a number of means, including the quasi-legal detainment of activists in several Russian regions (Horvath 2013, 194–195).

In the days preceding the planned rally, law enforcement officials searched and confiscated the computers of the editorial office of a local newspaper. Sometime later, prosecutors launched criminal proceedings against the newspaper's editor-in-chief. Officially, the law enforcement officials conducted the raid on suspicions of unlicensed software. According to the editor, however, they rather intended to paralyze the activity of the newspaper, as it was one of few local media outlets willing to mobilize readers for the Dissenters' March. The officials also raided the news agency next door, presumably to stop them from lending the newspaper the necessary hardware to continue publishing. The leader of the news agency was unsure whether the agency's political attitudes influenced the decision to take away their computers, but she was positive that the raid was based on improvisation and not part of any prearranged plan. In contrast to the raid on the newspaper, it seemed unorganized and lacked an official permit. Instead, according to this interviewee, the raiders provided a backdated court permit some days later.

Almost simultaneously, another NGO in the city was subjected to similar treatment. In the same way as sketched out above, its office computers were confiscated on alleged suspicions of copyright violations, and a case was opened against its leader. The NGO's staff was locked out of the premises without access to their documents and hardware. Like the above editor, the NGO's leader was also a well-known critic in the area. Before the rally, she became involved in the conflict by criticizing how the police tackled the situation of rising tensions. One day when the rally drew near, she was informed that a special police unit had just been raiding the NGO's office.

Although these raids were presumably part of an initiative to suppress the Dissenters' March, the quasi-legal pressure against the two main targets of the raids was sustained after the event ended. Criminal proceedings against the editor were carried on for more than two years, and the computers were held back. The newspaper was not able to function without hardware and ceased publishing. Criminal investigation against the head of the news agency was dropped sooner, but another case was soon opened against the agency in which its leader had official status as a witness. As for the NGO leader, the criminal procedures were cancelled in a matter of months, but both she and other NGO staff experienced continued harassment. In the interview, she suggested that someone had hopes of paralyzing the organization's ability to monitor elections the same year. While the case against her had been closed, nobody informed her of this until March of the next year, two days after the presidential elections. While the crackdown seemed triggered by the Council of Europe summit, this is only part of the story.

As the editor explained, he and his newspaper had always been a "bone in the throat" of the regional government.

The interviewees' perceptions of informal criteria in general fit with the core rule as formulated above. Beyond that point, however, the answers bear witness to the complexities of informal schemes. The unwritten rules are never fixed, so we must always interpret them in the complex context in which they are acted upon. A skilful player in this game will understand the applicability and implication of both formal rules and informal norms under any given circumstances. Within the interview setting, the interviewees were encouraged to articulate these complexities that are often unspoken, and the informal criteria thus became more tangible for outsiders who want to put labels on them. Yet, the triggers for selective law enforcement are contingent upon a more complex background. This makes it difficult to isolate the informal criteria from the broader context.

In the case of selective registration denials, some interviewees also repeated the by-now-familiar claim that candidates from the opposition and candidates that have a reputation as troublemakers will have a particularly hard time being registered. In addition to these criteria, however, there was a widespread view that opposition candidates would "get special consideration from the committee" if they had some weight to throw around. Regardless of policy preference or political stance, candidates may be removed from the race if they appear to stand a fair chance of winning against incumbents or friends of the incumbents. When the Duma party Just Russia was denied participation in some municipal elections in Vladimir oblast, its leaders took this almost as a compliment: "We had a quite strong team, they just feared us". These findings echo Maria Popova's (2012) research on election disputes, which uncovered a significant statistical correlation between election disputes and competitive districts where more than one candidate had real chances of winning. Competitiveness increases the incentives not only for more active campaigning and thus more violations, but also for getting the main competitor de-registered before Election Day so as not to risk defeat.

Precisely whom the candidate is running *against* is particularly important in single-mandate districts. If you are serious about challenging an important incumbent from the ruling party or a favourite of the governor in a single-mandate district, the chances are good you might be targeted and you may want to start readying yourself for an appearance in court. One candidate was young and rather unknown in the region, as were his personal attributes and political views. According to this candidate, his registration was blocked only when the incumbents realized that he might actually win the seat. The ruling elites could not afford to lose this seat to an outsider, explained his political advisor, because the governor's favourite in this single-mandate district was a director of an energy company and "one of the sponsors" of the political regime. Another candidate who incidentally had ties to the same company was seemingly in agreement with the regional leadership about his candidacy. He reportedly fell out of favour, however, when his opponent's business associates in Moscow used their channels to convince the governor to change his priority.

Perceived motives

Most of the interviewees of this study rejected any suggestion that the legalistic veneer was intended to prop-up the harassment with popular support, as façade theories would imply (see Chapter 1). One activist reacted in disbelief when I hinted in this direction.

> *No, no, no, they are not trying [to look legitimate]. Why? Everybody understands! Come on! It is funny, because when you speak to the public you don't have iron clad proof that this is selective [law enforcement], but to say that [the prosecution] is done for the sake of protecting somebody's rights [would be] simply unbelievable ... The majority of the people says that this is bullshit.*

Once again, the façade theories have a poor fit with my findings on the ground. Instead of interpreting their experiences in terms of deception and hidden repression, the interviewees tended to talk about selective law enforcement in the context of power relations. They did *not* speak explicitly in terms of informal rules and their enforcement – this terminology is my own extension for purposes of concept development. Yet, the way interviewees framed the issues seemed to me clearly reminiscent of a rule enforcement perspective. They speak about "scaring" (deterrence), "setting an example for others" (general deterrence), and "hindering" the agenda of an organization (preventive acts). The communicative aspect of rule enforcement is also evident in their statements.

Just as the informal rules that guide selective crackdowns are complex and context-bound, the related perceptions of *motivations* behind selective law enforcement are similarly multi-faceted. If we exclude the special case of selective denials of election registration (the purpose of which is often straightforward), most interviewees that had experienced legal attacks believed that the prosecution had several motives. "I think it was 80% to prevent young people from taking part in such actions and 20% against me personally", said the young man prosecuted for aggravated hooliganism. One of the human rights activists from southern Russia had her computers confiscated and was charged with copyright violations and with "creating, using and distributing" illegal software.[1] Simultaneously, she was investigated for possible extremist activities. According to her interpretation, the initiators wanted:

> *to grab the information from my laptop and personal computers to see how much to expect from me, to divert me from human rights activities, and to engage me in[to] self-protection at the expense of my mission. I think [the*

> *proceedings] were [intended] to make me busy with something else rather than making projects and working … They wanted to scare [me], they wanted to stop me. The best scenario for them would be that I went away from the region, which actually I am on the brink of doing because I don't want to follow Karastelev*[2] *and be beaten up.*

Several of the interviewees used the term '*davleniye*' (pressure) when describing the motives they saw behind the legal acts. In two separate cases, the state agency for media monitoring, Roskomnadzor, issued formal warnings for extremist content to at least two branches of the same newspaper. "It [the warning] is a way to keep us under pressure, so that we don't get too deep into these issues", explains a representative of the newspaper's federal edition in Moscow. A part-time journalist for the other of the two editions expressed a similar view, but with a greater stress on the informal criteria. "It is a way to pressure", he explained; "You see, this is also a signal that if you are going to criticize the authorities [*vlast'*], we can arrange for a second warning".[3] By adding pressure, the selectors discourage unwanted behaviour in the future. In other words, the meaning of the term '*davleniye*' is strongly related to the theoretical concept of deterrence.

As discussed above, easily fabricated 'suspicion' allowed law enforcers to conduct searches and confiscate documents and computer hardware, not least on the pretext of enforcing copyrights. In these cases, some interviewees held that the gathering of information could indeed have been an important goal of the law enforcers or their patrons. As the interviewees saw it, the raiders did not primarily seek unlicensed software or signs of extremism – which may have been the pretext for the raids – but rather tried to find internal documents or correspondence that could give them some form of leverage in ongoing or future political conflicts.

The gathering of information (not least *kompromat*) and the exertion of pressure are connected in the Russian term *povesit' na kryuchke* (to hang on the hook). When a troublemaker attracts the attention of the ruling elites, legal investigations may both communicate a warning and help to gather information on the subject. The information obtained from raids may give the law enforcers a possible edge in a conflict, and the opened case makes it easier to pull (*potyanut'*) the hook when or if necessary. The investigations against the activist charged for both extremist activities and cybercrime were eventually closed as she went into internal exile in Moscow. However, as she said, "they open and close criminal cases just like that. If I go back and become active [again], they may reopen it. They already did it three times, [so there is] no guarantee there won't be a fourth, a fifth, and so on".

In the case of an ecologist from the Volga region, the law enforcers confiscated a computer in an initial raid. After the initial raid, the case had hardly moved forward when I conducted the interview several months later. "In Russian, this is called to keep (*derzhat'*) on the hook", explained the ecologist. "They know if they bring the case forward at this time, they will probably lose. At the same time, they do not want to close the case". We recall the case in which a news agency head had status as a witness. According to a local source, this was also a political move – a way to "keep her on the hook". It would not be hard to change her status back to accused in the middle of the investigation, the source explained.

The 'selectors'

In general, the interviewees of this study did not believe that actors within the law enforcement structure initiated cases on their own account. There were exceptions, however. When a court sentenced a blogger to a penal colony for various extremist activities, for instance, his lawyer believed that the FSB initiated and pushed the case informally because they were themselves targets of the blogger's criticism. Two of the interviewed activists also found reasons to believe that the FSB was involved in initiating legal processes against them. At the same time, both of them also stressed the role of regional authorities in the background. In some cases, the FSB seems to act as the intermediary between the state administration and the less politically active law enforcement agencies. In the spectacular case from a small town, we noted previously in this chapter how the court chair himself repeatedly tried to get an engineer-turned-activist convicted, amongst other things for planning terrorist attacks. More commonly, however, interviewees believed that the legal actors participated in the schemes on behalf of patrons or networks external to the formal law enforcement structure.

In the majority of the examined cases, the interviewees linked their problems to powerful figures in the regional administration, typically governors or their close associates. Some insisted that the head of the region had directly issued an order; others mentioned names of bureaucrats or advisors within the administration. More than one electoral candidate denied registration in Perm, for instance, claimed that a certain individual within the governor's team (*komanda*) arranged the selective registration denials. Yet other interviewees were less specific in their accusations. They had little knowledge or interest in these details or were hesitant to make personal accusations.

A point worth noting is the degree and nature of the Kremlin's alleged involvement in the regional conflicts in which selective law enforcement was used. None of the interviewees suspected that the president or prime minister were personally initiating a case against them. One of the interviewees even held that criticizing Putin in general was safe, while criticizing local authorities could be fatal. That being said, many of the interviewees claimed that top political figures were involved in the informal schemes leading up to their prosecution, including not only the regional elite and governors, but also other higher federal officials and the Presidential Administration. The interviewees leave us with the impression that the links between the rulers in Moscow and the regional elites do not follow a simple chain of command but take many different forms.

Several interviewees suggested that federal interests were at stake in the March 2010 elections in Vladimir, in which the election committees denied registration to a large number of serious candidates. A local journalist suggested that a central figure within United Russia orchestrated the purge (*zachistka*) by himself.

> *He acts as if he is the ruler (*khozyain*) of all Rus'.*[4] *He comes here and starts to whisper and everyone for some reason fears [him] ... He headed the staff, so therefore everything went through him – all these lists, whom to purge, whom to crush.*

Prior to the elections, many territorial election committees in Vladimir received additional support from officially neutral advisors, hired from various parts of the country. Part of their work was directly concerned with the registration process. These "highly qualified lawyers knew all the election laws ... and they approached the opposition candidates in a very scrupulous way and tried to deny them registration", the journalist claimed. In a short article for Golos in Vladimir, Lyudmila Eshanu (2011) suggests that these lawyers in fact worked unofficially for United Russia and for money from outside the city.

In the crackdown against several offices in Nizhniy Novgorod in 2007, Moscow was allegedly involved, but in an indirect fashion. According to one fieldwork source, the governor had travelled to Moscow to get clearance from a top figure in the Presidential Administration for the use of 'active measures' against a number of organizations. The plan was already developed locally, and a list of organizations was apparently ready in advance. The eventual raid and confiscation of hardware took place the same year and in a manner outwardly similar to the one in Samara. Among the targets was a well-known human rights activist. In his opinion, the decision to crack down may have been cleared with Moscow, but the tactical details on how to engage the task must still have been decided locally. Another interpretation of how higher politics is involved in selective law enforcement was formulated by a journalist charged with extremist activities in a small Russian city. The journalist maintained that the legal cases against him had been undertaken on local initiatives. At the same time, he suspected that Moscow provided protection (*krysha*) to his antagonists and blocked his efforts to resolve the conflict within the formal system.

In many cases, the interviewees stuck to regional explanations and did not mention Moscow at all. In the examined claims about selective registration denials in Perm, nobody mentioned federal elites, and several activists presented their problems as locally constituted. One even reported to feel "more or less safe" in the capital, where she had gone into internal exile. Although she believed that her problems originated with regional authorities and the highly centralized FSB, her antagonists seemed to lack the influence or willingness to act outside of their own region. In general, the interviewees depicted regional elites as very capable of independently pulling the strings of law enforcement and administration in their region. Moscow could have been involved in many cases, but not in the classical notion of a power vertical or chain-of-command. Instead, federal interests played a multitude of roles. In short, nothing in the research material suggests that selective law enforcement takes place according to an unwritten master plan. Whatever patterns we may discover in the material, we should rather interpret as more or less uncoordinated actions based on the same rules of the game.

The centralization of the quasi-legal realm we observed in Chapter 3 does not imply that the Kremlin pulls all the strings, but rather that it has worked to align incentives and strengthened its ability to monitor and keep control with regional elites. Similar incentives give birth to behavioural patterns and thus perceptions of unity. The individuals, networks, or institutions that the interviewees believed were behind their cases were primarily interpreted as representatives of *vlast'* – the ones in power. These perceptions of unity produce the effects associated with rule enforcement on a higher level of abstraction. Even if many believed the initiatives had local origins, it would be reasonable to expect the federal elites to take action when they find regional rulers who act beyond their (informal) mandate and in conflict with Moscow's interest. Even if a case is initiated by regional law enforcement, administration, or private interests, the initiators may act with the intention of impressing their patrons in the Kremlin. The perceptions of one activist and opposition politician may illustrate the point. In an interview, he suggested that a local political leader initiated the legal case against him. At the same time, he interpreted this action as dictated by the logics of power: If this person had not taken action then someone else would have and the former would have lost his job. When needed, the central elites can engage more directly in regional conflicts and make things happen.

From my methodological perspective, it is hard to tell whether the regional actors acted as they did with the explicit or implicit blessing of Moscow. Moreover, we should be careful about inferring more general conclusions based on limited material. For instance, we cannot rule out that centralized and large-scale repressive campaigns do in fact take place. The findings do remind us, however, that we should not be tempted to reify the ruling elite in authoritarian systems – the ruling elites do not behave as a collective entity. When we are studying authoritarian or autocratic regimes, non-transparency and popular myths make an exaggerated belief in central authority and control especially tempting. Even the tsars, however, were not as autocratic as they wanted to be. Although Putin has introduced a centralistic form of governance, the huge, non-transparent, and highly corrupt country is by no means easy to rule, whether by formal, informal, or quasi-formal means.

The lines of communication

As was laid out in the previous chapter, the laws that underlie many cases of selective law enforcement seem to grant legal actors broad or at times almost indefinite discretion in decision-making. This is however an illusion, since law is not the only practical limit to the legal actors' discretion. Discretion is strongly compromised by a range of influences, including professional, social, and political expectations. In Russia, the latter set of expectations are also backed by quasi-formal sanctioning mechanisms, reproducing the logic of selective law enforcement within the broader legal system and bolstering core compliance with the central regime's interests.

In the cases examined, the interviewees claimed that the legal actors passed on most of their decision-making power to their patrons within the regime hierarchies, letting the political preferences of these insiders determine against whom legal acts should be targeted. What power the discretionary or incoherent legal rules allocated to the legal actors, then, was in these cases largely illusory. In the narratives of interviewees, correspondingly, the legal actors predominantly operated as cogwheels in an authoritarian machinery. In another words, the initiators of selective law enforcement not only instrumentalize laws, but also the manpower of the law enforcement system. Subservient legal actors are a key prerequisite for selective law enforcement to be effective.

A catch-all legal framework, corruption within the system, and a culture of legal manipulation provide incentives to instrumentalize the legal system. These incentives are, however, in theory present to any actor. The political leadership needs to ensure that selective law enforcement takes place in a way not contrary to its own interests. The discretion must somehow be controlled and delimited, and the activities of legal actors coordinated with the interests of the ruling elites. In order to be successful, selective law enforcement is in other words dependent upon the legal actors' ability to distribute punishment effectively and accurately, according to the interests of the ruling elite and according to the informal rules of which these elites are the main beneficiaries. In other words, the ability to constitute a consistent link between the informal rules of political conduct and the formal legal acts is dependent upon both the coercive and the cohesive capacity of the regime. The coercive ability is a direct function of law enforcement capacity that we have seen increased under Putin's period of dominance, not least with regard to the anti-extremist and copyrights enforcement. The cohesion is measured as the degree to which the political leadership is able to control the direction and severity of selective law enforcement.

In my interviews, I asked the self-perceived victims of selective law enforcement to share their perceptions on how the selectors' motivations are translated into concrete legal acts. As is the case with most of my other questions, I inquired about the interviewees' personal experiences of selective law enforcement, but did not stop them from voicing opinions of more general relevance. I sought to explore not least whether the law enforcement system had internalized the political bias or remained dependent on telephone justice – explicit suggestions or commands from higher up in the hierarchy.

A considerable proportion of the interviewees explicitly stated that the cases against them were initiated by means of direct commands from office-holders in political or administrative positions. In other words, they perceived the mechanism to work according to the logics of telephone justice in a narrow sense. In cases of selective denials for election registration, this view was particularly evident. "There were direct orders, of course", said a former mayor of a mid-sized town and a politician with considerable experience in regional politics. The above-mentioned journalist shared this interpretation of the regional and local elections in Vladimir: "the lawyers had direct orders to purge this, this, this, and this [candidate]". In Perm, one of the candidates claimed that the selections before elections were organized in a very simple and manual fashion: "They just call and say: 'Hello, this man needs to be rejected'".

Outside of the election registration context, a part of the interviewees similarly believed that regime insiders controlled the selective initiation of legal cases by means of clear-cut orders. "[There were] direct commands. They don't talk to each other in other ways", said one of the human rights activists. He continued, "it's very simple. They called and said that [our organization] had to be closed. They sent lawyers to show up in courts and the judge did what he had to". In another case, an individual served a sentence in a penal colony for extremism-related crimes and slander against a regional leader. As the offended party, the leader was personally involved in the case. A source close to sentenced man, however, believed that somebody associated with the regional power exerted pressure from outside of the courtroom: "I think that here we have something called telephone justice when everything is decided by telephone calls". We can find another example of perceived direct commands in the Nizhniy Novgorod raids in 2007, where the governor allegedly operated with a list of specific organizations that needed attention.

In other situations, the interviewees depicted a less direct transmission of informal agendas from the political actors to the law enforcers. "I don't think [the case] has a direct link [to regional authorities]", said one of them. "Instead, it shows the general attitude and the environment – the general flow of things in the region. It is a silent agreement between the regional authorities and the law enforcement agencies". In the hooliganism case, a friend of the accused believed that the police feared that their careers might have been in danger if they had not taken action in response to the riots: "[the Governor] said that they had to find the person that did this, but he did not say who. They just needed a scapegoat". Moreover, neither of the two interviewed representatives of the Moscow newspaper believed that there were any explicit political orders to issue an extremist warning to them. Rather, they contended it was Rozkomnadzor's initiative to "please the Kremlin", as one of them formulated it.

Finally, several interviewees took a third position between the other two, focusing on signals and political discourse. One of the journalists stressed how political signals often are more subtle:

> *[Selectivity] is a primary characteristic of the whole political system in Russia. These commands are not just given when somebody calls somebody else. A political will is expressed and spread to all the [administrative] branches. [The branches] accept this and work in the way that they think necessary.*

In another city, an interviewee explained how administrative leaders might provide public signals that agencies interpret as start flags: "Such a signal sounded from the President's representative (*federal'nyy inspektor*) in Samara oblast ... And naturally, the lower part of the vertical reacts to such signals in its own way and executes a persecution". In the particular case, the interviewee pointed to a newspaper article and some anonymous Internet postings that warned against spies and saboteurs in relation to the upcoming EU-Russia Summit. These postings explicitly mentioned names of individuals who later became targets of quasi-legal attacks.

To summarize, the interview material suggests that both direct commands and internalized practices among legal actors are relevant to the workings of quasi-legal repression. Notably, there is no real contradiction between the direct commands stressed by some interviewees and the vaguer signals from above emphasized by others. Rather, the different explanations reflect particular cases and tell different parts of the same story. The two forms of communication are complementary rather than conflicting. The core rules of Russian authoritarian politics ensure a certain level of 'automated' repression of regime critics. They also dictate, however, that the law enforcement agencies must adjust to signals or direct commands from above. On the level of the political regime, therefore, the combination of internalized bias and the continued practice of telephone justice makes perfect sense. Although heads of law enforcement agencies are politically aware in their work, the political leadership will still need to encourage and direct this bias by pulling strings manually from time to time. To have a successful career in law enforcement, the rules of the game dictate not only that you must be aware of the political signals and take active measures to curb political dissent, but they also dictate that you are ready to serve your patrons more directly when prompted, even when this may contradict the law. One source in particular voiced a similar interpretation: "[The election committees] know there is a general arrangement, let's say you should never register Yabloko under any circumstances. Here there is no need for telephone justice. They will do this on their own". The candidate, who was not himself associated with Yabloko, moved on to explain a more complex case where an earlier member of United Russia had been denied registration. "Here", he concluded, "we have an outright order. Here, of course, we have telephone justice".

Finally, we should note that any direct order from a patron is likely to influence the client's interpretations of the future situation. For this reason, direct commands will also influence the institutionalization of patterns and expectations about how selective law enforcement works within the political regime. In other words, direct orders are strong normative expressions and for this reason have ramifications: They are carriers of informal rules.

The smoking gun: Indicators of selectivity

What I call indicators of selectivity are basically what others would call circumstantial evidence for ulterior motives. The latter conceptualization would suggest that the indicators of selectively are the result of law enforcers' failed attempts to hide their real motivations from us. In light of my conceptualization (Chapter 5), however, this interpretation would be misleading and not give the indicators of selectivity the attention they deserve. The indicators of selectivity are in fact completely fundamental to the practice. They are the manifestation of the link between informal politics and law enforcement as interpreted by the interviewees. It is these indicators that determine how targets and observers alike come to interpret legal acts as motivated by particularistic and extra-legal interests. Without them, in other words, selective law enforcement would not deter.

This section shows some examples from the interview material on how this flag is set up (consciously or not) and identified in actual cases. Even though the ruling elites and law enforcers often deny personal or political motives publicly, my research indicates that legal actors in Russian make little if any attempt to hide the informal underpinnings. While the exact reasons for initiating these cases may sometimes be difficult to ascertain and the ulterior motives hard to prove legally speaking, the cases look like anything but apolitical. As noted in Part I of this book, the findings do not give much support to façade theories that would see selective law enforcement as a smoke screen to hide repression from observers.

- **Extraneous elements**

The targets of selective law enforcement may sense political motivations by identifying what they see as extraneous political elements in a given setting. As the argument goes, if a legal case had not been politically initiated, it would not have been paid attention to by political actors. In an interview about what she considered politically motivated tax charges against the human rights NGO where she was working, a lawyer explained her suspicions towards the regional authorities in part by referring to their awkward presence at a press conference:

> *When we arranged a press conference in relation to this case [on police violence], many journalists arrived and the victims [of the beatings] came too. They explained how everything happened, and the journalists listened.*

> *The head of the Internal Security Agency[5] in the region also arrived at this press conference, though what he wanted to do there is not known. The deputy head of the regional press service of the ministry of interior came too, and also others … A cop filmed the whole thing … Why would employees on such high level come to some [minor] press-conference?*

In another case, an editor detected a political element in the composition of the law enforcement group that raided their editorial office:

> *One of them, I don't know what he would do in that delegation, was connected with the agency that fights against terrorism and extremism … He was one of the threats for oppositional activists in [the city], always doing his best in order to make problems for those who try to work in the political sphere.*

While such incidents in theory may occur for several reasons and need not necessarily signify anything in isolation. Typically, however, the incidents appear in concert with other signs of ulterior motives.

- **Timing and coordinated crackdowns in related cases**

Interviewees commonly referred to the timing of events when they explained why they see a case as triggered by extra-legal criteria. As one human rights worker noted after the occurrence of subsequent raids and interrogations: "all these inquisitional acts related to this case happened against us precisely when we arranged some kind of event". For the purpose of communicating informal criteria or rules, the timing of crackdowns with specific events has the advantage of showing rather precisely what action is considered unwanted and *de facto* punishable.

A similar result can be achieved by coordinating crackdowns upon several organizations sharing a similar critical profile or operating in the same sphere. This was not least the case in Samara and Nizhniy Novgorod, where political interpretations of the affair naturally became popular.[6] One source in Nizhniy also notes that the law enforcement officials produced identical documents to sanction the raids against all three organizations, something he found peculiar.

Quasi-legal cases do not need to coincide in time in order to be interpreted as related. In some cases, it may be sufficient that they follow similar trajectories. As we have seen, one activist saw her own case in relation to another conflict between regional authorities and Vadim Karastelev, who experienced legal charges and later was hospitalized after severe beatings.

> *I see that in my situation the succession of events is the same. It is some kind of informal scheme. If a person is not easy to approach to make him loyal and less critical, they make a check-up against his organizations or open criminal cases against him in person. And if that doesn't work, they beat him up.*

Given several similar organizations and individuals experience crackdowns on formally unrelated grounds gives observers a reason to seek out the informal criteria by looking at what characteristics the targets have in common. The coordinated crackdowns provide a signal as to what elements of civil society are currently moving beyond the borders of what the authorities see as acceptable. In this way, the informal rules are communicated by means of enforcement patterns.

- **Consistent harassment**

Whereas in the campaigns discussed above law enforcers hit many targets at the same time, campaigns may also take another form. In many cases, the same target is instead hit again and again. This not only makes the target of persecution preoccupied. It also sends a signal to everyone that a legal case is part of a broader harassment campaign, not in reality intended to enforce law. Many informants have found themselves in a situation in which a number of punitive measures are initiated against them at the same time, be it legal charges, harassment by police officials, smear campaigns in mass media, or physical attacks by unidentified assailants.

"In short, it was such a nightmare", said the wife of an imprisoned man.

> *I don't want to think about it. Every day, court bailiffs packed at our doors saying that he [the husband] had not paid aliments. They wrote some kind of drivel and posted some kind of porn clips [on the Internet] in which he allegedly participated.*

The smear campaign was made public through local newspapers and Internet portals belonging to a media corporation associated with the regional government. Later, the wife recollected, it became physical: "They attacked him in the parking lot by the house and beat him up. He was hospitalized". She explained how she lost her job, and how even relatives of the couple were experiencing serious pressure. We can find another example of consistent harassment among the copyright cases, where one of the targets experienced a number of 'coinciding' activities. Uniformed police warned neighbours about her purported "drinking and troublemaking" (*chto ya p'yu i deboshiryu*) and suggested that she may be spreading extremist literature. In the investigation that originated in claims of unlicensed software, the investigator had her examined for mental illness and drug abuse. At the time of the interview, she said, she still got strange looks on the street.

The persecution of a NGO leader concerned with human rights violations in the Chechen Republic was rather notorious within the human rights community:

> *In the beginning of 2005, the process of destroying the organization had begun. It started with a criminal case initiated against me, where I got a two years*

> *suspended sentence and the organization was liquidated for extremism in 2006. We registered a new organization, but there were also serious tax attacks. In short, it was such a war.*

After the interview, the war escalated further. To show how the various forms of harassment are interrelated, the NGO leader explained how an international event his organization tried to organize was "torn apart" (*sorvana*) by various means.

> *Firstly, all our guests who arrived from Great Britain, the USA and Spain were informed that all pre-booked rooms allegedly leaked water from the ceiling. Repairs began immediately and nobody was allowed to move into the hotel … A similar disaster struck in the hall we had rented for the conference and press conference. One hour before the event, we were suddenly notified that the lights were out and that the keys to the [seminar] room had accidentally been lost … In addition, the car that we used was confiscated, purportedly because it was on a list of stolen cars … On the first day of the conference, I was summoned for urgent interrogations related to my criminal case. When I refused to testify, they did a new search to get documents and possible hard drives with piracy software that could've been at the office, and in short to not let us work. The search went on for about three hours, and at the same time the whole day a car from the OMON[7] circled [our building].*

The concurrence of selective law enforcement with (other) harassment techniques is important for several reasons. First, campaigns like these obviously serve as a very strong indicator of selectivity, leaving no doubt about the extra-legal nature of the conflicts. As the interviewee himself concludes: "This whole circus was very telling". Second, the concurrence of selective law enforcement with other forms of *low intensity coercion* illustrates how selective law enforcement is not merely a high-profile issue concerning diplomatic rows over political prisoners. In its more common form, selective law enforcement may be less dramatic (drowned out by even more serious attacks), yet over time strongly contributes to deter civic activism. Finally, to see selective law enforcement in this context goes a long way towards explaining why Russians tend to see the practice as not fundamentally different from other means of repression, including those of a purely illegal nature.

- **Blackmailing**

We have seen a multitude of ways that insiders may signal that extra-legal interests are at stake when they prosecute a target by quasi-legal means. The informal rules, however, can be transmitted in a more direct fashion through blackmail. Through more or less overt threats, the prosecuted party will get to know in more detail what criteria may unleash legal acts and sometimes who is behind the initiatives.

One of the interviewees who had been charged with extremism reports that in the very first meeting he and his colleagues had with the regional authorities, the persons he met with "offered (*predlagali*) us their cooperation and said that if we would not cooperate, they would use the law on extremism against us. They said this to us themselves". Another had just been blackmailed for half a million roubles by a man previously unknown to him when the court chair (and leader of a criminal network) called to make him understand: "I am the one sending people to prison in this town, and not you". The specific sum the interviewee was blackmailed for was presumably a reference to an earlier legal claim made against him in relation to a conflict at work, thus serving to link the cases. In yet another case, a police officer told one of the interviewees directly:

> *That he would do anything to get me jailed … They said specifically that they would initiate a criminal case against me if I did not stop writing … They beat me up after the meeting where I said openly that our city authorities steal money […] They beat me up just there at the meeting – three thousand witnesses [watched] and not one of them reacted.*

Other cases show that the direct communication does not simply come in the form of blackmail. When there is a mutual understanding of informal motives, the various actors do not necessarily take any care to pretend they are not engaging in blackmail. To make it even easier, some political leaders personally file requests to the Procuracy to initiate criminal cases against their critics. In this form, anti-extremism has in part taken the form of an extended defamation suit where there is a *general* agreement between the prosecutors and the targets of what acts caused the law enforcement. There are, however, also cases in which the criticized individuals initiate cases formally unrelated to the criticism. The court chair, for instance, not only blackmailed the man in question but also personally filed requests to the Procuracy to take action against him.

A third form of direct communication would be to provide hints of why a reaction already has taken place in order to stop similar things from happening in the future. The interviewees of this study actually fell short of mentioning this possibility. In conclusion, while the practice of blackmail is not insignificant in the observed cases, it does not seem to be a corner stone for the promulgation of informal rules as was suggested for instance in Darden's (2001) study of Ukraine under Leonid Kuchma.

Some concluding notes on communication

Making law enforcers act in specific ways and according to certain patterns is obviously central to the mechanism of selective law enforcement. Knowledge about how the internal communication takes place may contribute to our understanding of how well selective law enforcement is institutionalized. The interviewees were divided with respect to whether direct orders or political signals provide the primary form of transmitting informal criteria downstream in their individual cases. Instead of seeing this division as different interpretations, we may see them as different sides of the same coin. To interpret informal rules correctly is an important skill for employees in the Russian state machinery, including law enforcement officials and judges, The law enforcers understand political agendas and are pro-active and sensitive to political winds (Ledeneva 2013). This political awareness presumably make the actors more open to direct interference with their work as well.

This chapter has again shown that the importance of communication in rule enforcement is twofold. First, the ruling elites must providc guidance to legal actors on how to implement the law selectively. Second, they also need to communicate the rules so that the targets, and potential critics in the future, interpret the legal acts in a way that makes them reconsider their political activity and oppositional stance. To some degree, however, the two communitive tasks may be approached by the same means. If legal actors are ready to interpret political signals, so also is the more politically conscious part of the citizenry. The core rule of Putinist repression, as formulated by Marie Mendras, (2012, 231–2) is loyalty – "expressed in the negative [passive] – do not criticize or hinder the center of the constellation, and in the positive [active] – take action against disloyal actors". The citizenry, used to Russian patronal authoritarianism, are ready to interpret political signals within this frame of understanding. As one interviewee said:

> *People here they have a vast Soviet experience in understanding the general line of the ruling group, not from legal books but from the front page on the Pravda newspaper. So when we see something, or hear, that Putin as president said something about those Western spies or something like that – everybody will understand what will happen next.*

While the Russian media is less than free, the active citizen still has the means to get to information about the political connotations of selective law enforcement. The politically interested public does not need to frequent underground clubs in dark basements or read illegal periodicals to get information on selective law enforcement. The political context of the above-mentioned raids for instance, were discussed openly in the mass media locally, domestically, internationally, and even in scholarly works, in addition to various reports, blogs, forums, and websites. Whereas a few may possibly see the crackdowns as an offensive against counterfeit software, most interested individuals will quickly interpret the situation in a political light. Because the political interpretations circulate more or less freely, the informal rules are also spread horizontally. This in fact eases the job of rule promulgation for the authorities. Yet, popular frustrations with this form of power abuse may also trigger mass protests as for instance happened following the arrest of Navalny in spring 2018.

When properly institutionalized, this indirect means of signalling is a very powerful tool of control for the government. Society may react to the mass media's headlines as Americans in the Wild West would react to a Wanted poster: Most will hide, but some will go bounty hunting. The above-quoted interviewee finished his line of thought:

> *... The prosecutors also know this. So they do not need formal orders to take action. They understand that this is a new line in politics, and [that] they have to do something. If they do not have orders they will not be too enthusiastic of course, but at least they will do something. If they do get orders, they will of course do anything [requested of them].*

I thus arrive at a model of communicating informal rules that may be lubricated by path dependencies, but whose existence is dependent upon both encouragement and enforcement from above to keep the wheel spinning (Figure 8.1).

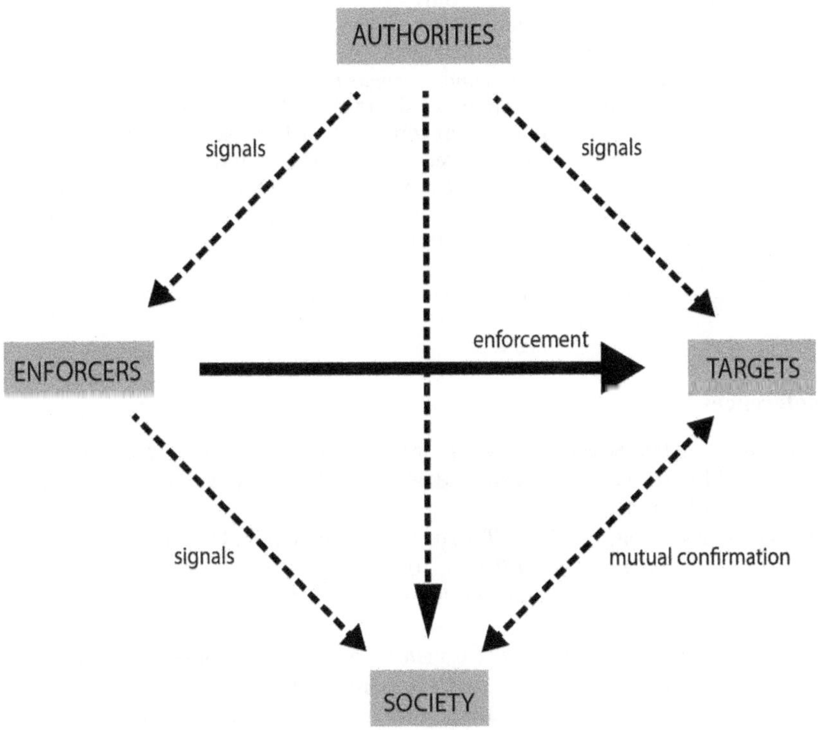

Figure 8.1 Communication of informal rules.

Once again, my evidence does not support a façade interpretation. As Mendras (2012, 220) put it: "no effort has been made to keep up appearances. The crushing of opponents is shown on television". Though Mendras takes an active stance against façade interpretations, I would suggest taking Mendras' argument one step further: When opponents are crushed on television, it suggests that the regime *does* care for its domestic appearance – the publicity of the violent action is actually an integral part of promulgating informal rules. The overt suppression of certain elements in society does not therefore necessarily indicate a careless attitude. More likely, they are part of an active policy to demarcate the political limits to constitutional freedoms.

Notes

1. The Criminal Code, Article 146.3 and 271.3, respectively.
2. Vadim Karastelev is an activist who worked in the same region and was subjected to anti-extremist charges before being beaten and hospitalized. See OMCT (2010).
3. While a first warning for extremist activity from the media monitoring agency Roskomnadzor has no direct legal effect, a second warning will open the way for liquidation procedures in court.
4. "Ruler of all *Rus*" is a reference to early eastern Slavic tribes and the medieval Russian/Ukrainian state.
5. *Glavnoye upravleniye sobstvennoy bezopasnosti MVD RF.*
6. To deny the political selectivity of the raids in Nizhniy Novgorod, the police claimed that hundreds of organizations had been searched for unlicensed software this year, and that a bread factory had been raided the same week as a critical newspaper. Unlike the more standard answer of the Samara police, who pulled the discursive switch (see Chapter 5) and referred to legal violations, the Nizhniy police thus actually attempted to deny the accusations of selectivity.
7. *Otryad militsii osobogo naznacheniya,* Russian special police units.

References

Bækken, H. 2009. Selective Law Enforcement against Russian NGOs. Pursuing Informal Interests through Formal Means. *NUPI report*. Oslo: Norwegian Institute of International Affairs.

Darden, K. 2001. Blackmail as a Tool of State Domination. Ukraine under Kuchma. *East European Constitutional Review,* 10, 67–72.

Eshanu, L. 2011. Spetsy zachistki Byulleteney. *GOLOS Novosti, Vladimirskaya Oblast*, 04.02.2011.

Horvath, R. 2013. *Putin's Preventive Counter-Revolution. Post-Soviet Authoritarianism And the Spectre of Velvet Revolution*. Oxon: Routledge.

Ledeneva, A. 2013. *Can Russia Modernise? Sistema, Power Networks and Informal Governance*. Cambridge: Cambridge University Press.

Mendras, M. 2012. *Russian Politics. The Paradox of a Weak State*. London: Hurst & Company.

OMCT (World Organization Against Torture), 2010. Russian Federation. Violent Assault and Judicial Harassment against Mr. Vadim Karastelev. 16.03.2010. Available at: http://www.omct.org/human-rights-defenders/urgent-interventions/russia/2010/03/d20595/ [accessed 06.12.2017].

Popova, M. 2012. *Politicized Justice in Emerging Democracies. A Study of Courts in Russia and Ukraine*. Cambridge: Cambridge University Press.

9 The impact of quasi-legal repression

I have defined selective law enforcement as a rule enforcement mechanism. In the previous four chapters, I have argued that the phenomenon fits this conceptualization well, and showed how its various components fit together and makes the practice what it is. What is still missing is an examination of to what degree selective law enforcement actually brings about any consequences for the targets or for society in general. If the mechanism is indeed a rule enforcement mechanism, it ought to enforce rules. While most interviewees would not admit to being deterred from continuing their oppositional and critical activities, the material still suggests that the suppression of constitutional rights is substantial. Below, I detail and discuss the interviewees' perceptions of the effects of selective law enforcement. The chapter proceeds to discuss the impact of the practice from a societal perspective, drawing on findings from many of the previously presented chapters.

Punishment as experience

Unsurprisingly, many of the cases of alleged selective law enforcement presented here resulted in legal sanctions. In the legal issue area of election registrations, court rulings in the examined cases validated the election committees' decisions to deny registration. Various administrative and criminal punishments were enacted against some of the interviewees. The two newspapers that received formal warnings for extremist activities failed to overturn the warnings in the judicial system. In two other cases examined, the targets had already been imprisoned for their purported extremism before the interviews took place, and I could only interview other sources close to the case. In a number of cases that were eventually closed, the pre-trial phase involved legal sanctions. At least two of the acquitted activists were held in pre-trial detention for many weeks, and in other cases travel bans were issued while investigations were pending. In other words, examples of formal sanctions resulting from controversial cases are plentiful.

At the same time, a number of the examined cases were never taken beyond the investigative phase, and some were eventually closed by court decision due to a lack of evidence. Several of the interviewees who were charged with using unlicensed software not only escaped formal punishment, but also received official apologies and financial compensation. The activist charged with hooliganism was acquitted and the prosecutors' appeal rebuked, which greatly surprised him. A court also decided that he had the right to receive compensation for moral damages, though the money reportedly never materialized. Even when charges are dropped, and even if the targets of crackdowns are later compensated for prosecutorial misconduct, however, they still have little reason to celebrate. While observers at times suggest that won cases are 'celebrations of justice', most of the interviewees would probably object. While legal sanctions would presumably be even worse on most occasions, the legal processes are harmful even when won. For this reason, even 'successful' cases can be considered lost, and there might be more to come around the corner. The activist charged with hooliganism, for instance, only had a few months as a free man before he was sentenced to several years in a penal colony in the Bolotnaya-trials. Some interviewees even suggest that the very aim of the processes is not to win cases, but to sustain pressure and keep the targets preoccupied.

> *I understand this criminal case as one attempt in a series of other attempts … simply not to let the organization work by any means. The task was not so much to put me in prison, for instance, as it was to torment me with these actions every day, every hour.*

As posited in Chapter 5, the litmus test of what can be considered punishment is whether non-compliers are put in worse situations than those who comply. The legal acts can evidently bring about both punitive and preventive effects, even when they are not officially recognized as punitive. In many and perhaps all examined cases, the various law enforcement agencies of the executive branch successfully imposed *de facto* punishment without the support of the judicial system. The newspaper in Samara had to close when the criminal procedures dragged on and the confiscated computers were not returned. The newspaper in Nizhniy Novgorod also had to stop publishing temporarily. The conflict with regional authorities induced two of the activists to resettle in a different part of Russia, and their organizations stopped functioning. It is not difficult, then, to see why selective law enforcement may work to enforce rules even in cases in which no official punishment is enacted.

Most interviewees assured me that they would keep on challenging the regime despite the troubles associated with their actions. Several of them were hardened critics who expected no less harassment than they received. Some of the interviewees, however, contended that the obvious incentives to change could not simply be ignored.

> *First of all, I will try to do less journalism, and in particular of the investigative type … I quit because I have now been through all the stages. They*

> *have threatened me and beaten me up, and the next stage would be ... simply to kill me and that's it. Why would I want that? I want to live!*

In cases like the one above, quasi-legal repression seems to be of secondary importance to even more serious threats. In many other cases, it is impossible to discern what effect may be caused by quasi-legal practices and what is rather a consequence of other types of harassment.

- **"It simply takes years off our lives"**

If the legal system and enforcement apparatus through its acts cannot deter its selected targets, it may still have the capacity to curb their efficiency by keeping them preoccupied. The Vladimir journalist was among those who by no means were satisfied even when candidates were able to get registered for elections after several rounds with committees and courts. After all, she said, "the candidates have lost time, energy and often considerable sums of money – everything to fight off some absurd charges". Many interviewees report similar problems of time and resources spent on legal processes: "It simply takes years off our lives", said one. "It just deprives us of so much time and energy", said another - "it would be much easier to pay some bribes or sign some papers about cooperation with police of FSB".

One of the NGO workers explained how repeated episodes of a quasi-legal nature had made an already strained situation almost unbearable:

> *We already had very limited resources, depleted from this judicial war with everyone. At the end of the day, we faced this question: Should we appeal all the unlawful decisions and try to fight this criminal case or should we concentrate all our efforts to finish this monograph [on human rights violations in Chechnya]. We considered the preparation of this book to be our most important task so we had no possibility to get involved in all of these episodes. After half a year, they once again took our equipment on some other pretext. In the end, we had to finish the work from our private apartments.*

Researchers know the importance of working undisturbed. It is easy to imagine how constant inspections, interrogations, and requirements to produce documentation for investigators will make effective work considerably more difficult, not least when the hassle comes in addition to already burdensome standard requirements of registration and reporting. Add to this the possibility of confiscated hardware, the occasional beating with subsequent hospitalization, and the harassment of your family and staff. The eventual legal sanctions come on top of this form of pressure. One interviewee regretted the fact that he could give me little information on the latest developments in recent proceedings against him. He explained how he simply refused to let these pretexts distract him from his work and take more of his time than they already had.

The initiators of selective law enforcement have little to lose if they act within the informal mandates of their patrons. If a case fails, the state will pay the cost, and it will at least serve the purpose of harassment and an informal warning. If a case happens to lead to a legal sanction, it may very well be considered a bonus. In the case of election registration denials, a legal sanction (a denial) would presumably be a clearly favoured outcome for the initiator. Yet, even in this field and even if the denial is rejected, there are indirect benefits to be reaped from instrumentalizing the legal system. To quote a handbook of 'political technology':

> *We are talking about legalistic attacks on the competitor on absolutely every move he makes ... Here it is not important if he wins all the processes. The important thing is that it will wear out his nerves ... The important thing is to keep him in suspense and make him careful. He will refuse to participate in some plans and events, and act more modestly or restricted in others. This is all in our favour ... And of course nobody can exclude the possibility of some case ending up in success and you will finally have succeeded in denying registration to your competitor. (Matveychev and Novikov 2003)*

- **Additional pressure for legal compliance**

An indirect effect of selective law enforcement is an additional and informally constituted pressure to comply with law. While extra incentives to comply with law at first glance may look like a healthy side effect of selective law enforcement, they actually contribute to suppressing criticism. If the violations of informal rules increase the risk of a law being enforced, a link between the informal rules and the final punishment has been established. If legal regulations are enforced selectively against a certain segment of the population, this segment will have stronger incentives for complying strictly with these regulations. The bias will lead to an unequal situation, and the additional incentive to comply will work to enforce the informal rules.

The situation of the opposition party Yabloko in Perm provides an illustrative example. Because the party expected extraordinary scrutiny on the legality of their campaign, they spent a considerable amount of time preparing for every eventuality. When I visited the party at their premises, one of their members showed me some flyers showing two hands holding an apple.[1] Because the regional election committee had earlier denied registration to another opposition candidate because of unlicensed use of photos in the pre-election campaign, Yabloko had made sure to get all the documentation necessary to verify that their campaigning material was strictly in accordance with the law on copyrights. To be on the safe side, they obtained a written permission from the person whose hands were on the photo, the party representatives explained. Considering the tremendous problems surrounding both copyright violations and election campaigns in Russia, the extra-legal pressure for compliance ensures an uneven playing field even when no crackdown takes place.

The problem is not limited to party politics or election registration. When officials raided various regime critics in Samara in purported search for pirate software, human rights activists all over the country reportedly rushed to make sure that their software was licensed (Finn 2007). The behaviour of the activists in this situation suggests that there were two important factors determining their decisions. First, their increased efforts to follow the law suggest that they perceive this as a meaningful defence against quasi-legal charges. At the same time, it is obvious from the timing of the human rights activists' sudden care for licenses that it was not the legal prohibition as such that prompted them to take action. Rather, they may have thought the risk of enforcement had increased because they shared some informal characteristics with the organizations that were targeted in Samara.

This behaviour indicates the semi-institutionalization of informal rules, and how broadly selective law enforcement may affect the relevant actors. It also shows how running an oppositional party or a critical NGO requires more resources than working in less contentious fields. As we can see, extraordinary pressure for compliance in effect eats into the organizational resources of regime critics and political opposition. It should be noted that the extra time and resources Yabloko spent on getting documentation for the legality of their apple photo were a direct outcome of an increased risk perception stemming from challenging the incumbents.

- **Recruitment and stigmatization**

One of the self-imposed exiles continued to work on human rights issues even after he moved to Moscow, and in a form similar to what he did before. In his experience, however, cases like the ones against him and his organization have serious impacts upon society:

> *[After the crackdown] organizations fear controls, fear that they may be closed. [...] Now they stopped working with [these matters], or they started to work for the administration. [People] are generally not criticizing nowadays. They have gone either into business or they work with children, with pensioners, with the handicapped. Well, with any topics not connected with criticism [of the authorities].*

The effect of *general* deterrence hits a broader segment of society, and in principle any possible perpetrator aware of the rule and its enforcement (Friedman 1975, 72–73). Recruitment to the sphere of political or human rights oriented activity may therefore be considerably limited by the kind of deterring measures presented in this study. Most young professionals would not want to work in a human rights organization only to fend off selective legal claims against the organization itself. In this way, we can see that even preventive acts carry a deterring potential. By means of systematically targeted suppression, the state apparatus makes organizations with a critical mission become less attractive workplaces. Youth that know how the state *de facto* punishes political disobedience have strong incentives to make the most of the situation *within* the system instead of challenging it. In addition comes the economic uncertainty of working under constant threat of quasi-legal bombardments and the possible liquidation of one's place of work. A life of such uncertainty is obviously not attractive to most.

Selective law enforcement may hit the social environment of the targets like bad news on the stock exchange, as the surrounding actors with less political ardour withdraw their support. In at least two cases, not only the targets of quasi-legal repression lost their jobs, but family members also lost theirs. With reference to a standard, non-selective judicial system, Harold Garfinkel (1956) has called the criminal trial 'a status degradation ceremony'. The legal punishment is often just the tip of the iceberg for convicted criminals, and the shame associated with legal prosecution leads to social ostracism and stigma that may linger on for longer than it takes to serve a sentence. We may assume, however, that this effect is weaker in Russia. Or put in a different way, the stigmatization comes from a different source. As Garfinkel (1956, 423) noted, for the status degradation ceremony to be successful, the prosecutor has to convince the audience that he or she is condemning on the basis of commonly shared norms and not for his own sake. If the prosecutor cannot do this successfully, the status degradation ceremony will misfire. Because the informal backdrop of the cases is obvious to most relevant observers, also stigmatization must be understood with reference to the informal rules. We have already seen that the law in itself has limited normative power in Russia, and particularly so when cases are interpreted as belonging to the 'jurisdiction' of the prerogative regime rather than the normative state system.

Thus, in the case of selective law enforcement, observers do not shun prosecuted individuals because they believe them to be criminals. Even if they indeed had believed in the charges, most Russians would care little as to whether an NGO has infringed on the copyrights of Microsoft or Adobe. Instead, society shuns the prosecuted critics because Russians understand the political links and want to stay clear of trouble. In this sense, the selective law enforcement has the effect of stigmatizing the targets as *troublemakers*. To Russian society, the prosecution signifies a controversy with the ruling elites and the power networks – with *vlast'*. The golden rule, as Mendras (2012, 191) maintains, is to "keep away from anyone in trouble, because the machine is likely to also destroy those who express their support for the victims".

Capacity and willingness: Explaining non-sanctions

From the last section, we can conclude that many targets of selective law enforcement are formally sanctioned for alleged legal violations. Others experience to be punished even if no formal punishment takes place.

In some cases, the consequences of official sanctions are similar to the indirect consequences of quasi-legal or other forms of harassment. From an outcome perspective, it may be less important to involved actors whether an organization is liquidated in court or forced to cease its operation for other reasons.

That being said, the cases that have *not* lead to legal sanctions are worth considering. To the extent that the issue of judicial independence was discussed in my interviews, interviewees tended to assess the courts in an extremely negative light. Judges were, in the same way as all other legal actors, regarded as pawns in the hands of the regime: "Absolutely, absolutely. One hundred percent. It is not even a question for the courts of first instance. They are completely subordinated". Indeed, that Russian courts are vulnerable to pressure when handling politically salient cases is an established fact among observers of the country. Chapter 3 laid out several ways the ruling elites may compromise the formal empowerment and jurisdiction of judges. Yet, despite the interviewees' harsh judgment of the Russian courts, the judiciary actually refused to convict some of the targets and even granted them compensations. Even in cases with political overtones, it seems that the subordination of courts is not complete.

In the research material, some of the cases that involved the most flagrant violations on the part of the law enforcement agencies, such as fabricated copyright violations or the production of fake witnesses, ended up in acquittals. The fact that these cases did not pass successfully through the judiciary may suggest that legal concerns are not completely irrelevant when a politically initiated case is considered. At the same time, several interviewees found that poor or non-existing legal foundations sometimes led to formal sanctions. Commenting on the legal background for election registrations, Lyubarev suggests that while the election committees seek a sound legal basis for their denials, more casual or even invented foundations may also work at times:

> *As candidates turn more and more experienced and more and more careful to align their documentation [to the requirements], the election committees will see that there are no clear errors and start to look through and through in search of non-existing insufficiencies or sometimes just think up something.*[2]

We get the impression that the more the election committees can do by legal means, the better. Put differently, selective law enforcement is favoured over purely informal means, and denials based on good legal foundations are better than denials based on poor legal foundations. A veteran in this game, however, suggested in my interview that the legality or illegality of political technologies is not necessarily the most relevant attribute in the minds of 'technologists.' More important, he maintained, was the amount of *noise* a technology would make when employed. If someone wants to remove a candidate from an election, he explained, the actor would start with the most 'silent' (*tikhiye*) technologies: Informing the candidate about the situation and adding soft pressure behind the scenes. If these attempts do not work, "then they will 'turn on' (*vklyuchat'*) the level of committees and lawyers who must find some hook or pretext to deny registration to the unwanted candidate. If this also fails, then the political technologists may 'plug in' (*podklyuchat'*) absolutely illegal stuff". The authorities will never hesitate to use any form of pressure, the interviewee assured: "If they have to use them, they will use them. If they don't need to, they will not".

The legality of many cases is often up in the air as the secondary rules on jurisdiction and legal procedures are also subject to interpretation. A case many contain many elements and practices that are perhaps odious, yet not always bluntly illegal. Examples include far-fetched 'interpretation' of vague formulations, formalistic enforcement, disproportional punishment, dubious expert analysis, election committees' failures to provide due warnings, the selection of judges to preside over a case, and the initiation of copyright raids on thin evidence. To summarize, it may seem like substantial legal backing makes it easier for prosecutors to get a selectively initiated case through court. We also see, however, that the borders of what is legal or not are sometimes unclear and that a solid legal foundation is not a prerequisite for formal punishment in all instances.

In the researcher's black box is another factor that we cannot ignore, namely the possibility that the targets of selective law enforcement (or their associates and defenders) engage in informal bargaining with other actors behind the scenes. If the charges are pro forma, so are perhaps also the decisions to abandon them. Some actors may have been able to come to an agreement on their own, or they may have persuaded actors higher up on the ladder to intervene on their behalf. We can also imagine how a case may be counteracted at the initiative of political forces higher up in the system if these forces see the level of manipulation becoming exaggerated or the signals being misinterpreted. In other words, won cases may be the product of informal 'counter-interventions', with or without the complicit involvement of the targets themselves. In one examined case, the regional FSB turned the heat on the criminal group headed by the court chair and perhaps saved the interviewee's life. When different concerns combine, all sorts of arrangements may be agreed upon. Since the issue of informal bargaining is beyond the reach of this book, I can only point to the caveat and restate a suggestive statement by a human rights worker from a previous study: "We are all experts with higher education – we know how to adapt to Russian realities" (Bækken 2009, 96).

Capacity, willingness, and cost of interference

Even if certain actors have the *capacity* to intervene in legal processes it does not mean that they have the *willingness* to do so, particularly not when there are costs involved. In a revealing study of politically sensitive cases in Russian and Ukrainian courts in the years 2002 and 2003 respectively, Popova (2012) found a significantly greater bias in the judicial *output* of the Ukrainian cases. Because there is little in her study to indicate that Ukrainian incumbents had greater capacity to interfere with judicial decision-making than had the Russian incumbents, Popova suggests that the reason for the difference must be sought elsewhere. In Ukraine, the period was marked with great political strife and huge political stakes, providing actors with strong incentives to manipulate courts in order to tilt the balance in their favour. In Russia, on the contrary, the authorities had less interest in interfering much (or often) in legal processes because their political dominance was already consolidated. This finding may be relevant on a more general level as well. Both capacity and willingness to interfere are thus relevant in explaining bias in judicial output.

In cases of selective law enforcement, the willingness to interfere with legal processes is implicit. While the willingness to initiate a case on a political basis is given, however, the *degree* and *level* of interference is not. There are after all a myriad of ways to harass your rivals, and often your goals can be achieved solely by using the upstream law enforcement agencies. This point is particularly relevant in a situation in which the judiciary shows some degree of autonomy. Because the Russian judiciary has a certain level of autonomy and because the laws are not irrelevant in Russia, pushing a poor case through the legal system may be possible but might imply significant costs. These costs include organizational resources but also the risk of scandalizing the regime, which after all is not immune to popular sentiment. To let flagrant falsifications pass is *in general* not acceptable within the current regime and would require considerable political will (Mendras 2012, 147). For the political leadership, I posit, this is a pragmatic solution as it helps curb unwanted interference on local levels. The formal state, as I laid out in Chapter 4, serves to safeguard the informal prerogatives of the powerful because it keeps these prerogatives exclusive.

Compared to the courts, it is both easier and less controversial to control law enforcement agencies through formal and informal incentive structures. The upstream law enforcement is more directly subordinated to the executive branch and more readily accessible. The very fact that observers so often speak about interference with judicial independence presupposes that there indeed is something to interfere with. The dependence of law enforcement and administrative agencies is largely taken for granted, and thus less of an issue in academic or political discourse. The mandates of these agencies are also more flexible than those of the judicial system. Law enforcement agencies may initiate investigations or raids on vague suspicions, and they have a work force and broad mandates that make it easy for them to engage in harassment. While a full-scale politicized show trial implies multiple actors and a significant organizational effort, no clever conspiracy is needed to initiate a bit of police harassment on local levels.

Small but multiple incidents may still influence the choice of a politically interested public not to engage in oppositional activities. The consistent harassment by law enforcement agencies may successfully restrain the targets' abilities to conduct activities that are unwanted by the regime, and scare others away from conducting similar activities. Moreover, these types of acts have a relatively low potential to mobilize protests. While harassment may lead to some negative publicity now and then, criminal proceedings and severe sentences may produce national or even international headlines. When confronted by critics, accusations of selective investigations, interrogation, or otherwise soft reactions will presumably be easier for initiators to dismiss as paranoia than would a sentence. The less tangible the harassment, the less potential it has to scandalize the regime.

Finally, when the Russian judiciary acknowledges cases of prosecutorial misconduct and awards compensation, these cases are less likely to be considered in the European Courts of Human Rights (ECHR). Since many cases are poorly founded, and the victims and their support networks often appeal legal sanctions to the ECHR, many end up with international embarrassment for the Russian judiciary. The Russian leadership has taken this issue quite seriously (Bowring 2005; Solomon 2008b). This may therefore in part explain why authorities often seem hesitant to pressure courts to make decisions with no legal backing. Ledeneva (2013, 251) even sees the ECHR as a possible source of change to the deeper dynamics of the current system of governance – an external challenge to pervasive quasi-legality. Recent decisions to reduce the impact of international courts on Russian decision-making may of course have reduced any such effect, but these considerations clearly remained relevant during the examined period of 2007-2011. In general, the logic can be comprehended in terms of low intensity coercion – the tendency of modern authoritarians to favour relatively silent means of repression, sending signals without creating big scandals. Conclusively, the relative empowerment of the Russian judicial system and the associated costs of political interference may serve to explain cases in which no legal punishment is imposed on the targets. Perhaps the most important reason why legal sanctions are not always imposed, however, is that selective enforcement may work effectively even without engaging the judicial branch.

The predictability of quasi-legal coercion

I have shown how a conceptualization of informal rules as analogous to formal rules may be useful for understanding selective law enforcement. I have suggested that informal rules can (or must) be promulgated and that they may or may not guide behaviour, be complied with, or be followed in the same way as formal rules. Moreover, we have seen that the analogy between formal and informal rules may help explain how the practice distorts and deflects criticism. Finally, we have seen how the interviewees describe the purposes of selective law enforcement in ways that conforms to ideas of prevention and deterrence.

This is not to deny there are serious differences between the two notions of formal and informal rules.[3] Informal rules are by definition opaque rules of thumb, and by necessity in flux even though the core rules are usually highly resistant to change. For this reason, the interpretation of informal rules will always be a matter of context. If formulated at all, they will be formulated either on a high level of abstraction, or alternatively be identified through their implications in individual cases. For these reasons, it makes little sense to talk of the enforcement of this or that particular informal rule, as if they were formal. I therefore prefer to discuss informal rules in the plural form, alternatively in terms of rule sets. The idea of informal rules serves to illustrate how the cases of selective law enforcement have certain commonalities that Russians interpret within an existing understanding. It is the sum of these commonalities that constitutes the informal rules as observable entities, and their practical entrenchment that constitutes the institutionalization of selective law enforcement.

Institutions increase predictability. Indeed, to increase predictability is perhaps their most fundamental attribute (North 1990). For this reason, institutionalized selective law enforcement does in itself not make the ruling of Russia more arbitrary or unpredictable, as is sometimes suggested. To be more precise, we must consider the degree of arbitrariness and unpredictability relative to other arrangements. Whereas it may tend to yield a less predictable and coherent outcome than would a well-functioning system of rational-legal governance, selective law enforcement may indeed increase the level of predictability if the legal system is dysfunctional. After all, selections are done according to a pattern and not by throwing dice. Friedman illustrates this point through a hypothetical example reflecting his time:

> *Even if rules were meaningless or totally ignored, it would not follow that chance and caprice would govern the courtroom. It would mean only that something other than the official rules – the judge's attitude and values, for example – would determine decisions. Imagine a secret, fanatical Marxist taking office as a judge in a non-Marxist country … his ideology would decide his cases for him. The outcomes would not be random or accidental; once one cracked his code, they might be easy to predict. (Friedman 1975, 43)*

Certainly, the outcome may differ from that of the other judges in the same country. Yet, for an expert on Marxism at least, the sentences would be no less predictable. A person not acquainted with Marxism will need some time to predict the rulings of the Marxist judge. In the same way, an observer would have to be acquainted with the ordinary jurisprudence in the country if he or she were to predict the behaviour of a more conventional judge. In the case of selective law enforcement, this fact is germane. The informal rules that guide Russian politics may be non-transparent to outsiders and may therefore appear as more unpredictable than they actually are for insiders (also see Hendley 2009). Something *not* expressed by the interviewees of this study is surprise.

With regard to the core rule of authoritarianism, the interests of the various insider actors are well aligned. The core rule of political obedience by necessity favours those in power. The central authorities are left with the task of making sure that actors further down the hierarchy do not overextend their mandates and make moves that either challenge the regime or create scandals that are not worth the efforts. As I laid out in the first part of the book, Putin's regime has approached this task in a twofold consolidation of repressive capabilities. First, it has boosted the political regime's cohesion by formal institutional reform, but also by unofficial recruitment policies and coercion against dropout and powerful outsiders. In a second and related move, it has centralized access to law enforcement capabilities and judicial decision-making. Yet, we have also seen that there are limits to this centralization. It seems that from the perspective of the interviewees, at least, the connections to Moscow are often indirect when selective law enforcement is concerned. In Chapter 6, we also saw that the Supreme Court has occasionally tried to curb abusive practices of quasi-legal character, including those obviously political in nature. While we cannot know whether the quasi-legal acts or the Supreme Court resolutions represent the real intensions of the power holders in Moscow, the battle of interpretation at least indicates diverging views within the system. Despite the significant centralization processes and growing authoritarianism, there are limits to the Kremlin's reach.

A regime of repression

Despite their indisputable importance, the coercive features of authoritarian systems are reportedly underrepresented in research on regime trajectories (Levitsky and Way 2010, 54–7). One explanation for this lack of representation may lie in the stabilizing role of effective coercion: Who wants to do research on something that *prevents* change? Explaining non-action may perhaps encourage functionalist and statist models of society. To a considerable degree, however, the difference between dissatisfaction with a regime and open revolt against it may indeed lie in the effectiveness of the coercive apparatus. "If the state's coercive apparatus remains coherent and effective, it can face down population disaffection and survive significant illegitimacy", Eva Bellin (2004, 143) observes, paraphrasing Theda Skocpol's (1979) seminal work on revolutions. The ability and willingness of the coercive apparatus to serve the regime is not only a prerequisite for clamping down upon legitimate mass protests. It is also needed to prevent dissent to be vocalized and to deter against protests on an everyday basis. The willingness and ability to employ low intensity coercion effectively is therefore important for the long-term survival of authoritarian regimes, not least for the modern and hybrid variants (see Chapter 1).

In consolidating the enforcement apparatus and intensifying the suppression of dissent, the political leadership under Putin gradually strengthened a *regime of repression,* as coined by Mark R. Beissinger.[4] According to him, the regime of repression is

> *... a set of regularized practices of repression and the internalized expectation about the ways in which authority will react punitively toward challenging acts that result from these practices. Repression exercises its effect in part because it functions as habitus. That is, part of the effect of repression occurs because individuals "have internalized, through a protracted and multi-sided process of conditioning, the objective changes they face"[5] in challenging authority and what types of penalties they would most likely suffer on the basis of prior responses of authority to challenge. (Beissinger 2002, 326)*

For selective law enforcement to be institutionalized, it is of course important that the informal rules be promulgated to the effect that both law enforcers and legal subjects understand them. For a regime of repression to be established, Beissinger (2002, 327) contends, the practices involved need to be institutionalized so that they may reproduce shared expectations of how the system will react to challenges. We have seen that selective law enforcement takes many different forms, yet that it is still marked by a level of "consistency, regularity, and predictability with which repression occurs, the internalized discipline that emerges as a result, and the institutional resources necessary to produce such patterning" (ibid.).

By means of systemized and consistent distribution of preventive and punitive acts, the activities of the opposition movement and other activists are suppressed. At the same time, however, the movement is also radicalized. The harsh suppression of dissent leaves little space on the barricades for ordinary people. To be active in the protest movement in Russia is therefore no longer possible as a side activity, but turns into a lifestyle. A regional Golos coordinator, for instance, claimed that the FSB had blocked his opportunities to pursue his academic career, and he did not see any alternative other than to keep fighting for democratic elections and cross his fingers for change. In this way, the regime's way of dealing with criticism as if it were extremism has in one sense become a self-fulfilling prophesy – criticism *is* in a sense politically extreme in Russia because of how it is dealt with. As Robert Horvath (2013, 207) remarks, it takes a serious narrowing down of political space to "lend revolutionary pathos to the opposition's demands for the unshackling of the mass media, the observance of the constitution, freedom to demonstrate, and the return of free and fair elections".

While some societal elements may be radicalized, however, there may be more of those who will be deterred by the systematic crackdowns on attempts to hold the regime accountable. Selective law enforcement may therefore be part of the explanation for the political apathy that has long been observable in Russia. The lack of political initiatives from below is not exclusively a cultural phenomenon but is also the result of actions from above by a regime that discourages such initiatives unless they happen to fit with its informal agendas. It has been pointed out that a key to the survival of Putin's regime (and the apparent popularity of its president) has been the lack of alternatives. While this is true, the dearth of alternatives is not a product of chance. What is sometimes attributed to loyalty is at least in part "a form of submission stemming from the fear of trouble" (Mendras 2012, 195). As stressed by Hale (2015), expectations are paramount in patronal systems. The system works, he claims, because everyone expects it to. If the mirage breaks, it may lead to mass defections (Robertson 2011).

As the coercive practices illustrate, these expectations of the system do not reproduce themselves in an automatic fashion. Rather, the obedience of citizens is in part a result of active and persistent enforcement of the rules of the game on all levels of politics and society. For externally enforced rules to survive through time, their enforcement through punishment cannot halt. The fact that the rules of political conduct are indeed enforced by quasi-legal (and other) means suggests that they are in no way self-enforcing or 'natural' to Russia. Quasi-legal abuse, however, has long been intrinsic to Russian legal culture. From a general perspective, its institutionalization embodies the interests and preferences of the ruling elites as a group.

Notes

1. The name of the party, *Yabloko*, means apple in Russian.
2. Arkady Lyubarev. Author's interview, 2.6.2011, Moscow.
3. For a critique of the analogy, and of the notion of informal rules in general, see Ledeneva, 2006, 14–22.
4. The use of Beissinger's term for contemporary Russian politics is an idea I borrow from Taylor (2011).
5. Here Beissinger quotes Bourdieu and Wacquant (1992, 130).

References

Bækken, H. 2009. Selective Law Enforcement against Russian NGOs. Pursuing Informal Interests through Formal Means. *NUPI report*. Oslo: Norwegian Institute of International Affairs.

Beissinger, M. R. 2002. *Nationalist Mobilization and the Collapse of the Soviet State*. Cambridge: Cambridge University Press.

Bellin, E. 2004. The Robustness of Authoritarianism in the Middle East. Exceptionalism in Comparative Perspective. *Comparative Politics*, 36.

Bourdieu, P. & Wacquant, L. 1992. *An Invitation to Reflexive Sociology* Chicago, University of Chicago Press and Polity.

Finn, P. 2007. Russia Casts a Selective Net in Piracy Crackdown. *The Washington Post*, 14.11.2007. Available at: http://washingtonpost.com/wp-dyn/content/article/2007/11/13/AR2007111302070.html [accessed 06.12.2017].

Robertson, G. B. 2011. *The Politics of Protest in Hybrid Regimes. Managing Dissent in Post-Communist Russia*. Cambridge: Cambridge University Press.

Friedman, L. M. 1975. *The Legal System. A Social Science Perspective*. New York: Russell Sage.

Garfinkel, H. 1956. Conditions of Successful Degradation Ceremonies. *American Journal of Sociology*, 61, 420–424.

Horvath, R. 2013. *Putin's Preventive Counter-Revolution. Post-Soviet Authoritarianism And the Spectre of Velvet Revolution*. Oxon: Routledge.

Ledeneva, A. 2006. *How Russia Really Works. The Informal Practices That Shaped Post-Soviet Politics and Business*. Ithaca: Cornell University Press.

2013. *Can Russia Modernise? Sistema, Power Networks and Informal Governance*. Cambridge: Cambridge University Press.

Levitsky, S. & Way, L. 2010. *Competitive Authoritarianism. Hybrid Regimes after the Cold War*. Cambridge: Cambridge University Press.

Matveychev, O. A. & Novikov, V. J. 2003. *Predvybornaya kampaniya. Praktika protiv teorii*. Ekatarinaburg: Izdatel'stvo Uralskogo universiteta.

Mendras, M. 2012. *Russian Politics. The Paradox of a Weak State*. London: Hurst & Company.

North, D. C. 1990. *Institutions, Institutional Change and Economic Performance*. Cambridge: Cambridge University Press.

Skocpol, T. 1979. *States and Social Revolutions. A Comparative Analysis of France, Russia, and China*. New York: Cambridge University Press.

Taylor, B. D. 2011. *State Building in Putin's Russia. Policing and Coercion after Communism*. Cambridge: Cambridge University Press.

Concluding remarks

Throughout modern history, personal bonds have been crucial to power relations in Russia. In Soviet times as well as today, the image of a strong state has coexisted with a reality where the selected few have enjoyed the prerogatives to interfere in legal processes and use the state for their personal or group interests. As this book documented, it would be simplistic to call the strong state rhetoric a façade. Indeed, the legal state has been built even in periods where repression and quasi-legality were also on the rise. This was true under Stalin in the 1930s, Brezhnev in the 1970s, and again under Putin since the early 2000s. The political system of Russia today has developed through an intensification of these two tendencies, and created a system of governance partly capable of exploiting the benefits of rational-legal mechanisms while retaining authoritarian prerogatives to interfere in them. Because the ultimate logics of the normative and prerogative subsystems of Russian governance are in conflict, neither ambitions can be completely satisfied. Indeed, Putinism can as a system be defined exactly by how it solves the dilemmas resulting from the interactions between these two logics, navigates between contradicting rule sets, and gradually develops and renews its very own sense of hybridity.

In this book, my primary concern has been to widen and deepen our understanding of how and why laws are being used selectively against critics of the Putinist regime, and how this practice makes sense within the broader politico-legal system. Throughout the chapters, arguments have been put forward and conclusions reached. I started out by considering the rationale of hybrid governance in authoritarian regimes, and why limited legal autonomy makes sense in the Russian case. For better or worse, Putinism represents an effort to avoid some of the pitfalls of informal rules, while clinging eagerly to others (Chapter 1). I continued by considering the Russian politico-legal tradition, pointing out the persistent traits of instrumentalism, formalism, and disconnect from moral values in Russian legal culture. I showed how these traits have played out in the repression of political dissent over time, and how the persistent manipulation of law has fed into a low trust spiral that it is now hard to pull out of (Chapter 2). Under Putin, Russia witnessed a consolidation of both formal and informal power under new super elites.

This development, I concluded, has had important implications for how quasi-legal practices have been utilized in political repression. While Putin certainly did not initiate each and every case of selective law enforcement in person, the regime's consolidated control with legal and quasi-legal tools have made the practice increasingly aligned with the interests of the ruling elites (Chapter 3). Furthermore, I have taken into consideration the genuine legal reforms, and argued that today's politico-legal system is fundamentally dual – marked by a split jurisdiction where political and ordinary legal cases are dealt with according to fundamentally different rules and serve different functions. Whereas improvements in bulk justice are perhaps more important to most people and contribute to explaining the popular approval of the regime, it is the political cases that inform us about the real power relations in society. Authoritarian systems have nothing to lose by granting their general population access to fair arbitration when settling their internal disputes. Indeed, for a multitude of reasons, the contrary is the case. Yet, when a statement or an action is seen as beyond the informally recognized limits of what the regime accepts, the impersonal principles can evidently be set aside (Chapter 4). The *de facto* limitations to constitutional freedoms are fluid. They are regulated not only by law and social norms, but also by the raw power of elites with access to sanctioning mechanisms.

Part II produced more detailed insight with regard to selective law enforcement. I argued that selective law enforcement is perhaps best comprehended as a mechanism to enforce informal rules, implying *inter alia* that signalling and deterrence effects are crucial to how it works. I suggested a model for how actors can instrumentalize the ambiguity of overlapping formal and informal rules to distort and deflect criticism even when faced with popular disbelief. To achieve the desired effect, the political significance of selectively initiated cases is not hidden. Instead, the opposite is the case: it is flagged. At the same time, both political and legal actors can flatly deny any interference with reference to the impersonal nature of state justice and the autonomy of courts (Chapter 5). I also presented three legal issue areas where the laws have been frequently abused for political purposes. I showed how different legal contexts can encourage selective law enforcement in different ways (Chapter 6). I laid out how formal rules can contribute to quasi-legal scheming by means of vagueness, strictness, or by other characteristics, and concluded that the politico-legal environment is what ultimately decides how these characteristics work in practice. This environment consists of both semi-permanent (cultural) and more fluid (political) elements. Whereas their dependence on structural conditions helps explain the persistence of quasi-legal schemes in Russia, the more fluid elements explain why their attributes can change relatively quickly (Chapter 7).

I have also presented stories and perceptions about informal politics behind the legal scenes, as experienced and interpreted by Russian actors involved with oppositional politics, critical journalism, or various forms of activism (Chapter 8). While some insights were presented in this discussion, its main purpose was to underpin my conclusions of previous chapters. Finally, I looked at the outcomes of selective law enforcement from both an individual and a societal perspective. As their continued activities indicate, Russian veteran activists may be incredibly hard to scare away from their mission. Presumably, experiences of quasi-legal repression may even strengthen the determination of some activists to continue their fight. If the goal of punishment is to get this hard core of regime critics to reconsider their critical attitude, it is likely to backfire. We have seen, however, that the restrictive aspect of rule enforcement is still operative in these cases. The effect of general deterrence, moreover, has a much broader impact. I have therefore argued that we need to comprehend the phenomenon broadly to understand its stifling effect on Russian politics. As it seems, the informal rules of authoritarian politics gradually become internalized by the population (Chapter 9).

Together, the lines of argument and tentative conclusions constitute my answer to the chief questions posed in the introduction: How and why laws are being used selectively against critics of the Putinist regime, and how this practice makes sense within the broader political-level culture. Perhaps the most important answer lies within the definition of selective law enforcement as a mechanism of repression aimed at enforcing informal rules of political conduct through selective legal acts. This definition is the epicentre of the analysis. In a way, it is also its conclusion – a condensed answer to my question of what selective law enforcement *is* and a hint towards how it *works*.

What can be said about the place and role of quasi-legality in Russia's development in the years to come? While legal abuse was rife in the 1990s, and while quasi-legal rule was prominent under the Soviet regime, selective law enforcement has become a symbol of Putinism. A new standard was set with the prosecution of several oligarchs in Putin's first term of presidency. Gradually, selective law enforcement became a popular tool to suppress the activities of less distinguished targets. It was frequently employed in relation to the fight against dissent that followed in the wake of the so-called coloured revolutions, and its use was again intensified in recent years. By means of selective law enforcement, the authorities have touched spots that neither the contemporary legislation nor batons could reach. Not only street protest, but also journalists, bloggers, editors, human rights organizations, ecologists, and other critics fell victim to the practice. In a stage of siege, imagined or real, the regime has spent large amounts of resources on this form of censorship. Not only are alternative views and oppositional voices restrained, but also information on what crimes have been committed by individuals within the incumbent regime, not least with regard to claims of corruption, have been suppressed. On a broader scale, the impact of this repression is hard to measure; the number of opinions that were never publicly voiced is literally speaking uncountable. After almost two decades of Putinism, selective law enforcement has long been one of its hallmarks.

The children born in Putin's first term as Russia's president are now coming of age. While some take to the streets to cry out that "Putin is not our tsar" and similar slogans, the President has certainly acquired a dominating position both in domestic and foreign policy. The sheer longevity of the regime itself makes it increasingly hard to speculate on alternatives. The lack of alternatives is a major source of the regime's legitimacy and longevity. Beyond the wave of protests, the pressures towards constitutionalism are relatively weak. The ruling elites have obvious interests in the *status quo*, and constitutional freedoms are continuously undermined by ordinary legislation, left unenforced by the court system, and frustrated by repeated abuse of law enforcement structures for private or group gain.

As noted by Popova (2017), it would be theoretically possible that Putin and his closest associates would push for constitutionalism to protect their spoils from quasi-legal pressure. This need not come in democratic from, but could also take authoritarian shape. In an authoritarian constitutional system, law can be used in a straightforward fashion to suppress opposition parties, independent media, and critics within civil society (Rajah 2012). In such a system, "oppositionists are sanctioned in accordance with the laws that limit opposition activity, rather than imprisoned on other charges" (Popova 2017, 67).

Considering how some rules that used to be unwritten in recent years have been formalized, a change towards authoritarian constitutionalism may already be underway. Homosexual propaganda, for instance, used to be cracked down upon by quasi-formal means before it was turned into federal law in 2013. Gay parade participants knew they should never cross the street on red lights, because the Russian police had been known to use this infringement as a pretext to crack down on such events. Similarly, Russian NGOs financed from abroad complained about being harassed by means of an extraordinarily high level of scrutiny with regard to all sorts of formal requirements (Bækken 2009). In 2012, the stigma was formalized by means of the 'foreign agent' label. In some spheres, then, limitations on constitutional freedoms have come out in the open.

In Russia, however, a considerable drift towards constitutionalism in any form seems implausible. After all, the repeated political interventions build upon centuries of informal penetration of the legal sphere. Quasi-legality is simply too entrenched to disappear from Russian politics short to mid-term. Even in the 'openly restrictive' legal issue areas, laws still tend to be used in a way that is "arbitrary, expedient, and instrumental, rather than predictable and principled" (Popova 2017, 65). A gradual weakening of the regime seems a more likely scenario, in which we may witness an intensified quasi-legal crackdown against anything and anyone seen as a threat – a development we are perhaps seeing today. Late Putinism, therefore, may very well be a more violent version of the system than what we have seen so far.

Many of the qualities of the regime are structural and sticky – they are not likely to change even with a considerably different president. Even political revolutions can take place without rocking the foundations quasi-legality builds upon – patronalism, legal nihilism, and high personal stakes. Whereas it has undergone political upheavals greater than most countries, many of Russia's fundamental characteristics have survived them all. Even opposition politicians are not immune to the patronal culture that pervades Russian politics. In future periods of legal reform, moreover, there will be thousands of powerful and wealthy individuals ready to resist change and refusing to let go of the prerogatives they are used to. Even a sincere champion of law cannot easily break off the low trust spiral in Russian law, especially not when the nihilist are plentiful within the legal administration. Liberal reform initiatives under Gorbachev and Yeltsin provide examples of how difficult the task may be.

A red line through this book concerns patterns and institutionalization. Expectations become rules when their generalizations get entrenched and influence human conduct by their very capacity of being rules. A mechanism that has been institutionalized has independent weight and a regularity that shapes actors' expectations and allows it to run more smoothly. The institutionalization of selective law enforcement makes legal actors aware that they should take informal agendas into account and be more willing to bend when powerful actors interfere and voice their preferences. The fact that powerful individuals even consider this tool as a means to solve their problems is also a product of its institutionalization. Because law enforcers, targets of the practice, and society as a whole share roughly the same expectations of politicized justice, the institutionalization of the practice also lubricates the promulgation of informal rules. I have argued that the practice in its institutionalized form resembles what Beissinger (2002) called a 'regime of repression.' The Putinist system still requires a great deal of hands-on management. When rules of the game become increasingly entrenched and stable, however, quasi-legal repression can gradually become routine and thus operate in a more automatic fashion – until the foundations of the regime are shook and the rules shift once again.

Russians have a mutual understanding that ordinary and exceptional cases are dealt with according to different logics. Because Russian citizens understand that political cases are exceptional, the rational-legal functions of the system as a whole are not seriously hurt. In addition, exactly because they understand that the exceptional cases are political, the informal rules are effectively enforced instead of the formal. Selective law enforcement stabilizes the regime, at least in the short term, by enforcing the status quo and reproducing existing power relations. While parts of the elites pull in the direction of more Rule of Law and effective governance, others are set to sabotage such efforts and perhaps extract even more rents instead. Following Robinson (2017), this division of interests has kept the neo-patrimonial regime in a form of balance throughout the Putinist period in spite of considerable policy shifts.

The combination of strong statism and bureaucratic formalism on the one hand, and clientelistic politics and low trust in formal institutions on the other, create fertile grounds for selective law enforcement. Because selective law enforcement is an intrinsic part of a long standing legal culture, there are no reasons to believe that the practice will disappear overnight. What we need to remember, however, is that while institutions are associated with regularity, stability, and predictability, they do not imply stagnation or stalemate. On the one hand, the very definition of selective law enforcement as a rule enforcement mechanism implies that the rules need to be enforced. In other words, if the willingness or capability to employ force diminishes, so will selective law enforcement as a coercive tool. On the other hand, the longevity of the practice is also threatened from the 'opposite side.' Some anti-liberal policies that would seem politically impossible to formalize a decade ago have now found legal form. The practice is contingent on a much more complex set of factors that are yet to be clearly identified. We may expect that selective law enforcement will continue to evolve, yet our possibility to predicate how remains limited.

References

Beissinger, M. R. 2002. *Nationalist Mobilization and the Collapse of the Soviet State*. Cambridge: Cambridge University Press.

Bækken, H. 2009. Selective Law Enforcement against Russian NGOs. Pursuing Informal Interests through Formal Means. *NUPI report*. Oslo: Norwegian Institute of International Affairs.

Popova, M. 2017. Putin-Style 'Rule of Law' & the Prospects for Change. *Dædalus*, 146, 64–75.

Rajah, J. 2012. *Authoritarian Rule of Law. Legislation, Discourse and Legitimacy in Singapore*. New York: Cambridge University Press.

Robinson, N. 2017. Russian Neo-patrimonialism and Putin's 'Cultural Turn'. *Europe-Asia Studies*, 69, 348–366.

Index